Professional Certificate in Marketing

STUDY TEXT

Marketing Information and Research

Valid for assessments up to June 2014

The Chartered
Institute of Marketing

BPP
LEARNING MEDIA

First edition July 2012

ISBN 9781 4453 9143 4

e-ISBN 9781 4453 7616 5

British Library Cataloguing-in-Publication Data
A catalogue record for this book
is available from the British Library

Published by

BPP Learning Media Ltd
Aldine House, Aldine Place
142-144 Uxbridge Road
London W12 8AA

www.bpp.com/learningmedia

Printed in the United Kingdom by CPI Antony Rowe Ltd

Bumpers Lane
Bumpers Farm Industrial Estate
Chippenham
SN14 6LH

Your learning materials, published by BPP Learning
Media Ltd, are printed on paper obtained from
traceable sustainable sources.

We are grateful to The Chartered Institute of Marketing for
permission to reproduce in this text the unit syllabus.

Lead Author: Richard Bakare

Contents

Page

Introduction

Studying for The Chartered Institute of Marketing (CIM) qualifications ▪ The Professional Certificate Syllabus ▪ Assessment ▪ The Magic Formula ▪ A guide to the features of the Study Text ▪ Additional resources ▪ Your personal study plan

v

Chapters

1 Studying for The Chartered Institute of Marketing (CIM) qualifications

There are a few key points to remember as you study for your CIM qualification:

(a) You are studying for a **professional** qualification. This means that you are required to use professional language and adopt a business approach in your work.

(b) You are expected to show that you have 'read widely'. Make sure that you read the quality press (and don't skip the business pages), *Marketing*, *The Marketer*, *Research* and *Marketing Week* avidly.

(c) Become aware of the marketing initiatives you come across on a daily basis; for example, when you go shopping look around and think about why the store layout is as it is; consider the messages, channel choice and timings of ads when you are watching TV. It is surprising how much you will learn just by taking an interest in the marketing world around you.

(d) Get to know the way CIM write their exam papers and assignments. They use a specific approach (the Magic Formula) which is to ensure a consistent approach when designing assessment materials. Make sure you are fully aware of this as it will help you interpret what the examiner is looking for (a full description of the Magic Formula appears later).

(e) Learn how to use Harvard referencing. This is explained in detail in our CIM Professional Certificate Assessment Workbook.

(f) Ensure that you read very carefully all assessment details sent to you from CIM. There are strict deadlines to meet, as well as paperwork to complete for any assignment or project you do. You also need to make sure have your CIM membership card with you at the exam. Failing to meet any assessment entry deadlines or complete written work on time will mean that you will have to wait for the next round of assessment dates and will need to pay the relevant assessment fees again.

2 The Professional Certificate Syllabus

The Professional Certificate in Marketing is aimed at anyone who is employed in a supporting marketing role such as Marketing Co-ordinator or Executive. You may also be a manager with a senior role within a small or medium-sized company where marketing only forms part of a wider work remit. Or you may be looking to move into your first marketing role or to specialise.

The aim of the qualification is to provide a strong foundation of marketing knowledge. You will develop the breadth of knowledge of marketing theory but also appreciate issues faced within the organisation as CIM qualifications concentrate on applied marketing within real workplaces.

The complete Professional Certificate qualification contains four units:

- Unit 1 Marketing Essentials
- Unit 2 Assessing the Marketing Environment
- Unit 3 Marketing Information and Research
- Unit 4 Stakeholder Marketing

CIM stipulates that each module should take 40 guided learning hours to complete. Guided learning hours refer to time in class, using distance learning materials and completing any work set by your tutor. Guided learning hours do not include the time it will take you to complete the necessary reading for your studies.

The syllabus as provided by CIM can be found below with reference to the coverage within this Study Text.

Unit characteristics - Marketing Information and Research

This unit focuses on the importance of marketing information in gaining a more in-depth understanding of both the market in which the organisation operates and the customers it seeks to serve.

It aims to provide an understanding of how marketing information supports marketing decisions within the organisation and how information contributes to the overall marketing process. The unit explores different research methodologies and encourages consideration of complementary approaches to collecting a range of market and customer information.

The unit also considers the role of databases in information management, the nature and scope of the research industry, and of various research methodologies linked to the collection of primary and secondary data.

By the end of the unit, students should be able to demonstrate a thorough knowledge and understanding in the ways of collecting and manipulating information to support and justify key marketing decisions.

Overarching learning outcomes

By the end of this unit, students should be able to:

- Identify appropriate information and marketing research requirements for marketing decision making

- Evaluate the importance of customer databases and their contribution to providing detailed market information to support marketing decisions

- Review the processes involved in establishing an effective database

- Explain the nature and scope of the research industry and discuss the importance of working in line with the industry's code of conduct

- Explain the process for selecting a marketing research supplier, in domestic and international markets, and developing the criteria to support that selection

- Explain the process for collecting marketing and customer information, utilising appropriate primary and secondary sources

- Appraise the appropriateness of different qualitative and quantitative research methodologies to meet different research situations.

 The Chartered Institute of Marketing

SECTION 1 – The importance of marketing information (weighting 20%)

		Covered in chapter(s)

1.1	Discuss the need for information in marketing management and its role in the overall marketing process:
	
	   ▪ Information on customers
	   ▪ Information on competitors and other organisations
	   ▪ Information on the marketing environment
	   ▪ Descriptive v comparative v diagnostic role of information
		1

1.2	Evaluate the impact of information technology on the marketing function and discuss the challenges facing organisations in collecting valid, reliable and measurable information to support the decision making process:
	
	   ▪ Growth in information sources (The Information Explosion)
	   ▪ The Internet/Intranet
	   ▪ Consumer generated media eg, on-line communities/blogs
	   ▪ Customer databases
	   ▪ Internal reporting system, scanning/inventory control etc
	   ▪ Validity and reliability of different information sources
		1

1.3	Explain the concept of a marketing decision support system and its role in supporting marketing decisions:
	
	   ▪ Definition
	   ▪ Components (data storage, reports and displays, analysis and modelling)
	   ▪ Types of information held
	   ▪ Manner in which it can assist decision-making
		1

1.4	Review the key elements and formats when reporting or presenting marketing information to decision-makers:
	
	   ▪ Understanding the audience/audience thinking sequence
	   ▪ Physical and online research report format
	   ▪ Oral presentation format
	   ▪ Using tables and graphs
		10

SECTION 2 – The role of databases in information management (weighting 20%)

		Covered in chapter(s)
2.1	Demonstrate an understanding of the role, application and benefits of customer databases in relation to customer relationship management (CRM):	2
	▪ Types of customer data (behavioural data, volunteered data, attributed data)	
	▪ Role in profiling customers	
	▪ Role in marketing intelligence testing campaigns/forecasting	
	▪ Role in determining life-time value	
	▪ Role in personalising offerings and communications	
	▪ Role in building relationships	
2.2	Identify and explain the different stages in the process of setting up a database:	2
	▪ The importance of evaluating software and what is needed to ensure it works properly	
	▪ Evaluating software	
	▪ Identifying needs of users of a database	
	▪ Processing data (formatting, validation, de-duplication)	
2.3	Explain the principles of data warehousing, data marts and data mining:	2
	▪ Understanding how databases can be used to select, explore and model large amounts of data to identify relationships and patterns of behaviour	
2.4	Explain the relationship between database marketing and marketing research and explain the legal aspects of data collection and usage, including the Data Protection Legislation:	2
	▪ Data protection legislation	
	▪ List brokers	
	▪ Profilers and their offerings (eg, Acorn, Mosaic etc)	
	▪ Issues involved in merging marketing research and customer database information (transparency, aggregation of data, using customer databases for marketing research purposes)	

The Chartered Institute of Marketing

SECTION 3 – The nature of marketing research (weighting 25%)

		Covered in chapter(s)
3.1	Discuss the nature and structure of the market research industry: ■ Marketing research departments v marketing research agencies ■ Types of marketing research agency ■ Scale of industry ■ Professional bodies and associations in the marketing research industry	3
3.2	Explain the stages of the market research process: ■ Identification of problems and opportunities ■ Formulation of research needs/the research brief ■ Selection of research provider/the proposal ■ Creation of research design ■ Collection of secondary data ■ Collection of primary data ■ Analysis of data ■ Preparation and presentation of research findings and recommendations	3
3.3	Evaluate a range of procedures and criteria used for selecting a market research supplier in domestic and international markets: ■ Short-listing criteria ■ The research proposal ■ Supplier assessments (Pitch) ■ Selection criteria	3
3.4	Explain how best to liaise with the research agency on a day to day basis to leverage best levels of service, support and implementation and high quality information to support the business case development: ■ Monitoring working arrangements using quality and service standards	3
3.5	Explain the stages involved in order to develop a full research proposal to fulfil the brief which support the information needs of different marketing projects: ■ Content of proposal covering background, objectives, approach and method, reporting and presentation procedures, timing, personal CVs, related experience, contract details	3
3.6	Evaluate the ethical and social responsibilities inherent in the market research task: ■ Need for goodwill, trust, professionalism, confidentiality ■ Codes of marketing and social research practice (eg the Market Research Society Code of Conduct) ■ Responsibilities to respondents (Use of information/protection of vulnerable groups such as children, etc) ■ Responsibilities to clients (transparency, data reporting, etc)	3

SECTION 4 – Research methodologies (weighting 20%)

		Covered in chapter(s)
4.1	Evaluate the uses, benefits and limitations of secondary data: ■ Benefits ■ Limitations ■ Sources of secondary data ■ Internet search strategies ■ Integrating secondary data with primary data	4
4.2	Evaluate the various procedures used for observing behaviour: ■ Categories of observation (natural v contrived, visible v hidden, structured v unstructured, mechanised v human, participant v non-participant) ■ Audits and scanner-based research ■ Television viewing measurement ■ Internet monitoring ■ Mystery shopping	5
4.3	Identify and evaluate the various techniques for collecting qualitative data: ■ Types of research most suited to qualitative research ■ Individual depth interviews ■ Group discussions (including basic guidelines on group moderation, stimulus material and projective techniques) ■ Using the Internet for qualitative research (online group discussions, chat rooms, blogs) ■ Overview of approach to the analysis of qualitative research	6
4.4	Identify and evaluate the various techniques for collecting quantitative data: ■ Face-to-face survey methods ■ Telephone interviews ■ Postal surveys ■ Online surveys ■ Omnibus surveys ■ Forum voting (pressing voting buttons)	7
4.5	Identify and evaluate the various techniques for undertaking experimentation: ■ Hall tests ■ Placement tests ■ Simulated test markets	5

The Chartered
Institute of Marketing

SECTION 5 – Research tools (weighting 15%)

		Covered in chapter(s)
5.1	Design a **basic** questionnaire and discussion guide to meet a project's research objectives: ■ Discussion guide format ■ The questionnaire design process ■ Question and response formats ■ Scaling techniques (Likert and semantic differential) ■ Sequence and wording ■ Design layout and appearance ■ Questionnaire-generating software	6 & 9
5.2	Explain and evaluate different **basic** sampling approaches designed to maximise the benefit of market research activities: ■ The sampling process ■ Difference between probability and non-probability samples ■ Knowledge of convenience, judgement and quota samples ■ Determining sample size ■ Sampling and non-sampling error ■ Panels	8

3 Assessment

The unit covered by this study text (Unit 3 Marketing Information and Research) is assessed by an assignment. In order to help you focus specifically on your assignment we have also written a Professional Certificate in Marketing Assessment Workbook which is available either through your usual book retailer or our website www.bpp.com/learningmedia.

4 The Magic Formula

The Magic Formula is a tool used by CIM to help both examiners write exam and assignment questions, and you, to more easily interpret what you are being asked to write about. It is useful for helping you to check that you are using an appropriate balance between theory and practice for your particular level of qualification.

Contrary to the title, there is nothing mystical about the Magic Formula and simply by knowing it (or even mentioning it in an assessment) will not automatically secure a pass. What it does do, however, is to help you to check that you are presenting your answers in an appropriate format, including enough marketing theory and applying it to a real marketing context or issue.

The Magic Formula for the Professional Certificate in Marketing is shown below:

Figure A   The Magic Formula for the Professional Certificate in Marketing

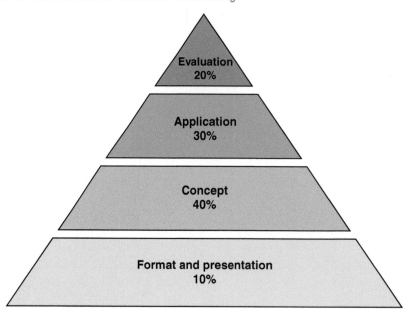

You can see from the pyramid that for the Professional Certificate marks are awarded in the following proportions:

- Presentation and format – 10%

   You are expected to present your work professionally which means that assignments and projects should **always** be typed. Even in an exam situation attention should be paid to making your work look as visually appealing as possible. CIM will also stipulate the format that you should present your work in. The assessment formats you will be given will be varied and can include things like reports to write, slides to prepare, emails, memos, formal letters, press releases, discussion documents, briefing papers, agendas and newsletters.

- **Concept – 40%**

  Concept refers to your ability to state, recall and describe marketing theory. The definition of marketing is a core CIM syllabus topic. If we take this as an example, you would be expected to recognise, recall and write this definition to a word-perfect standard to gain the full marks for concept. Understanding marketing concepts is the main area where marks will be given within your assessment at the Professional Certificate level.

- **Application – 30%**

  Application-based marks are given for your ability to apply marketing theories to real life marketing situations. For example, a question may ask you to discuss the definition of marketing and how it is applied within your own organisation. Here you are not only using the definition but are applying it in order to consider the market orientation of the company.

- **Evaluation – 20%**

  Evaluation is the ability to asses the value or worth of something, sometimes through careful consideration of related advantages and disadvantages, or weighing up of alternatives. Results from your evaluation should enable you to discuss the importance of an issue using evidence to support your opinions.

  For example, if you were asked to evaluate whether or not your organisation adopts a marketing approach you should provide reasons and specific examples of why you think they might take this approach, as well as considering why they may not take this approach, before coming to a final conclusion.

5 A guide to the features of the Study Text

Each of the chapter features (see below) will help you to break down the content into manageable chunks and ensure that you are developing the skills required for a professional qualification.

Chapter feature	Relevance and how you should use it
Introduction	Shows why topics need to be studied and is a route guide through the chapter
Syllabus reference	Outlines the syllabus learning outcomes covered in the chapter
Chapter topic list	Study the list, each numbered topic denotes a numbered section in the chapter
Key Term	Highlights the core vocabulary you need to learn
Activity	An application-based activity for you to complete
The Real World	A short case study to illustrate marketing practice
Exam tip/Assessment tip	Key advice based on the assessment
Chapter roundups	Use this to review what you have learnt
Quick quiz	Use this to check your learning
Further reading	Further reading will give you a wider perspective on the subjects you're covering

6 Additional resources

To help you pass the entire Professional Certificate in Marketing we have created a complete study package. The **Professional Certificate Assessment Workbook** covers all four units for the Professional Certificate level. Practice questions and answers, tips on tackling assignments and work-based projects are included to help you succeed in your assessments.

Our A6 set of spiral-bound **Passcards** are handy revision cards and are ideal to reinforce key topics for the Marketing Essentials and Assessing the Marketing Environment exams.

7 Your personal study plan

Preparing a Study Plan (and sticking to it) is one of the key elements to learning success.

CIM have stipulated that there should be a minimum of 40 guided learning hours spent on each unit. Guided learning hours will include time spent in lesson, working on fully prepared distance learning materials, formal workshops and work set by your tutor. We also know that to be successful, students should spend approximately an additional 60 hours conducting self study. This means that for the entire qualification with four units you should spend 160 hours working in a tutor-guided manner and at least an additional 240 hours completing recommended reading, working on assignments, and revising for exams. This Study Text will help you to organise this 60-hour portion of self-study time.

Now think about the exact amount of time you have (don't forget you will still need some leisure time!) and complete the following tables to help you keep to a schedule.

	Date	Duration in weeks
Course start		
Course finish		Total weeks of course:
Assignment received	Submission date	Total weeks to complete

Content chapter coverage plan

Chapter	To be completed by	Considered in relation to the assignment?
1 The role of information in marketing		
2 Customer databases and CRM		
3 The market research industry		
4 Secondary data		
5 Observation and experimentation		
6 Qualitative research		
7 Quantitative research		
8 Sampling		
9 Questionnaire design		
10 The presentation of results		

The role of information in marketing

Introduction

The CIM defines marketing as 'the management process responsible for identifying, anticipating and satisfying customer requirements profitably'. This chapter outlines the vital role that information plays in the marketing management process. The first section discusses the need for information at every stage of the marketing management process and its role in equipping managers for effective decision making.

The second section evaluates the impact of information technology on the marketing function and discusses the challenges facing organisations in collecting valid, reliable and measurable information to support the decision-making process. The growth in information sources during the past two decades has significantly increased the quantity and quality of information available to marketers. Information needs to be collected, organised and made available to marketing managers at the right time and in the right form. The third section explains the concept of a marketing decision support system and its role in supporting marketing decisions.

The final section defines marketing research and the systems that are used for gathering and interpreting relevant information from the business and its environment.

Topic list

Marketing and information	(1)
Information technology and marketing	(2)
Marketing decision support systems	(3)
What is marketing research?	(4)

1.1	Discuss the need for information in marketing management and its role in the overall marketing process: ■ Information on customers ■ Information on competitors and other organisations ■ Information on the marketing environment ■ Descriptive vs comparative vs diagnostic role of information
1.2	Evaluate the impact of information technology on the marketing function and discuss the challenges facing organisations in collecting valid, reliable and measurable information to support the decision-making process: ■ Growth in information sources (the Information Explosion) ■ The Internet / Intranet ■ Consumer-generated media eg online communities, blogs ■ Customer databases ■ Internal reporting system, scanning / inventory control, etc ■ Validity and reliability of different information sources
1.3	Explain the concept of a marketing decision support system and its role in supporting marketing decisions: ■ Definition ■ Components (data storage, reports and displays, analysis and modelling) ■ Types of information held ■ Manner in which it can assist decision-making

1 Marketing and information

1.1 The marketing management process

▶ Key term

"Marketing is the **management process** responsible for identifying,, anticipating and satisfying customer requirements profitably" (CIM, 2010)

There are several key points in this definition:

■ **Marketing is a management process** – It is something that managers do in the course of running the operations of the business on a day-to-day basis. Like other management activities, it requires the application of management skills in analysis, planning, implementation and control.

■ **Marketing identifies customer needs** – It involves finding out who your customers are and getting to know them. This usually involves using market research to obtain more information about customers so that companies can tailor their products or services to meet their customers' needs.

■ **Marketing anticipates customer needs** – It involves not only monitoring customer needs and trends, but understanding them so well that suitable products and services can be developed in advance. This requires a proactive approach to understanding customer needs so that a company can achieve a competitive advantage in its industry.

The Chartered Institute of Marketing

I buy mineral water. What need am I fulfilling?

Write down as many as you can think of...

- **Marketing satisfies customer needs** – It is about giving customers the right product or service at the right price, in the right place and at the right time. Products and services should match customer needs in terms of quality, pricing, availability and service standards.

- **Marketing fulfils customer requirements profitably** – Where profitability is an objective of the organisation, marketing activities should be conducted to ensure that it is achieved.

Not only is marketing a philosophy (being customer-centric) but it also is a function with a role of a 'management process', which includes:

- Identifying customer needs and wants
- Satisfying customers
- Identifying market opportunities
- Targeting the 'right' customers
- Staying ahead in dynamic markets
- Knowing and pre-empting competitors
- Using resources effectively
- Enhancing profitability.

To achieve this range of activities, marketing is broken down into four manageable stages: analysis; planning; implementation and control (Kotler, 1994).

- **Analysis**. 'Managing the marketing function begins with a complete analysis of the company's situation. The company must analyse its markets and marketing environment to find attractive opportunities and to avoid environmental threats. It must analyse company strengths and weaknesses, as well as current and possible marketing actions, to determine which opportunities it can best pursue. Marketing analysis feeds information and other inputs to each of the other marketing management functions.'

- **Planning**. 'Through strategic planning, the company decides what it wants to do with each business unit. Marketing planning involves deciding on marketing strategies that will help the company attain its overall strategic objectives.'

- **Implementation**. 'Good marketing analysis and planning are only a start toward successful company performance – the marketing plans must be carefully implemented. It is often easier to design good marketing strategies than put them into action.

- People at all levels of the marketing system must work together to implement marketing strategy and plans. People in marketing must work closely with people in finance, purchasing, manufacturing and other company departments. And many outside people and organisations must help with implementation – suppliers, resellers, advertising agencies, research firms, the advertising media. All must work together effectively to implement the marketing programme.'

- **Control**. 'Many surprises are likely to occur as marketing plans are being implemented. The company needs control procedures to make certain that its objectives will be achieved. Companies want to make sure that they are achieving the sales, profits, and other goals set in their annual plans. This control involves measuring ongoing market performance, determining the causes of any serious gaps in performance, and deciding on the best corrective action to take to close the gaps. Corrective action may call for improving the ways in which the plan is being implemented or even changing the goals.

- Companies should also stand back from time to time and look at their overall approach to the marketplace. The purpose is to make certain that the company's objectives, policies, strategies, and programs remain appropriate in the face of rapid environmental changes. To do this, good quality marketing information is essential.'

The diagram below outlines these four stages and adds details about exactly what they involve and the inputs required in terms of actual marketing activities that will need to take place.

Figure 1.1   The stages of marketing

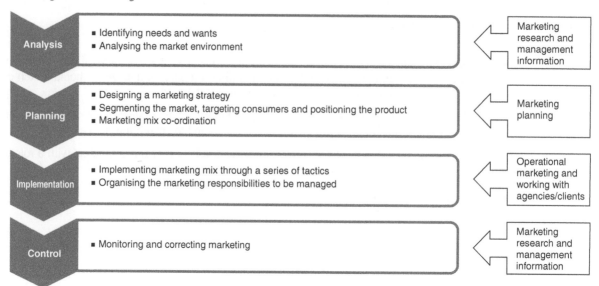

On the right-hand side of the diagram you will see that the inputs which are needed at each stage include marketing research and management information, marketing planning and actual operational marketing activities, which includes day-to-day activities. The list of day-to-day activities will be enormous and dependent on the actual job role of the individual marketing team members, but it could include anything from day-to-day sales forecasting, writing press releases, booking ad space, dealing with customer complaints, monitoring a customer web forum or working with a design agency to ensure the exact colour specification for artwork. Marketing research enables marketers to make decisions more easily and is an activity that may be ongoing in many organisations.

To carry out marketing management activities, **marketing managers need information**. They need to:

- Anticipate changes in demand
- Introduce, modify or discontinue products or services
- Evaluate profitability
- Set prices
- Undertake promotional activity
- Plan budgets
- Control costs.

1.2   The need for marketing information

> ▶ **Key term**
>
> **Information** is 'data that has been verified to be accurate and timely, is specific and organised for a purpose, is presented within a context that gives it meaning and relevance, and that can lead to an increase in understanding and decrease in uncertainty' (CIM, 2010).

Information is a **marketing asset**. It impacts on performance in several ways.

- It helps to increase **responsiveness** to customer demands.

- It helps to identify **new customer opportunities** and new product/service demands.

- It helps to anticipate **competitive attacks** and threats.

 The Chartered Institute of Marketing

Overall, marketers need information to help them to make decisions.

In a **knowledge-based economy** organisations compete by obtaining **superior information**. The more information that a firm can obtain about competitors and customers, the more it should be able to adapt its product/service offerings to meet the needs of the market place.

There's nothing new about using information to get things done, but you will often hear that we now live in the **'Information Age'**. That suggests that information is more important than ever before – perhaps **the** most important thing in modern life.

- At one time organisations could be successful simply by investing in physical resources – bigger and better factories, nearer to customers than their competitors' factories, for example. The problem was producing enough to satisfy demand.

- As competition has increased and become more global there is no significant difference between, say, a Ford factory in Chicago and a Nissan factory in Wales. The problem now is creating enough demand in the first place.

In a **knowledge-based economy** economic factors such as land and capital are not vital for success. Organisations now compete by **knowing** more about the markets they serve, who the best suppliers are, how to do things, and – above all – by having the best new ideas. In other words they compete by **gathering information** and **using it intelligently**.

Firms are becoming increasingly aware of the competitive advantage that may be achieved through the use of information. Information systems can affect the way the firm approaches **customer service** – the very essence of the **marketing concept** – and can provide advantages over competitor approaches. Superior customer service can only be achieved by being able to anticipate and satisfy customer needs. In order to meet this objective, **information** which is **up-to-date**, **accurate**, **relevant** and **timely** is essential.

Here is a list of questions that marketing managers might need answered.

- **Markets.** Who are our customers? What are they like? How are buying decisions made?

- **Share of the market.** What are total sales of our product? How do our sales compare with competitors' sales?

- **Products.** What do customers think of our product? What do they do with it? Are our products in a 'growth' or 'decline' stage of their life cycle? Should we extend our range?

- **Price.** How do our prices compare with others: higher, average, lower? Is the market sensitive to price?

- **Distribution.** Should we distribute directly, indirectly or both? What discounts are required?

- **Sales force.** Do we have enough/too many salespeople? Are their territories equal to their potential? Are they contacting the right people? Should we pay commission?

- **Advertising.** Do we use the right media? Do we communicate the right message? Is it effective?

- **Customer attitudes.** What do they think of our product/firm/service/delivery?

- **Competitors' activities.** Who are our competitors? Are they more or less successful businesses? Why are they more or less successful?

- **Environmental factors.** What factors impact on marketing planning (PESTEL factors)?

Another way of viewing information needs in marketing management is to consider the **four key strategic questions**.

Table 1.1   Four key strategic questions

Question	Examples of information needed	Sources of information
Where are we now? Strategic, financial and marketing analysis	Current sales by product/market Market share by product/market Competitors' market shares Customer attitudes and behaviour Corporate image versus competitors' image Company strengths and weaknesses	Accounting system Customer database Market analysis/surveys Competitor intelligence Customer surveys Internal/external analyses
Where do we want to be? Strategic direction and strategy formulation	Market forecasts by segment Environmental changes Growth capabilities Opportunities and threats Competitor response New product/market potentials	Industry forecasts/surveys PESTEL analysis PIMS (Profit Impact of Market Strategy database) Competitor research Product/market research
How might we get there? Strategic choice and evaluation	Marketing mix evaluation Buying behaviour New product development Risk evaluation Alternative strategic options	Internal/external audits Customer research Concept testing/test marketing Feasibility studies/competitor response modelling/focus groups/marketing mix research
How can we ensure arrival? Strategic implementation and control	Budgets Performance evaluation	Internal accounting, production and human resource systems Marketing information systems Marketing audit Benchmarking External (financial) auditing

We can think about this in terms of three key areas where marketing decisions are required. Three key questions exist:

- How can we satisfy customer needs?
- How do we ensure we are competitive within the market?
- What external factors are likely to affect us?

To address these questions we need to gather information on customers, competitors and the marketing environment. The table below outlines the broad issues and then focuses on some of the detail that marketers will need to consider.

Table 1.2   Information requirements

Customer information required	Information required on competitors and other organisations	Information required about the marketing environment
Who are our customers? Can our customers be segmented in any way? Are customers B2B or individual consumers or both? Do we have groups of key customers or a broad market appeal?	**Competitor activity** Who are competitors? What are their core competences? What share of the market do they have? What additional threat do they pose?	**Macro environment** What are the PESTEL factors to impact us? Is our market growing or in decline? Are we likely to remain profitable in the current and future market conditions?

The Chartered Institute of Marketing

Customer information required	Information required on competitors and other organisations	Information required about the marketing environment
Where are customers found? Location? Frequent visitors to where? Online presence, sites visited? Where can we be available at their convenience?	**Performance benchmarking** Who should we measure ourselves against? What metrics should be used to provide a meaningful analysis?	**Micro environment** How effective is our internal market? Are we working with the right partners, suppliers etc? Internally are we organised as best as we can be to meet customer needs? Do our people understand our customers and how to best meet their needs?
How do we build a relationship with customers? Are our customers exclusively loyal? Are we part of a portfolio of brands that our customers purchase? How do our customers like to communicate with us? What is our history with our customers? How do customers perceive us?	**Partner organisations and marketing networks** What referral markets should we belong to? Are we making the most of the networks that we belong to? How can we partner with other organisations for mutual gain?	
How do customers make purchases? What is the decision-making process for consumers? What reference groups are important? What decision-making units are involved in the purchase? Do customers regard purchases as high or low involvement?		
How do we satisfy customers' needs? Have we correctly identified what customer needs are? How does our offering meet their needs? What are satisfaction levels? How can satisfaction levels be improved?		
What are the behaviour patterns of customers? Do customers relate to our product/service individually or within a group? What is the influence of third parties on the behaviour of customers with regard to our product / service?		

Think about your own organisation and the following questions for **one** aspect of your job:

(a)   What information do you use on a regular basis?
(b)   Where does this information come from?
(c)   What do you use this information for?
(d)   Who else uses the same information?

1.3   The role of marketing information

Marketing information is used in different ways by marketing managers to provide solutions to marketing problems:

- **Descriptive information** answers straightforward questions such as which products are customers buying, what level of knowledge do clients have about our services, when are customers most likely to use our services and what promotional activities have customers been exposed to. It addresses the **what**, **where** and **when** questions.

- **Comparative information** examines how one factor compares with another and is generally used for performance management purposes. It addresses questions like *How does the performance of our product compare with the competition?* and *How does the customer's experience of our dry cleaning services compare with their previous experience?*

- **Diagnostic information** attempts to analyse and explain customer behaviour by asking the '**why**' questions. It addresses questions like *Why do customers buy our product rather than a cheaper alternative? Why are some clients dissatisfied with our services?* and *Why do customers buy more of our products during a particular period of the year?*

Marketing research plays the following roles within modern organisations:

- Enables an organisation to know its buyers: Marketing research helps an organisation to know more about the individuals and groups that are willing to pay for its products and services.

- Enables the organisation to measure the impact of its promotional efforts: Modern organisations employ a wide range of promotional tools. Accurate information about which tools are most effective and which constitute a waste of resources is valuable in improving the effectiveness and efficiency of its marketing activities.

- Enables the organisation to understand customer response: Marketing research enables firms to know how customers will respond to new products / services and changes to the marketing mix.

- Enables the organisation to master external forces: Every organisation needs reliable information about competitors' moves, the company's share in the market, developments in foreign markets, government policies, technological changes, and consumer incomes to devise and implement effective marketing strategies.

Try to find three examples each for descriptive, comparative and diagnostic information needs. You can think of your own organisations for the purpose of this activity.

The Chartered
Institute of Marketing

2 Information technology and marketing

Information and communications technology (ICT) is changing the way markets are structured and it has created **new marketing techniques** and **new marketing channels**.

Take the clothing industry as an example. It is now possible for a retail organisation in England to develop designs and production specifications which may be sent electronically to a remote manufacturer off-shore. The manufacturer will put the garments into production, organise transportation, inform the customer, invoice the customer and despatch the goods – all within a matter of days rather than the weeks or months that this might have taken not so long ago.

This not only opens up new market opportunities but may also present competitor threats. New technologies increase the opportunities to develop **global markets** for what once may only have been local products or services.

ICT has also created new **marketing techniques** and new **marketing channels**. As we'll see in much more later in this book, **database marketing** allows vast amounts of customer data to be stored and analysed and used to produce more accurate targeting as well as other marketing tactics. This is significant when a firm is able to gain an advantage over competitors by accessing and applying technologies that the competitor has not yet developed, information that the competitor does not possess, and ideas that have not occurred to others.

2.1 Growth in information sources

There is no substitute for effective judgement to be used to make decisions by the marketer. IT solutions cannot and possibly never can be capable of making decisions on behalf of a human. They can however, if used appropriately, help to store, organise, sort and assist decision making by enabling easier access to information. The growth in IT has also opened up the accessibility of information and the ability for disparate groups of individuals to publish materials online. The net effect is that we can access information faster, from a wider range of sources and more conveniently than ever before.

Most decisions however are still based on incomplete information. All possible information is not available. Beyond a certain point, the gathering of more information would not be worth the extra time and cost of obtaining and analysing it.

Too much information also makes decision making harder rather than easier, as 'information overload' takes effect.

The diagram below shows just some of the information which is available to marketers to assist in decision making.

Figure 1.2   Sources of information

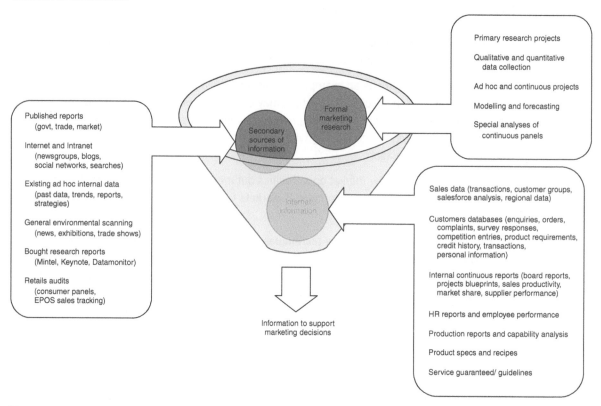

Figure 1.2   Sources of information

You will see from the diagram that, far from being short of information, the average marketer has a wealth of data at his or her disposal. The trick however is being able to cut through the data, process it and establish some real meaning. Most of the problems associated with the ability to make decisions are actually a result of the inability of marketers to filter the relevant data from the explosion of information.

Technological advances have fuelled the information explosion. The internet, for example, has opened a wealth of opportunities, not only as a way of gathering information but also by observing how consumers behave online, recording transactions efficiently to build more powerful databases and opening communications with customers through forums. More recently the use of Web 2.0, online survey tools, voting buttons added to sites, analysis of social networks and virtual worlds have not only enabled new data collection methods but continue to add to the banks of information available to organisations.

THE REAL WORLD

Marketing author and consultant Jack Trout, writing in his column for the US magazine Forbes, and reported by *Research*, cautions against too much reliance on data and research. He feels that commonsense is in danger of being disregarded, as we suffer from too much 'overload' of data, some of which he feels to be confusing. He cites, in particular, research which uses visual ethnology, galvanic skin response and neuroscience. A surfeit of data shouldn't 'wash away your common sense and your own feelings for the market', he says. Before you accept offers to conduct lots of heavily science-based surveying and research, do pause and consider how necessary the data will be, and whether you can be sure it has proven validity – rather than just being the latest gimmick.

(*Research*, 2008)

2.2 Intranet / extranet

▶ **Key term**

An **intranet** is a mini-version of the internet accessible only within a company. Intranets can be used for a wide variety of information-sharing purposes. It is an internal network used to share information. Intranets utilise internet technology and protocols. The firewall surrounding an internet fends off unauthorised access.

Intranets use a combination of the organisation's own networked computers and internet technology. Each employee has a browser, used to access a server computer that holds corporate information on a wide variety of topics, and in some cases also offers access to the internet.

Potential applications include company newspapers, induction material, online procedures and policy manuals, employee web pages where individuals post details of their activities and progress, and **internal databases** of the corporate information store.

Most of the **cost** of an intranet is the **staff time** required to set up the system.

The **benefits** of intranets are diverse.

- Savings accrue from the **elimination of storage**, **printing** and **distribution** of documents that can be made available to employees online.

- Documents online are often **more widely used** than those that are kept filed away, especially if the document is bulky (eg training manual) and needs to be searched. This means that there are **improvements in productivity** and **efficiency**.

- It is much **easier to update** information in electronic form.

- Wider access to corporate information should open the way to **more flexible working patterns**, eg material available online may be accessed from remote locations.

An **extranet** is an intranet that is accessible to authorised outsiders.

Whereas an intranet is accessible only to people who are members of the same company or organisation, an extranet provides various levels of accessibility to outsiders.

Only those outsiders with a valid username and password can access an extranet, with varying levels of access rights enabling control over what people can view. Extranets are becoming a very popular means for **business partners to exchange information** for mutual benefit.

Extranets therefore allow better use of the knowledge held by an organisation – by facilitating access to that knowledge.

THE REAL WORLD

Continuous market research providers such as Nielsen and SymphonyIRI rely on extranets to provide faster information as part of an added-value service proposition. Retailers and grocery product manufactures who make up these organisations' core clients log on to dedicated extranet sites using bespoke passwords. Once logged onto the system, they are able to access information based on scanned EPOS data and responses from panels of consumers who scan products they purchase and then proceed to complete lifestyle surveys.

Log onto the general websites and look at the types of services that these organisations offer: http://www.nielsen.com/uk/en and http://www.symphonyiri.co.uk

2.3 IT-influenced data collection

- The capture of transaction data via **barcodes** and scanners is commonplace these days. The combination of Electronic Point of Sale (**EPOS**), Electronic Funds Transfer at Point of Sale (**EFTPOS**) and possibly a **loyalty card** scheme enables individual transactions and individual purchasers to be tracked, identified and linked. This helps to build up a very detailed picture of the buying habits of individual customers, as well as serving the practical purpose of updating stock records and financial accounts.

- Barcode technology is well-established and is especially suitable for retailers, but the capture of data is still so time-consuming and expensive for many organisations that new applications and developments will continue to emerge.

- The **internet** offers the possibility for customers to do all the data entry themselves as well as allowing organisations to track browsing behaviour. You may think that the internet is a familiar tool, but Tim Berners-Lee, the 'inventor' of the World Wide Web, still considers the technology and the possible applications to be at infant stage. Certainly, the developments in web use are one of the key areas to impact businesses; management consultants McKinsey identify it as one of the eight business technological trends to continue to watch (Manyika *et al*, 2008). Web 2.0, social networks and online collaboration are all examples which will be covered later in the text.

- **Voice recognition software** already enables computers to interpret and respond to human speech to a limited extent and the technology is steadily improving.

- Better 'seeing' devices and software will capture **visual information** in ways that computers can interpret. This will enable machines to carry out surveillance, checking and inspection activities with less human supervision.

2.4 Validity & reliability of marketing information

Valid data is data which represents that which it is supposed to; eg if you were collecting information about the number of cars parked within a town during weekends, data collected during weekdays would not be valid.

Reliable data is data which would look similar if it were collected in exactly the same way in the future. In other words, consistent results would be found if there were no other confounding factors. If different researchers conducted the count of cars in a different way (cars stopping for less than a minute being considered 'parked' by one researcher, but only cars which stop for more than ten minutes are defined as 'parked' by another researcher) then the data will not be reliable.

All data collected should be evaluated using the following criteria.

- Is the data relevant to the purpose for which it was collected?
- Is it up-to-date?
- Is it reliable and accurate?
- Is the source of the data credible and objective, or unbiased? Look for the following.

Figure 1.3   Evaluating data

- Is the data subject to confirmation, or comparison with data from other sources? Are you prepared to risk basing decisions on uncorroborated data? The term triangulation refers to the ability to produce similar findings from multiple sources. If once source verifies another, the findings are viewed as more credible.

- Is the data based on a large and representative statistical sample of the relevant population (the group or issue under investigation)?

- Has the data been gathered in a way that makes it meaningful and reliable? Has the same question been put to all respondents? Were all terms consistently defined? Did researchers lead or suggest 'right' answers? Were the respondents influenced by the researcher, or each other, or the desire to be nice?

- Has the data collection and analysis been worthwhile? Has it fulfilled its purposes at a reasonable cost in money, time and effort?

3 Marketing decision support systems

> **Key term**
>
> **Decision support systems** help managers to consider and evaluate alternative answers to problems that cannot be reduced to rules.

Decision support systems are used by management to assist them in making decisions on issues which are not clear-cut. The objective is to allow the manager to consider a number of **alternatives** and **evaluate** them under a variety of potential conditions.

A **marketing decision support system** is a co-ordinated collection of data systems, tools and techniques with supporting **software and hardware** which is used for gathering and interpreting relevant information from the business and its environment, which may be used as a basis for marketing decisions and action. It is used by management to aid decision making on unstructured, complex, uncertain or ambiguous issues.

Figure 1.4   A marketing decision support system

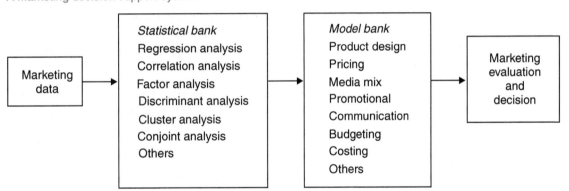

In fact, a simple **spreadsheet** 'what if' model, using data extracted from an accounting package, is one form of decision support tool: you may have devised one of your own without realising how clever you were being! However, there are also many specialised software packages that enable **computer modelling** of **complex marketing management problems**.

A typical marketing decision support system will include internal measures of:

- Sales

- Operational measures (in a car rental chain these may include the rate at which different classes of vehicles are rented out, the frequency of vehicles being unavailable, etc)

- Customer satisfaction levels

- Advertising expenditure

- Customer complaints

- The effectiveness of previous promotional campaigns

- Marketing research reports from previous studies.

The system will also contain external information on the main factors impacting on the marketing environment, competitors and market trends.

4 What is marketing research?

Marketing research is defined by the MRS (2010) as:

'The collection and analysis of data from a sample of individuals or organisations relating to their characteristics, behaviour, attitudes, opinions or possessions. It includes all forms of marketing and social research such as consumer and industrial surveys, psychological investigations, observational and panel studies.'

As you can see and as you might expect, it is much more technical. It covers techniques and sector applications.

Do not worry now if you do not understand terms like 'sample', or 'observational and panel studies'. You will by the time you finish this text!

Less formally the MRS (2010) says that:

'Research is one of the most useful tools in business, any business. It is the way in which organisations find out what their customers and potential customers need, want and care about. This involves the collection and interpretation of confidential data concerning people, products, services and organisations. The key elements in obtaining good research material are that researchers talk to a few people to get the views of many, and that it only works if they talk to the right number of people, ask the right questions and interpret the results correctly.'

Research has a variety of uses, from the testing of new products to employment and customer satisfaction surveys, to social and opinion research. It can help organisations and individuals identify new market areas and assess the scope and potential success of a particular advertising/marketing campaign and develop new policies and future activities.

One of the biggest growth areas for research over the past few years has been in the field of opinion research – understanding more about the public's view on social topics such as politics, the environment, religion, and moral issues.

Wilson (2012) outlined key characteristics of marketing research as a discipline:

- Marketing research provides commercial and non-commercial organisations with information to aid marketing decision making
- Marketing research involves the collection of information using a wide range of sources and techniques.
- Marketing research involves the analysis of information
- Marketing research involves the communication and dissemination of information.

Mintel to examine Chinese consumer behaviour

Mintel is planning to launch a series of monthly reports that examines different aspects of Chinese consumer behaviour. The reports will cover the FMCG, food service, retail and lifestyle sectors and combine primary consumer research with market analysis and data.

Primary research will be conducted in China's tier 1, 2 and 3 cities.

Mintel wants to use the new series of reports to deliver unique insight into the world's most complex and exciting consumer market, so that its global clients can understand, evaluate and anticipate developments in the Chinese consumer marketplace.

(*Research*, 2012)

▶ **Assessment tip**

The December 2008/March 2009 assignment contained a task on the importance of marketing research and database information for your chosen organisation.

- Marketing is the management process responsible for identifying, anticipating and satisfying customer requirements profitably.

- Marketing management involves analysis, planning, implementation and control.

- Managers need information to anticipate changes in demand, introduce, modify or discontinue products and services, evaluate profitability, set prices, undertake promotional activity, plan budgets and control costs.

- Marketing managers use descriptive, comparative and diagnostic information.

- Information and communication technology is changing the way markets are structured and has created new marketing techniques and new marketing channels.

- Decision support systems help managers to consider and evaluate alternative answers to problems that cannot be reduced to rules.

- Marketing research is the gathering and analysis of data relating to market places or customers; any research which leads to more market knowledge and better informed decision making.

FURTHER READING

Chapter 1 of each of the following books:

Bradley, N. (2010) *Marketing research: Tools & techniques*. 2nd edition. Oxford, Oxford University Press.

Wilson, A. (2012) *Marketing research: An integrated approach*. 3rd edition. Harlow, Financial Times Prentice Hall.

REFERENCES

Kotler, P. (1994) *Marketing Management: Analysis, planning, implementation and control*. New Jersey, Prentice Hall.

Manyika, J., Roberts, R. P. and Sprague, K. L. (2008) 'Eight business technology trends to watch'. *McKinsey Quarterly*, 00475394, Issue 1.

Trout, J. (2008) Avoid 'the research trap', author warns. *Research*, http://www.research-live.com/news/avoid-the-research-trap-author-warns/3004656.article [Accessed May 2012].

Verrinder, J. (2012) Mintel to examine Chinese consumer behaviour. *Research*, http://www.research-live.com/news/news-headlines/mintel-to-examine-chinese-consumer-behaviour/4007138.article [Accessed May 2012].

Wilson, A (2012) *Marketing research: An integrated approach,* 3rd edition. Harlow, Financial Times Prentice Hall.

The Chartered
Institute of Marketing

1   Define marketing.
2   What are the four manageable stages involved in marketing management?
3   In what ways does information affect marketing performance?
4   What are the four key strategic questions in marketing management?
5   What is an intranet?
6   What does it mean for data to be valid and reliable?
7   What are decision support systems?
8   What is marketing research?

ACTIVITY DEBRIEFS

Activity 1.1

You probably have a long list which might include the following:

- I am thirsty.
- I am hot.
- I am concerned about the chemical contents of tap water.
- I care for my family.
- I want a healthy lifestyle.
- I am buying packaged water for convenience.
- I am going to the gym and need to rehydrate.
- I like sparkling water with my meal.
- Buying this water says that I am sophisticated.
- I like the taste of this brand.
- I like the new packaging.
- It is cheaper than cola.

Activity 1.2

You will probably find that the information comes from a number of sources and that it is often quite complex pulling this all together. Think about the following example. A marketing executive of a small group of five private dental practices has been asked by the group managing director to monitor levels of patient satisfaction and to report this at monthly practice meetings. The marketing executive has responded to this activity using this aspect of their job.

(a)   What information do you use on a regular basis?

Patient satisfaction information

(b)   Where does this information come from?

(i)   Patient complaints received: online, by letter, verbal complaints recorded on a complaints database, discussions with dentists, nurses, reception staff.

(ii)   Patient satisfaction cards returned in the comments boxes within the practices.

(iii)   Feedback left on the group website and individual practice microsites.

(iv)   Patient numbers including number of visits, returns, length of registration with the practices, number of new patients for each practice.

(c)   What do you use this information for?

Information is processed to lead to direct measures such as the satisfaction cards and complaints received with the rest of the information being used to provide context and less direct indications of satisfaction. Satisfaction levels are monitored to ensure that we are meeting patient needs. As this information is tracked continuously, any issues that may arise within a practice are discovered quickly and the information is also useful to check whether there are any differences in the level of perceived service between practices. Any changes in practices such as redecoration, the introduction of new treatments etc can be monitored and compared with practices which have not undergone any change.

(d)   Who else uses the same information?

Nobody else uses this combination of information as it is processed and presented as a handout and slide to be used within monthly meetings by myself (the marketing executive). The final collation of the information is distributed to all staff members within the five practices via the group intranet. The finance director uses the same source of information used to identify patient numbers as this data also shows sales revenue.

In this example, there are many sources of information used to collect information to address one simple question 'how satisfied are patients each month?'. It is likely that you will have some aspect of your job where you are reliant on a number of diverse sources.

Activity 1.3

Using the same dental practice group as Activity 1.2, the following information needs are plausible examples:

Table 1.3   Sample information requirements

Role of marketing information	Example information needs
Descriptive information	What practice advertising have patients seen in the last six months?
	Where are the nearest competitor practices to our group practices?
	When do patients tend to book appointments?
Comparative information	How similar is the practice equipment compared to our nearest competitor?
	How do satisfaction levels differ between each of the group's practices?
	How regularly do patients attend for checkups compared to NHS patients?
Diagnostic information	Why do patients like to see fish in waiting rooms?
	Why do patients switch between different dentists within the group?
	Why is there not a large uptake of Saturday morning appointment times?

The Chartered Institute of Marketing

1   Marketing is the management process responsible for identifying, anticipating and satisfying customer requirements profitably.

2   Analysis, planning, implementation and control.

3   Increases responsiveness to customer demands, helps to identify new customer opportunities and helps to anticipate competitive attacks and threats.

4   Where are we now, Where do we want to be, How might we get there and How can we ensure arrival?

5   It is a mini-version of the internet accessible only within a company.

6   Valid data is data which represents that which it is supposed to. Reliable data is data which would look similar if it were collected in exactly the same way in the future.

7   Systems that help managers to consider and evaluate alternative answers to problems that cannot be reduced to rules.

8   It is 'the gathering and analysis of data relating to market places or customers; any research which leads to more market knowledge and better-informed decision making'. CIM (2010)

CHAPTER 2

Customer databases and CRM

Introduction

Having examined the importance of information to marketing management, this chapter introduces one of the main tools that is used to store and manage information in modern organisations – the customer database. We will discuss the importance of customer databases and their contribution to providing detailed market information to support marketing decisions. The first section explores the role, application and benefits of customer databases in relation to customer relationship management (CRM).

The second section outlines and explains the different stages in the process of setting up a database. The third section explains the principles of data warehousing, data marts and data mining. The fourth section explains the relationship between database marketing and marketing research.

The final section discusses the legal aspects of data collection and usage, which has significantly affected the activities of the marketing function and the market research industry in recent years.

Topic list

The customer database   ①

Setting up a database   ②

Data warehousing and data mining   ③

Database marketing, user-generated content and marketing research   ④

Data protection legislation   ⑤

2.1	Demonstrate an understanding of the role, application and benefits of customer databases in relation to customer relationship management (CRM):
	■ Types of customer data (behavioural data, volunteered data, attributed data)
	■ Role in profiling customers
	■ Role in marketing intelligence testing campaigns / forecasting
	■ Role in determining lifetime value
	■ Role in personalising offerings and communications
	■ Role in building relationships
2.2	Identify and explain the different stages in the process of setting up a database:
	■ The importance of evaluating software and what is needed to ensure it works properly
	■ Evaluating software
	■ Identifying needs of users of a database
	■ Processing data (formatting, validation, de-duplication)
2.3	Explain the principles of data warehousing, data marts and data mining:
	■ Understanding how databases can be used to select, explore and model large amounts of data to identify relationships and patterns of behaviour
2.4	Explain the relationship between database marketing and marketing research and explain the legal aspects of data collection and usage, including:
	■ Data protection legislation
	■ List brokers
	■ Profilers and their offerings (eg Acorn, Mosaic etc)
	■ Issues involved in merging marketing research and customer database information (transparency, aggregation of data, using customer databases for marketing research purposes)

1 The customer database

1.1 What is a customer database?

> ▶ **Key term**
>
> A **customer database** is 'A manual or computerised source of data relevant to marketing decision making about an organisation's customers.' (Wilson, 2012).
>
> **Database marketing** has been defined as 'an interactive approach to marketing, which uses individually addressable marketing media and channels to extend help to a company's target audience, stimulate their demand and stay close to them by recording and keeping an electronic database memory of customer, prospect, and all communication and commercial contacts, to help them improve all future contacts and to ensure more realistic planning of all marketing.'

Customer databases can contain a wide variety of information about the customer such as **contact details**, **transaction history**, **personal details** and **preferences** and so on. Information may come from a variety of sources besides transaction processing systems, including specialist geodemographic data and lifestyle information.

A marketing database can provide an organisation with much information about its customers and target groups. **Every purchase a customer makes has two information functions.**

- Provision of **sales revenue**
- Provision of **information** as to future market opportunities.

A typical customer database might include the following.

Table 2.1   Typical customer database contents

Element	Examples
Customer or company details	Account numbers, names, addresses and contact (telephone, fax, e-mail) details; basic 'mailing list' data, relationship to other customers. For business customers these fields might include sales contact, technical contact, parent company or subsidiaries, number of employees
Professional details	Company; job title; responsibilities – especially for business-to-business marketing; industry type
Personal details	Sex, age, number of people at the same address, spouse's name, children, interests, and any other relevant data known, such as newspapers read, journals subscribed to
Transaction history	What products/services are ordered, date, how often, how much is spent (turnover), payment methods
Call/contact history	Sales or after-sales service calls made, complaints/queries received, meetings at shows/exhibitions, mailings sent, etc
Credit/payment history	Credit rating, amounts outstanding, aged debts
Credit transaction details	Items currently on order, dates, prices, delivery arrangements
Special account details	Membership number, loyalty or incentive points earned, discount awarded, where customer loyalty or incentive schemes are used

The **sources** of information in a customer database and the **uses** to which it can be put are outlined in Figure 2.1.

Figure 2.1   Inputs and outputs of typical customer database

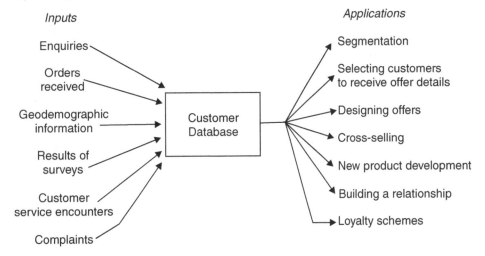

- The **majority of customer information** will be gleaned from the orders they place and the enquiries that they make. A relatively recent development in this area is the combination of cookies or user log-ins and server logging software, which enables **tracking and recording** of a customer's progress through a **website**, perhaps revealing interests that would otherwise have gone unnoticed.

- **Geodemographic** information relates to the characteristics of people living in different areas. Even simple postcode information can contain a lot of data about the customer.

- **Customer service** can be used to indicate particular concerns of customers. For example, in a DIY store, if customers have to ask service staff where items are stored, the volume of complaints might indicate poor signage and labelling.

- **Complaints** also indicate deficiencies in the product or the fact that customer expectations have been poorly communicated.

- The specific information held may **vary by type of market**. For example, an industrial database will hold data on key purchasers, influencers and decision makers, organisational structure, industry classification (SIC codes), and business size.

1.2   Types of customer data

Customer data can be categorised into four groups:

- **Behavioural data** which is collected by the organisation as a result of their interactions with the customer eg contact records, letters, complaints, competition entries, orders, payments, online enquiries, tracked web pages visited, discussion forums used, loyalty or membership cards swiped, etc

- **Volunteered data** is generated when customers complete forms, register with websites, request more information and provide their own details, respond to calls for more information, agree to be contacted by relevant third parties and update their online profiles.

- **Attributed data** is data generated as a result of a specific research project. This information is confidential and therefore individual respondents cannot be added to a database using their personal identity. The results of a research study, however, can be used to add more detail to your database. For example, a charity may have conducted some research into the type of communications message that is most likely to elicit a response from different groups of potential donors. If, for example, they found that a plea for help worked well with mothers aged between 20 and 40 years of age, then they could place a code next to individuals within that group on their database to show that they are best communicated using that type of message; professional men aged 40–50 may have been found to respond more to altruistic appeals and therefore males fitting this profile could be tagged accordingly. The next time the charity sent a piece of direct mail, they could then adapt their tone and send more targeted messages to the individuals on their database.

- **Profile data** is collected when it is linked with data from another source eg lifestyle databases purchased, corporate databases, geodemographic profiles. Profiling is explored in more detail later in the chapter.

  Databases may be populated by information that the organisation collects for itself or through information that is hired or purchased from data providers.

1.3   Benefits of customer databases

Databases can provide **valuable information** to marketing management.

- Computer databases make it easier to collect and store more **data/information**.

- Computer software allows the data to be **extracted** from the file and **processed** to provide whatever information that management needs.

- In some cases businesses may have access to the databases of **external organisations**. Reuters, for example, provides an online information system about money market interest rates and foreign exchange rates to firms involved in money market and foreign exchange dealings, and to the treasury departments of a large number of companies.

Other benefits of database systems might include:

- Increased **sales and/or market share** (due to enhanced lead follow-up, cross-selling, customer contact)
- Increased **customer retention** (through better targeting)
- Better use of **resources** (targeting, less duplication of information handling).

The Chartered Institute of Marketing

Databases enable marketing managers to improve their decision making, by:

- **Understanding customers** and their preferences
- Managing **customer service** (helplines, complaints)
- Understanding the **market** (new products, channels etc)
- Understanding **competitors** (market share, prices)
- Managing **sales operations**
- Managing **marketing campaigns**
- **Communicating** with customers.

A database built for marketing purposes will, like the marketing function itself, be **future orientated**. It will be possible to **exploit** the database to **drive future marketing programmes**, not just glory in what has happened in the past.

Find out what type(s) of database your organisation (or college) uses, and for what applications. If possible, get access to the database and browse through the index, directory or switchboard to see what databases/catalogues contain what database files or tables, queries, reports and forms, with what fields. If you can't get access to a database at work, try the local library, where you may find that the 'index card' system has been computerised as a database. Or use an internet search engine or browser to interrogate some online databases.

1.4 Database applications

The range of database applications include:

- Focusing on prime prospects
- Evaluating new prospects
- Cross-selling related products
- Launching new products to potential prospects
- Identifying new distribution channels
- Building customer loyalty
- Converting occasional users to regular users
- Generating enquiries and follow-up sales
- Targeting niche markets.

The most valuable information in a customer-focused organisation is its knowledge of its customers. The customer database has two uses in such an organisation:

- **Operational support** (for example, when a telephone banking employee checks that the password given by a caller is correct before giving out details of the account)

- **Analytical uses** (the analysis by the same bank of the customers who receive a certain amount into their account each month and so may be targeted with personal loans or other offers)

The database may be applied to meet a variety of objectives with numerous advantages over traditional marketing methods.

1.4.1 Identifying the most profitable customers

The Italian economist Vilfredo Pareto was the first to observe that in human affairs, 20% of the events result in 80% of the outcomes. This has become known as Pareto's law, or the 80/20 principle. It shows up quite often in marketing. For example, 20% of the effort you put into promotion may generate 80% of the sales revenue. Whatever the precise proportions, it is true that in general a small number of existing customers are 'heavy users' of a product or service and generate a high proportion of sales revenue, buying perhaps four times as much as a 'light user'.

A customer database which allows purchase frequency and value-per-customer to be calculated indicates to the marketer who the potential heavy users are, and therefore where the promotional budget can most profitably be spent.

1.4.2 Identifying buying trends

By tracking purchases per customer (or customer group) you may be able to identify:

- **Loyal repeat customers** who cost less to retain than new customers cost to find and attract

- **'Backsliding'** or lost customers, who have reduced or ceased the frequency or volume of their purchases. These may be a useful diagnostic sample for market research into declining sales or failing customer care.

- **Seasonal** or local purchase patterns (heavier consumption of soup in England in winter, for example).

- **Demographic purchase patterns**. These may be quite unexpected. Lower-income consumers might buy top-of-the-range products, which they value and save for. Prestige and luxury goods, which marketers promote largely to affluent white-collar consumers, are also purchased by students, secretaries and young families, who have been dubbed 'Ultra Consumers' because they transcend demographic clusters.

- Purchase patterns in response to **promotional campaigns**. Increased sales volume or frequency following promotions is an important measurement of their effectiveness.

1.4.3 Identifying marketing opportunities

More detailed information (where available) on customer likes and dislikes, complaints, feedback and lifestyle values may offer useful information for:

- **Product** improvement

- **Customer care** and quality programmes

- New **product development**

- **Decision making** across the marketing mix: on prices, product specifications, distribution channels, promotional messages.

Simple data fields such as 'contact type' will help to evaluate how contact is made with customers, of what types and in what numbers. Business leads may be generated most often by trade conferences and exhibitions, light users by promotional competitions and incentives, and loyal customers by personal contact through representatives.

Customers can be investigated using any data field included in the database: How many are on e-mail or have access to the internet? How many have spouses or children? Essentially, these parameters allow the marketer to **segment** the customer base for marketing purposes.

THE REAL WORLD

Counting footfall electronically

Electronic footfall counting technology begins by answering the retailer's most basic question 'What is actually driving our business: are changes in the volume of sales the consequence of a rise / fall in footfall levels or changes in the percentage of shoppers that make a purchase?' The system measures and reports upon customer numbers entering stores, building a factual picture of footflow for the retailer, hour-by-hour, week-by-week, month-by-month, year-on-year. Offered by Synovate subsidiary, Retail Performance, one system monitors more than 1.1 billion visits to over 6,500 retail premises and operating in more than 20 markets across Europe, the Americas and Asia Pacific.

(Ipsos, 2012)

The Chartered
Institute of Marketing

1.4.4 Using database information

The following is a summary of the main ways in which database information can be used.

- **Direct mail** can be used to:
    - Maintain customer contact between (or instead of) sales calls
    - Generate leads and 'warmed' prospects for sales calls
    - Promote and/or sell products and services direct to customers
    - Distribute product or service information

- **Transaction processing**. Databases can be linked to programmes which generate order confirmations, despatch notes, invoices, statements and receipts.

- **Marketing research and planning**. The database can be used to send out market surveys, and may itself be investigated to show purchasing patterns and trends.

- **Contacts planning**. The database can indicate which customers need to be contacted or given incentives to maintain their level of purchase and commitment. A separate database may similarly be used to track planned and ongoing contacts at conferences and trade shows and invitation lists to marketing events.

- **Product development and improvement**. Product purchases can be tracked through the product life cycle, and weaknesses and opportunities identified from records of customer feedback, complaints and warranty/guarantee claims.

1.4.5 Profiling customers and prospects

Building **accurate** and **up-to-date profiles** of customers enables the company to **extend help** to a company's **target audience**, to stimulate further demand, and to stay close to them. The company's own information can be enriched by collating it with geodemographic and lifestyle information from sources such as ACORN.

As we have seen, a database is a collection of available information on past and current customers together with future prospects, structured to allow for the implementation of effective marketing strategies.

Database marketing is a customer-oriented approach to marketing, and its special power lies in the techniques it uses to harness the capabilities of computer and telecommunications technology. Building **accurate and up-to-date profiles** of customers enables the company:

- To extend **help** to a company's target audience
- To **stimulate further demand**
- To **stay close** to their customers.

Keeping an electronic database of customers and prospects (and of all communications and commercial contacts) helps to improve all future contacts.

ACTIVITY 2.2

Explore the ACORN site from CACI (http://www.caci.co.uk/acorn-classification.aspx) and look at some of the tools they have available for marketers.

Then look at the government's database for national statistics (http://www.statistics.gov.uk/hub/index.html); look at 'regional statistics' section, then at 'local profile' and see how much information you can obtain for an area known to you – your home postcode, for example, or your office location. Check out education levels, numbers of crimes, income levels, etc. Being aware of what information is available – and where to access it quickly – can be of great value to the efficient marketer!

1.5 Customer relationship management and databases

Databases provide valuable **information** to assist with many marketing management tasks and decisions and can play a key part in **customer relationship management** because they permit **mass customisation**.

CRM is now commonly used as a label for marketing management software products. More precisely, however, customer relationship management consists of:

- Helping an enterprise to **identify** and **target** its **best customers**, manage marketing campaigns with clear goals and objectives, and generate quality leads

- **Allowing** the **formation of relationships** with **customers**, with the aim of **improving customer satisfaction** and **maximising profits**; identifying the most profitable customers and providing them with the highest level of service

- **Providing employees** with the **information** and **processes necessary** to know their customers, understand their needs, and effectively build relationships between the company, its customer base, and distribution partners

- Assisting the organisation to improve **sales**, **account**, and **sales management** by **optimising information shared**, and **streamlining existing processes** (for example, taking orders using mobile devices)

- Measuring and anticipating the lifetime value of customers.

The **database** is clearly key to CRM. For example, an enterprise might build a database about its customers that describes relationships in enough detail to allow management, salespeople, service staff and maybe customers themselves to access information, match customer needs with product plans, remind customers of service requirements and know what other products a customer had purchased, and so on.

The result is something called **mass customisation**, in which a large number of customers can be reached, but simultaneously these customers can be treated **individually**. It has been remarked how the traditional values of the 'corner shop' are returning with the resurgence of relationship marketing and customer focus.

THE REAL WORLD

Sainsbury's: 'Nectar data makes our c-stores stronger than rivals'

Sainsbury's believes Nectar data will set it above the competition in the increasingly competitive convenience market, as it will help shape marketing, product and store performance.

Speaking at the IGD Convenience conference yesterday (9 November) Helen Buck, convenience director at Sainsbury's, says that by using Nectar data, the retailer can understand customers and respond quickly in a way that other convenience retailers can't. She said: "There is lots of competition going on, we know that everyone is trying to up their game and watching Morrisons and Waitrose to see what they're doing. We are confident that we have some elements in our armoury that the others don't. "We're not complacent, but we're confident that we will retain a strong place in the UK convenience market."

Sainsbury's spends £150m a year on trying to understand its customers' behaviour and product and store performance through Nectar data and uses it to respond through local marketing, product development and cross promoting.

The supermarket, which currently operates around 400 c-stores, is opening 1 to 2 convenience outlets each week and says its £1bn small format division is growing at twice the rate of the rest of the business, which reported 1.9% like for like sales growth in the first half of the year. The IGD expects the convenience market to grow to £42.2bn in the next five years.

(*Marketing Week*, 2011)

The Chartered Institute of Marketing

Companies such as Tesco and Sainsburys, who use their database effectively, do so because they specifically target individual customers based on their behaviour. If you purchase anything through Amazon.com, note how quickly they are able to suggest other products you may like.

2 Setting up a database

Modern business databases are maintained on a central computer to enable **sharing of data** and avoid duplication. A typical relational database consists of a number of inter-related tables of records and fields.

A database need not be computerised. A paper address book that you keep in your briefcase is a form of database and so is a card index. However most modern business databases will be created and maintained **centrally on a computer**. This is obviously the most efficient method where **large amounts of data** are involved and for several important additional reasons:

- **Common data** for all users to share

- Avoidance of **data duplication** in files kept by different users

- **Consistency** in the organisation's use of data, and in the accuracy and up-to-dateness of data accessed by different users, because all records are centrally maintained and updated

- **Flexibility** in the way in which shared data can be queried, analysed and formatted by individual users for specific purposes, without altering the store of data itself

- **Speed** of data retrieval.

The collection of computer programs that process data is more properly referred to as a **database management system (DBMS)**.

Basic features of database packages allow you to readily perform the following activities:

- **Find particular records**, using any data item you know

- **Sort records alphabetically**, numerically or by date, in ascending or descending order

- **Interrogate records**, generating the selection of records based on a complex set of criteria, from one or more linked tables. (For example, you might specify that you want all customer records where the field 'City' equals London or Birmingham and where the field 'Product' equals Widget and where the field 'Purchase Date' is between January 2011 and January 2012. The query would generate a table consisting of customers in London and Birmingham who purchased Widgets in 2011.)

- **Calculate and count** data entries. For example if you wanted to find out how many customers had purchased each product, you could run a query that asked the database to group the data by the field 'product' and then count by field 'customer ID': it would count the number of distinct customer ID numbers linked to each product. You could also ask to 'sum' or add up all the values in a field: total number of purchases, or total purchase value.

- **Format** selected data for a variety of uses, as reports, forms, mailing labels, charts and diagrams.

2.1 User requirements and evaluating software

There may be a number of different users of the database management system, possibly within different departments. For example, a telecommunications company may have a basic marketing database with details of their home broadband customers. This database may have details such as:

- Name and contact details
- Duration of contract
- Interactions with the company such as calls to helpdesk, customer complaints, enquiries, changes in package
- Details of phone, mobile, mobile broadband suppliers used
- Payment details.

From looking at just this one brief example you may have realised that a number of departments within the organisation will find the information useful. The sales department may find it helpful to see if they could cross-sell other products. The customer services department may need the information to maintain customer satisfaction levels. The finance department may need the information to ensure that payments are processed efficiently. It is important therefore that from the outset, the objectives, needs and uses of the database are made clear and the software available is able to meet user demands. Frequently, the format that information can be obtained in may not be useful for all users and so an agreed **specification of requirements** should be made.

Software used for database applications should be evaluated for:

- Compatibility with existing software applications (eg you may wish to import and export data between applications)

- Ability to provide the required reporting formats

- Ease of use, bearing in mind the users of the system

- Software support and training

- Impact of the implementation of the software (eg will it be easily integrated into the existing working practices or will it be a complete change in procedures, causing significant disruption for a period)

- Ease of ongoing maintenance, updates and future-proofing.

In recent years, there has also been a growing willingness among people to express themselves in public and in the process reveal their habits, purchases and opinions. This has led to the significant growth in the amount of 'user-generated content' that is available to marketers. User-generated content involves the production of content by members of the public on the internet, usually in the form of personal opinion, daily news, ideas, photos and videos that are published as blogs and wikis on social networks, online communities and product / service review sites. For example, news organisations like CNN and BBC now invite their listeners to submit their own news, images and videos on breaking stories or other issues of interest. Social networks like Facebook, Twitter, Flickr, LinkedIn and You Tube provide an avenue for organisations to interact with customers in order to better understand their needs. Gone are the days when organisations monopolised the conversation in the public arena, customers are now able to talk back using online media channels that can reach thousands and potentially millions. The information that they put out represents an additional source of vital market research data.

2.2   Key components

There are two basic kinds of **computerised** database.

- A **flat file system** lumps all the data into single file. A single worksheet in a spreadsheet is an example.

- A **relational database system** allows greater flexibility and storage efficiency by splitting the data up into a number of tables, which are linked and can be integrated as necessary. For example, one table may contain customer names and another customers' payment histories. A linking field such as a customer ID number would allow the user to interrogate both tables and generate an integrated report on a particular customer's purchases and payments, or a list of customers who had made multiple purchases, or a list of those with a poor payment record.

Flat systems are easy to build and maintain, and are quite adequate for applications such as mailing lists or membership databases. **Relational systems** integrate a wider range of business functions, for invoicing, accounting, inventory and marketing analysis: they are, however, complicated to develop and use properly. If your organisation already operates a relational system, learn how to use it. If you are required to set up or build a relational system, get help: use a 'wizard' or template (in the database package) or ask an expert, at least the first time.

All databases have some kind of structure, otherwise you would never be able to retrieve information from them. For instance, a telephone directory stores entries in alphabetical order. Computer database packages store data as follows.

- **Fields** are the labels given to types of data. A simple customer database, for example, might include fields such as: Title, First name, Last name, Address fields, and other contact details. The fields are the **columns** in a tabular database.

- **Records** are the collection of fields relevant to one entry. So all the above data fields for a particular customer make up one customer record. The records are the **rows** in a tabular database.

Figure 2.2   Rows of a typical customer database

ID	Title	First name	Last name	Address 1	Address 2	Address 3	City	County	Postcode	Country	Telephone	Fax	Email
1	Mr	Kieran	Davies	25 Dill Street	Merton		London		SW17 4QF	UK	020 7884 1122		kieran.davis@virgin.net
2	Mrs	Shagura	Jumal	37 Nelson Road	Trafford		Manchester		M41 2BD	UK	01584 452291		sjumal@freeserve.com

- **Tables** are collections of records that describe similar data. All the customer records for a particular region or product may be stored in one table.

- **Databases** are collections of all the tables relating to a particular set of information. So your customer database may include tables for various regions, products and customer contacts.

2.3 Data cleansing

> **▶ Key term**
>
> **Data cleansing** is the process of amending or removing data in a database that is incorrect, out of date, incomplete, improperly formatted, or duplicated.

A key issue in setting up a database is **data cleansing**: ensuring that the information is correct, up-to-date and not duplicated. Much can be done at the data entry stage, but where data is imported from other systems a good deal of preparatory work may be needed to ensure that it is in the correct format.

Information systems are only valuable if they give **good** information, and that depends crucially on the accuracy of the data.

A typical organisation will have many years' worth of potentially valuable information and this will have got into the system in a variety of ways.

- It may have been typed in by hand – correctly or incorrectly
- It may have been scanned in from paper documents, but this depends on how good the scanning process is (accurate scanning of ordinary text has only been possible for a few years)
- It may have arisen from EPOS and EFTPOS systems
- It may have been imported from other systems in other parts of the organisation – perhaps in an incompatible format
- It may have been purchased from another organisation (for instance a mailing list broker) or have arisen as a result of a merger between two organisations.

All of these methods are liable to lead to incorrect, out-of-date, incomplete, improperly formatted, or duplicated data that needs to be 'cleansed'.

2.4 Cleansing new data

2.4.1 Form elements

A great deal can be done to ensure that **new data is clean** at the time when it is initially entered into a system. For instance, computerised forms for data entry can contain a variety of elements that help to avoid human error and bad data. These **pre-define the acceptable responses** and simply require the user to select the appropriate option rather than type anything.

- **Radio buttons** force the user to choose one and only one of a number of options.

Figure 2.3   Radio buttons

Would you like to receive further information?

○ Yes

○ No

- **Check boxes** typically allow more than one choice, but still from a limited range of options

Figure 2.4   Check boxes

Which newspaper(s) do you read every day?

☐ Financial Times

☐ Guardian

☐ Telegraph

☐ Mirror

- **List boxes** operate in a similar way to either radio buttons or check boxes, but the selectable option or options drop down instead of being written out (this saves space on screen).

Figure 2.5   Drop-down options

2.4.2 Validation

Validation is the application of pre-programmed tests and rules by the data entry program to make sure that **typed data input** is reasonable.

There are a number of different types of computer controls for validating a user's typed entries. Here are some examples.

- **Format checks** test the data in each input area against rules governing whether it should be numeric, alphabetic or a combination of the two and whether it should have a minimum or maximum number of characters. For example, the software would not allow alphabetic characters to be entered in a box designated for a telephone number. It would check an e-mail address to ensure that it contained the @ symbol and at least one full stop.

- **Range checks** test that the data is within an appropriate range, for example no products are priced at less than £10 or more than £100. This will prevent somebody keying in the price of a customer purchase for £22.99 as £2,299 in error. These checks can also be applied to dates: for instance, you should not be able to enter a date of birth of 31 February, or enter an 'account opened' date in 2013 if it is 2012.

- **Existence checks** compare the input data with some other piece of data in the system, to see if it is reasonable. For example a customer code might be compared with an existing list of customer records. If the code exists there will be no reason to duplicate data already entered. If the code does not exist the computer would give you the options of amending the code you entered (in case you typed it wrongly) or of creating a new customer account. Deliberately incorrect entries can also be prevented, or at least

discouraged, by this means: for instance the system may query a customer name entered as 'Mickey Mouse', although some kind of override will be necessary, in case that really is the customer's name.

- **Completeness checks** ensure that all required data items have been entered. For example if the system requires a contact telephone number you will not be able to save a record until you provide one.

2.4.3 Verification

Verification is the **comparison** of **input** data with the **source** document. Computers can't yet see in the way that humans can but they can encourage the person entering the data to check the accuracy of their inputs. For instance, if the user enters a post code the computer may automatically display a street name and a range of house numbers. If the displayed information is not the same as the information that appears in the data source this should alert the user that either he or she has made a mistake or the source data is unreliable.

2.5 Cleansing imported data

2.5.1 Format and consistency

Suppose you **acquire an existing database** of customer addresses arranged with fields for:

Title, Last Name, First Name, House Number, Street Name, Town, City, Postcode

Your own database may have fields for:

Title, First Name, Last Name, Address1, Address2, Address 3, Postcode

On the face of it the information is the same in both databases but there are small differences that will make it **impossible to 'cut and paste'** the acquired data into your existing data without some cleansing work.

In this example the order of the fields is slightly different, and the acquired database has two fields for your 'Address1' field. Even if you succeed in importing the new data much of it will end up in the wrong field as far as your database is concerned and produce nonsense results when analysed.

Similar problems will arise if the data you want to import includes options that are **not allowed** in your database (a title of 'Prof.' or 'Lord', say), or if the **maximum size** of the Last Name field is 100 characters in one database and 50 characters in the other, or if **dates** are in US format (MM/DD/YYYY) in the new data but UK format (DD/MM/YYYY) in yours, or even if tiny things like **spacing** or **punctuation** (eg DD.MM.YYYY) are different or if **foreign characters** are used.

Computerised databases are sensitive to differences in format in a way that human beings are not, because they need to **store** information as **efficiently** as possible for subsequent **high-speed analysis**. Before you can import data into your own database you need to ensure that it is in a format (the same order, the same field size and so on) that is consistent with your existing data. This can often involve a **considerable amount of preparatory work**.

A technology called **XML** is likely to alleviate many formatting problems, but most organisations have only just started down this path.

2.5.2 De-duplication

Duplication of entries in your database is one of the best ways of annoying your customers! Suppose your database contains a record for Mrs Jane Wordingham and another for Ms J. Wordingham. If you send 'both' of these people the same mailshot you may successfully reach two different customers ... or you may strongly irritate one.

Duplication can occur for a variety of reasons.

- The data may have been **acquired** from another part of the organisation, or from another organisation such as a list broker, and be recorded slightly differently. Different systems ask for different information (eg 'Initial' as opposed to 'First Name').

- **People are inconsistent** in the data they provide. For instance they may generally include their 'Town' when providing their address, but leave it out if they are in a hurry.

- Even if data is read in **automatically**, from a credit card, say, there is nothing to prevent someone using **more than one credit card** and having slightly different versions of their personal information on each.

Fortunately, it is usually a fairly simple matter to **identify duplicates**. The software should be able to **compare a common field** such as post code and either **delete** duplicates **automatically** or **generate a report** for further investigation. This may be more problematic in business-to-business marketing, where several different businesses may operate out of the same location, or the same business may operate out of multiple locations.

2.6 Database maintenance

A customer database should be **regularly and systematically** maintained.

- **New fields** can be added to the database design as new types of information become available.

- Any **updated, altered or new information** should be entered in the database: changes of address, customer status, product interests.

- Names which have received **no response** after a certain period of time or number of contacts, should be **deleted**.

- If mailshots are **returned to the sender**, they will often be marked with the reason for non-delivery: no longer at this address, not known at this address. Whenever this happens addresses and names should be checked, and amended if possible (common errors include misspelt names, missing lines of the address, or the wrong company name).

- **Requests from customers** to have their **details erased** from the database should be honoured. This is a **legal requirement**.

- Maintaining the functionality of the database as it grows will also need careful consideration and significant IT support. Over time, if new applications are found or additional inputs from alternative sources are available, the database may require restructuring. For this reason, making sure requirements are well defined from the start can help to future-proof the database and ensure compatibility between software programs.

---

3 Data warehousing and data mining

▶ **Key term**

Data warehousing involves extracting information from disparate organisational sources to build a coherent set of information available to be used across the organisation for management analysis and decision making. On-line analytical processing (OLAP) techniques allow the data to be viewed from many different perspectives.

Two techniques designed to utilise the **ever-increasing amounts of data** held by organisations are data warehousing and data mining.

3.1 Data warehousing

Data warehousing involves a centrally stored source of data that has been extracted from various organisational databases and standardised and integrated for use throughout an organisation. Data warehouses contain a wide variety of data that present a coherent picture of business conditions at a single point in time.

A data warehouse contains data from a range of internal (eg sales order processing system, nominal ledger) and external sources. If necessary, the user can drilldown to access transaction level detail. Data is increasingly obtained from newer channels such as customer care systems, outside agencies or websites.

The Chartered Institute of Marketing

Figure 2.6   Components of a data warehouse

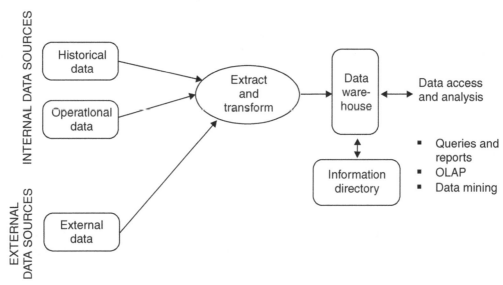

Data is copied to the data warehouse as often as required – usually daily, weekly or monthly. The process of making any required changes to the format of data and copying it to the warehouse is usually automated.

The result should be a coherent set of information available to be used across the organisation for management analysis and decision making. The reporting and query tools available within the warehouse should facilitate management reporting and analysis.

The reporting and query tools should be flexible enough to allow multi-dimensional data analysis, also known as on-line analytical processing (**OLAP**). Each aspect of information (eg product, region, price, budgeted sales, actual sales, time period etc) represents a different dimension. OLAP enables data to be viewed from each dimension, allowing each aspect to be viewed and in relation to the other aspects.

3.1.1 Data marts

Organisations may build a single central data warehouse to serve the entire organisation, or may create a series of smaller **data marts**. A data mart holds a selection of the organisation's data for a specific purpose.

A data mart can be constructed more quickly and cheaply than a data warehouse. However, if too many individual data marts are built, organisations may find it is more efficient to have a single data warehouse serving all areas.

3.1.2 Advantages of data warehouses and data marts

Advantages of setting up a data warehouse or data mart include the following.

- Decision makers can access data without affecting the use of operational systems.

- Having a wide range of data available to be queried easily encourages the taking of a wide perspective on organisational activities.

- Data warehouses have proved successful in some businesses for:

    - Quantifying the effect of marketing initiatives
    - Improving knowledge of customers
    - Identifying and understanding an enterprise's most profitable revenues streams.

Some organisations have found they have invested considerable resources implementing a data warehouse for little return. To benefit from the information a data warehouse can provide, organisations need to be flexible and prepared to act on what they find. If a warehouse system is implemented simply to follow current practice, it will be of little value.

Dunnhumby is the agency behind the interrogation of the massive Tesco Clubcard database containing purchase behaviour information of 13 million UK households.

When consumers make a purchase in store, online or through Tesco's partners in the scheme, information is stored and analysed in order to make decisions. Dunnhumby also sell analysis to manufacturer brands and will interrogate the data according to a specific brands needs.

(Dunnhumby, 2012)

3.2 Data mining

Data mining software examines the data in a database or data warehouse and discovers previously unknown relationships using complex statistical techniques. The hidden patterns and relationships the software identifies can be used to guide decision making and to predict future behaviour.

Data mining is a class of database applications that look for hidden patterns in a group of data. For example, data mining software can help retail companies find customers with common interests. The term is commonly misused to describe software that presents data in new ways. True data mining software does not just change the presentation, but actually discovers previously unknown relationships among the data. This can be used to guide decision making and to **predict future behaviour**.

The types of relationships or patterns that data mining may uncover may be classified as follows.

Table 2.2   Possible results of data mining

Relationship/Discovery	Comment
Classification or cluster	These terms refer to the identification of patterns within the database between a range of data items. For example, data mining may find that unmarried males aged between 20 and 30, who have an income above £50,000, are more likely to purchase a high performance sports car than people from other demographic groups. This group could then be targeted when marketing material is produced/distributed.
Association	One event can be linked or correlated to another event.
Forecasting	Trends are identified within the data that can be extrapolated into the future.

Most data mining models are either:

- **Predictive**: using known observations to predict future events (for example, predicting the probability that a recipient will opt out of an e-mail list)

- **Descriptive**: interrogating the database to identify patterns and relationships (for example, profiling the audience of a particular advertising campaign).

Some of the key statistical techniques used in data mining are described below.

- **Neural networks**: non-linear predictive models or formulas that adjust inputs and weightings through 'training'

- **Decision trees**: paths are followed towards a solution or result, branching at decision points which are governed by rules (is gender male? Yes/No) giving a complex picture of possible outcomes

- **Classification techniques**: assigning people to predetermined classes based on their profile data (in complex combinations)

- **Clustering**: identifying occurrences in the database with similar characteristics and grouping them into clusters.

Why might competitive pressures encourage data mining?

4 Database marketing, user-generated content and marketing research

Marketing managers must make a **distinction** between **information collected** in the **ordinary course of business** and **information collected via marketing research**. It is not acceptable to incorporate personal information derived from marketing research directly into a customer's record.

As we shall see in the next chapter when we discuss ethical and social responsibilities and codes of conduct, information collected by means of **marketing research** should **not be used** subsequently to create marketing databases that are used for **direct marketing**. Likewise direct marketing initiatives should not be disguised as marketing research, and customers should be given the opportunity to refuse to allow information they give you to be used for direct marketing purposes.

As a slightly frivolous example, let's say you discover, through the responses of willing participants in a **marketing research** study, that 87% of people who are over a certain weight prefer your company's Product A to Product B. That is probably useful information and it may legitimately be used for **general marketing purposes** such as designing advertising messages or choosing distribution outlets.

However, even though you may know that a particular customer of yours (who took part in the research) is not yet a purchaser of Product A, and you now know that he fits the weight criteria, it is considered **unethical** to add that specific data (the customer's weight) to that specific customer's record, and less ethical still to bombard him with brochures about Product A as a result of information that was not given to you with that purpose in mind. To do so would contravene the MRS Code of Conduct and not be compliant with data protection laws.

It is only acceptable to enrich a customer database with marketing research information so long as **personal data** is represented in an **anonymous** form and is **partly aggregated**.

▶ **Assessment tip**

The June 2010/September 2010 assignment contained a task on the importance to the organisation of having a customer database.

The availability of user-generated content posted on social media sites (Facebook & LinkedIn), blogs, micro-blogs (Twitter) and video-sharing sites (YouTube, Vimeo and Blip.tv) in recent years has provided valuable information that researchers can use to support market research data. User-generated content should also only be used to enrich a customer database as long as personal data is presented in an anonymous form and is partly aggregated.

5 Data protection legislation

Marketing researchers depend on the trust of their respondents. Most developed countries have **specific legislation** to **protect the privacy of individuals**. In the UK there is the Data Protection Act 1998 which establishes eight data protection principles.

Many people feel unhappy about their personal details being retained by commercial organisations. Here are some of the concerns that people have.

- **Incorrect details** may be entered, causing anything from minor irritation to significant financial problems
- A list or database may be **sold** to other organisations, who then try to sell various goods and services to the people on it
- 'Personalised' mailings may be **inappropriate** – they might be generated for people who have died, for instance.

5.1 The Data Protection Act 1998

Data protection legislation was introduced in the UK in the early 1980s to try to prevent some of these abuses. The latest version is the **Data Protection Act 1998**.

The Act is concerned with **'personal data'**, which is information about **living, identifiable individuals**. This can be as little as a name and address: it need not be particularly sensitive information. If it is sensitive (explained later) then extra care is needed.

The Act gives individuals (**data subjects**) certain rights and it requires those who record and use personal information (**data controllers**) to be open about their use of that information and to follow 'sound and proper practices' (the Data Protection Principles).

5.2 The eight data protection principles

Data must be:

- Fairly and lawfully processed
- Processed for limited purposes
- Adequate, relevant and not excessive
- Accurate
- Not kept longer than necessary
- Processed in accordance with individual's rights
- Secure
- Not transferred to countries that do not have adequate data protection laws.

If your organisation holds personal information about living individuals on computer or has such information processed on computer by others (for example, a data analysis or database agency) your organisation probably needs to 'notify' under the Data Protection Act 1998.

'Notify' means that the organisation has to complete a form about the data it holds and how it is used and send it, with an annual registration fee, to the office of the Information Commissioner.

The Data Protection Act 1998 also covers some records held in **paper** form. These do not need to be notified to the Commissioner, but they should also be handled in accordance with the data protection principles. A set of **index cards** for a personnel system is a typical example of paper records that fall under the Data Protection Act 1998.

The Chartered
Institute of Marketing

5.2.1 Fair processing, for limited purposes

These two principles mean that when an organisation collects information from individuals it should be **honest and open** about why it wants the information and it should have a **legitimate reason** for processing the data. For instance, organisations should explain:

- Who they are
- What they intend to use the information for
- Who, if anybody, they intend to give the personal data to.

5.2.2 Adequate, relevant and not excessive; accurate and no longer than necessary

Organisations should hold **neither too much nor too little** data about the individuals in their list. For instance, many companies collect date of birth or age range information from their customers, but in many cases all they actually need to know is that they are over eighteen.

Personal data should be **accurate and up-to-date** as far as possible. However, if an individual provides inaccurate information (for example lies about their age) the organisation would not normally be held to account for this.

There are only exceptional circumstances where personal data should be kept indefinitely. Data should be **removed when it is no longer required** for audit purposes or when a customer ceases to do business with you.

5.2.3 The rights of data subjects

Individuals have various rights including the following.

- The right to **be informed** of all the information held about them by an organisation

- The right to **prevent** the processing of their data for the purposes of direct marketing

- The right to **compensation** if they can show that they have been caused damage by any contravention of the Act

- The right to have any inaccurate data about them **removed** or **corrected**.

Organisations have obligations if they receive a **written request** from an individual asking to see what data it holds about them, or to obtain a copy of it, or to be given an explanation of what it is used for, or who it is given to. The organisation must deal with the request promptly, and in any case within 40 days. The organisation is entitled, if it wishes, to ask for a fee of (usually) not more than £10 in which case the 40 days does not begin until this is received.

5.2.4 Security

Organisations should make sure that they provide **adequate security** for the data, taking into account the nature of the data, and the possible harm to the individual that could arise if the data is disclosed or lost they need.

- Measures to ensure that **access** to computer records **by staff** is authorised (for instance a system of passwords).

- Measures to control **access** to records by **people other than staff**. For instance, care should be taken over the siting of computers to prevent casual callers to the organisation's premises being able to read personal data on screen. Also there should be procedures to verify the identity of callers (especially telephone callers) seeking information about an individual.

- Measures to prevent of the **accidental loss or theft** of personal data, for example backups and fire precautions.

5.2.5 Overseas transfers

If an organisation wishes to transfer personal data to a country **outside the European Economic Area (EEA)** it will either need to ensure there is adequate protection (eg a Data Protection Act) for the data in the receiving country, or obtain the consent of the individual.

All countries in the EEA already have suitable protection.

5.3 Sensitive data

The Act defines eight categories of sensitive personal data. If an organisation holds personal data falling into these categories it is likely that it will **need the explicit consent** of the individual concerned. It will also need to ensure that its security is adequate for the protection of sensitive data.

Here are the eight categories.

- The racial or ethnic origin of data subjects
- Their political opinions
- Their religious beliefs or other beliefs of a similar nature
- Whether they are a member of a trade union
- Their physical or mental health or condition
- Their sexual life
- The commission or alleged commission by them of any offence
- Any details of court proceedings or sentences against them.

5.4 Enforcement

If an organisation is breaching the principles of the Act, the Commissioner has various powers to force it to comply, including issuing an enforcement notice, and the power to enter and search their premises and examine equipment and documents. It is an offence to obstruct the Commissioner, and there are also fines and criminal penalties for holding data without being registered; for failing to comply with an enforcement notice; and for unauthorised disclosure of personal data.

The Chartered
Institute of Marketing

- Customer databases can contain a wide variety of information about the customer. Information may come from a variety of sources besides transaction processing systems, including specialist geodemographic data and lifestyle information.

- Databases provide valuable information to assist with many marketing management tasks and decisions.

- Modern business databases are maintained on a central computer to enable sharing of data and avoid duplication.

  A typical relational database consists of a number of inter-related tables of records and fields.

- A key issue in setting up a database is data cleansing: ensuring that the information is correct, up-to-date, not duplicated and so on.

- The company's own information can be enriched by collating it with geodemographic and lifestyle information from sources such as ACORN.

- Data warehousing involves extracting information from disparate organisational sources to build a coherent set of information available.

  Online analytical processing (OLAP) techniques allow the data to be viewed from many different perspectives.

- Data mining software examines the data in a database or data warehouse and discovers previously unknown relationships using complex statistical techniques.

- Marketing managers must make a **distinction** between **information collected in the ordinary course of business** and **information collected via marketing research**.

- Most developed countries have **specific legislation** to **protect the privacy of individuals**.

FURTHER READING

Chapter 8 of:

Bradley, N. (2010) *Marketing research: Tools & techniques*. 2nd edition. Oxford, Oxford University Press.

Chapter 3 of:

Wilson, A. (2012) *Marketing research: An integrated approach*. 3rd edition. Harlow, Financial Times Prentice Hall.

REFERENCES

Baker, R. (2011) Sainsbury's: 'Nectar data makes our c-stores stronger than rivals'. *Marketing Week*, http://www.marketingweek.co.uk [Accessed 12 June 2012].

Dunnhumby (2012) http://www.dunnhumby.com/ [Accessed 02 July 2012].

Ipsos (2012) About Ipsos. http://www.ipsos.com [Accessed 02 July 2012].

Wilson, A (2012) *Marketing research: An integrated approach*. 3rd edition. Harlow, Financial Times Prentice Hall.

1   What is a customer database?
2   Identify five elements that might be included in a customer database.
3   What are the four main groups of customer data?
4   Outline four ways in which databases enable marketing managers to improve their decision making.
5   Identify four ways in which database information can be used.
6   What is customer relationship management?
7   What are the two basic forms of computerised database?
8   What is data cleansing?
9   What is data mining?
10   What are the eight principles of the Data Protection Act 1998?

ACTIVITY DEBRIEFS

Activity 2.1

You need to do this hands on.

Activity 2.2

You may be quite surprised by the ACORN profile of your neighbours. Try to think about the reasons behind the profile. Next time you walk around your neighbourhood try to remember the ACORN profile to see if this sheds more light on the situation.

Activity 2.3

Data mining allows data to be used more productively through increased targeting and personalisation of the marketing mix. This assists with customer retention, which is crucially important in a highly competitive market.

1   It is a 'manual or computerised source of data relevant to marketing decision making about an organisation's customers' (Wilson, 2012)

2   Customer or company details, personal details, transaction history, credit / payment history and call / contact history.

3   Behavioural data, volunteered data, attributed data and profile data.

4   Understanding customers and their preferences, managing customer service, understanding the market, understanding competitors and managing sales operations.

5   Direct mail, transaction processing, market research and planning and contacts planning.

6   CRM describes the methodologies, software and internet capabilities that help a firm to manage customer relationships.

7   A flat file system and a relational database system.

8   The process of amending or removing data in a database that is incorrect, out of date, incomplete, improperly formatted, or duplicated.

9   Data mining is a class of database application that looks for hidden patterns in a group of data.

10   Data must be: fairly and lawfully processed, processed for limited purposes, adequate, relevant and not excessive, accurate, not kept longer than necessary, processed in accordance with individual rights, secure and not transferred to countries that do not have adequate data protection laws.

CHAPTER 3

The market research industry

Introduction

Now that we have an understanding of how organisations manage and use information about customers, we can explore the structure of the market research industry. This chapter explains the nature and scope of the research industry and discusses the importance of working in line with the industry's code of conduct. It also explains the process for selecting a market research supplier, in domestic and international markets, and developing the criteria to support that decision.

The first section discusses the nature and structure of the market research industry. The second section explains the different stages of the market research process. The third section evaluates a range of procedures for selecting a market research supplier in domestic and international markets. The fourth section explains how best to liaise with the research agency on a day-to-day basis to leverage best levels of service, support and implementation and high quality information to support the business case development. The fifth section examines the process involved in developing a research brief and a full research proposal which supports the information needs of different marketing projects.

The final section evaluates the ethical and social responsibilities inherent in the market research task.

Topic list

Nature and structure of the market research industry ⓵

The market research process ⓶

Selecting a market research supplier ⓷

Managing the agency relationship ⓸

The research brief and research proposal ⓹

Ethical and social responsibilities ⓺

3.1	Discuss the nature and structure of the market research industry: ■ Marketing research departments vs marketing research agencies ■ Types of marketing research agency ■ Scale of industry ■ Professional bodies and associations in the marketing research industry
3.2	Explain the stages of the market research process: ■ Identification of problems and opportunities ■ Formulation of research needs / the research brief ■ Selection of research provider / the proposal ■ Creation of research design ■ Collection of secondary data ■ Collection of primary data ■ Analysis of data ■ Preparation and presentation of research findings and recommendations
3.3	Evaluate a range of procedures and criteria used for selecting a market research supplier in domestic and international markets: ■ Short-listing criteria ■ The research proposal ■ Supplier assessments (Pitch) ■ Selection criteria
3.4	Explain how best to liaise with the research agency on a day-to-day basis to leverage best levels of service, support and implementation and high quality information to support the business case development: ■ Monitoring working arrangements using quality and service standards
3.5	Explain the stages involved in order to develop a full research proposal to fulfil the brief which support the information needs of different marketing projects: ■ Content of proposal covering background, objectives, approach and method, reporting and presentation procedures, timing, personal CVs, related experience, contract details
3.6	Evaluate the ethical and social responsibilities inherent in the market research task: ■ Need for goodwill, trust, professionalism, confidentiality ■ Codes of marketing and social research practice (eg the Market Research Society Code of Conduct) ■ Responsibilities to respondents (use of information/protection of vulnerable groups such as children, etc) ■ Responsibilities to clients (transparency, data reporting, etc)

1 Nature and structure of the market research industry

The information industry has changed dramatically over the last 20 years in line with changes in business generally. The business has internationalised, and the major organisations that supply research and database services to the market are among the largest organisations in marketing services.

The industry has embraced new technology and while it is still possible to carry out research without the use of a computer, much of the drudgery has been taken out of the process.

The emergence of the internet as a major channel and communications medium has meant that online research and research about online marketing is perhaps the fastest growing area.

In 2010, according to the organisation responsible for the research industry in Europe, ESOMAR, US$31.2 billion was spent on marketing research worldwide; of this, US$13.1 billion was spent in Europe. According to the Market Research Society (MRS), £2.06bn was spent on market research in the UK (MRS, 2011).

Global MR industry grew 2.8% in 2010, says Esomar

NETHERLANDS: The global research industry returned to growth last year with a 2.8% increase in revenue, according to industry association Esomar.

Research revenue in the 78 countries covered in Esomar's industry report rose to $31.2bn in 2010, up 5.2%, or 2.8% after inflation.

The softest recovery was in Europe, which saw inflation-adjusted growth of just 1% to $13.1bn. This was driven mainly by investment in central and eastern European countries, which now account for the top five fastest-growing markets in Europe.

North America returned to growth after two consecutive years of decline, increasing 3.1% to $9.9bn. Latin America was the fastest-growing region, with a 13.9% increase to $1.8bn, driven by an "outstanding" performance in Brazil. Asia Pacific and Africa also grew, with the Middle East the only area to record a decline, which Esomar blamed on "varied levels of stability".

(*Research*, 2011)

Research and database information can be produced internally or externally and the management task can be carried out in-house or externally.

Internal research departments within companies may be carrying out research themselves and commissioning agencies to carry out work on their behalf. They will usually be responding to requests for research support from internal departments or working alongside the marketing team providing a range of research-based services.

Advertising and direct marketing agencies also carry out a significant amount of work typically within the planning function. This may involve a combination of research-based activity and, increasingly, database analysis to support the creation of effective communications activity. These agencies may be carrying out work themselves or commissioning a range of external suppliers.

Market research suppliers differ according to whether they are in-house (within the organisation) or external suppliers. The diagram below which has been adapted from Malhotra (2004) depicts the industry structure.

Figure 3.1   Research suppliers

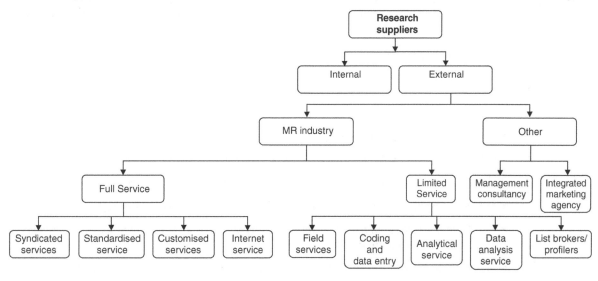

1.1 Internal marketing research departments

Research may be carried out in-house or using external specialists. The decision whether to plan and carry out research in-house, or use management consultants or a specialist research agency, depends on several factors.

External agencies offer several benefits:

- **Trained and experienced** staff, who can design appropriate programmes
- **Objectivity**, which may produce a clearer view of the questions to be asked
- **Security** and confidentiality: screened questioners, and respondent anonymity
- **Cost-effectiveness**, where the above are critical to the research's effectiveness.

Do-it-yourself research often makes sense, too:

- Where data is readily available to in-house staff
- Where in-house staff understand the nature of the problem and target audience
- Where the budget is very limited
- Where the confidentiality of the research is critical.

If a consultancy is used, they will need to be provided with a detailed written brief which explains:

- The **research problem** to which an answer is required
- The **intended use** of the data collected
- The **budgetary** constraints
- Any **background information** which will put the problem into context.

Most organisations will have somebody who is responsible for marketing research, even if that simply means liaising with external agencies who actually carry out the work.

Larger organisations that have a regular need for marketing research information (particularly FMCG organisations) are likely to set up their own **marketing research department**.

THE REAL WORLD

Left wing think tank Catalyst established its own pool of contract and freelance research assistants and consultants in an attempt to increase the number of policy areas it covers, including areas such as housing, transport and regional policy.

Catalyst said the research pool would 'facilitate the rapid identification and recruitment of researchers to work on specific projects where they arise at short notice'. The organisation was set up in 1998 with the purpose of developing and promoting 'practical policies for the redistribution of wealth, power and opportunity'. It is not affiliated to any political party but is funded in part by trade unions.

(MRS, 2012) and (*Research*, 2003)

1.2 Specialist agencies

Agencies include **specialist agencies** of various kinds (field agencies, data analysis agencies and so on), syndicated research agencies, list brokers, profilers, full service agencies and independent consultants.

As the name implies a specialist agency specialises in a particular type of work.

- Some agencies specialise in particular **markets** or market **sectors** or **regions**

- Others specialise in particular **research services** such as questionnaire design, or collection and analysis of qualitative information

- **Field agencies** have specialised skills in **conducting** personal or telephone interviews and **administering** postal or e-mail surveys

The Chartered
Institute of Marketing

- **Data analysis agencies** can be employed to code up, read in or input data collected (in questionnaires, say, or perhaps recorded in personal interviews) and analyse it using state-of-the-art hardware (for instance, highly accurate scanners) and software (for instance, highly specialised statistical packages)

- There are numerous **independent consultants** who will undertake a variety of tasks, usually on a **smaller scale**. Such people are typically ex-employees of larger research organisations or have gained their expertise in related disciplines such as IT or retail.

ACTIVITY 3.1

Use the internet to find market research companies that specialise in the following sectors:

- Food and drink
- Transportation
- Non-profit

1.3 Syndicated research agencies

A syndicated service is one that is **not conducted for any specific client**. Regular research is conducted into areas that the agency knows for certain many organisations will be interested in (for instance newspaper and magazine readership) and is then sold to anyone willing to pay the price.

THE REAL WORLD

Well-known examples of syndicated research agencies include **Datamonitor** (with products like MarketWatch: Drinks and MarketWatch: Food), and **Mintel** (http://www.mintel.co.uk) which has a huge number of regularly updated reports available on a subscription basis.

1.4 List brokers

▶ **Key term**

A **list broker** creates or acquires lists of potential consumers for the purpose of selling them on to companies who are interested.

Lists may be created from publicly available sources like the telephone book, yellow pages or the electoral roll but they will usually be **organised** for convenience, presented in **formats** that can be easily incorporated into client systems, and **checked** for accuracy and being up-to-date. The client could possibly do this in-house, but it would be very **time-consuming**. 'Names' are typically sold by the thousand at 10p to 20p each – it would almost certainly be more **expensive** for the client to find and record the information without help.

Lists that have arisen as a result of some other exercise, such as responses to mailshots or entry into a 'free' draw may also be **acquired** by list brokers. You have probably noticed that you are often asked whether you object to your details being given to **third parties** when you enter into correspondence with an organisation, or even just register on a website. Now you know that those third parties are likely to be list brokers!

1.5 Profilers

A profiler may also have access to other lists and be able to offer these to its clients, much like a list broker, except that the profiler has closer knowledge of the characteristics of the clients' existing customers and so the list may have more appropriate prospects.

1.6 Full service agencies

Well-known international examples are **BMRB** (http://www.tns-bmrb.co.uk), **Taylor Nelson Sofres** (http://www.tns-global.com) and **Ipsos** (www.ipsos.com).

Many full service **advertising agencies** also offer marketing research services, as do firms of **management consultants** like McKinsey (www.mckinsey.com).

1.7 Professional bodies

The main professional bodies are the **Marketing Research Society** and **ESOMAR**.

Apart from the CIM, many of whose members are involved in marketing research in some capacity, most countries have an association of some sort for market researchers. The largest is the **Market Research Society** (http://www.mrs.org.uk) based in the UK, but with international membership.

Likewise the **World Association of Opinion and Marketing Research Professionals** (**ESOMAR**: the 'E' originally stood for European) (http://www.esomar.org) has members all over the world. MRS works closely with the ESOMAR in some respects; later in this chapter we will look at the joint ICC ESOMAR Code of Practice for research workers, to which the MRS subscribes.

1.8 Marketing research departments vs marketing research agencies

There are a number of advantages and disadvantages to each alternative.

1.8.1 Using an external agency

- **Advantages**
  - External agencies **specialising** in research will have the necessary expertise in marketing research techniques. This should allow them to develop a cost-effective research programme to a **tighter timescale**
  - Skills in **monitoring and interpreting data** will allow the programme to be reviewed and modified as required
  - Nationwide or global agencies will be able to offer much **broader geographical coverage**
  - An external agency can provide an **objective input** without the bias which often results from a dependence on internal resources
  - **Costs** can be determined from the outset, allowing better **budgetary control**

The Chartered
Institute of Marketing

- **Disadvantage**

  Agency knowledge of the industry may be limited: a serious drawback if the agency needs a disproportionate amount of time to familiarise itself with the sector.

1.8.2 In-house programme

- **Advantages**

  - **Costs can be absorbed** into existing departmental overheads
  - It can **broaden the experience** and skills of existing staff
  - It might promote a **team spirit** and encourage a 'results-oriented' approach.

- **Disadvantages**

  - There is a danger of **overstretching current resources** and adversely affecting other projects

  - There is a risk of developing an **inappropriate programme**, yielding insufficient or poor quality data with inadequate analysis and controls

  - If additional **training or recruitment** is required this could prove expensive and time-consuming.

  - **Bias** could result from using staff with pre-conceived views

  - **Company politics** may influence the results

  - Considerable **computing resources** with appropriate software packages could be required to analyse the data

  - There may be a lack of **appropriate facilities**. For example, focus group research is often conducted off premises during evenings or weekends.

In view of the shortcomings of a purely in-house or external agency approach, a **combination** of the two might be more appropriate. For example, it might be deemed preferable to design the programme in-house but contract out certain aspects.

2 The market research process

If you read books on marketing research you will find many slight variations on the suggested 'stages' of the market research process, partly depending on whether the book is written from the point of view of a client or a market research agency. There is fairly general agreement, however, that the process will entail the following stages, in this order (the process spells **DODCAR**, if you like mnemonics!).

Stage 1	**Definition**: identify and define the **opportunity or threat**
Stage 2	**Objectives**: determine precisely what you need to know to deal with the opportunity or threat
Stage 3	**Design** the research and the methods to be used
Stage 4	**Collect** the data
Stage 5	**Analyse** the data
Stage 6	**Report** on the findings.

Where an organisation is using an agency or agencies to do the research it will send out a **research brief** at the end of Stage 2 and the various agencies that are asked to tender for the work will then submit **research proposals** (in outline, at least) covering Stage 3, explaining how they would do the work and why they should be chosen. Research proposals are discussed at more length in the next chapter.

The organisation will **select its preferred supplier(s)** based on the content and quality of their proposals (and on other factors such as cost, of course) and then Stage 3 will be completed in detail.

How long the overall process takes really depends on the nature of the problem under investigation. Longitudinal studies for example can take several years to collect the data. The majority of research projects however are planned and completed within six months. Hague *et al.* (2004) summarised a general view of the typical duration of ad hoc research projects and the individuals who tend to be involved in the process; the table that follows is adapted from this summary.

Table 3.1   Typical project personnel and timescales

What happens	Who is responsible	How long does it take
Idea generation – What is the problem to be investigated?	Organisation manager (client)	Days, a week, possibly a month
Internal debate / discussions. Further clarification of research problem	Client manager/ brand manager/ and internal market research manager (if there is one) and department / group heads or directors	A week or more
External debate and refinement of the research problem and research design	Client approaches agency to suggest a solution	One to two weeks
Data collection tool design and Information collection	Research agency	Four to twelve weeks

2.1   Stage 1: Identify and define the opportunity or threat

We've phrased this so that it reminds you of SWOT analysis, since the identification of a need for market research will usually arise from strategic and marketing planning processes and reviews.

- An **opportunity** is something that occurs in the organisation's environment that could be advantageous – a **change in the law**, say, or a **new technology** that could be exploited

- A **threat** is an environmental development that could create problems and stop the organisation achieving its objectives – a **new competitor**, perhaps, or an adverse change in **buying behaviour**.

In either case the organisation will **want to know more**. How can it best take advantage? What action is most likely to stave off or reverse the problem? The answers will depend on **how the market reacts** to different possible solutions, and the organisation can be much more sure about this if it conducts **research**.

Bear in mind that marketing research, however well organised, is not a substitute for decision making. It can help to reduce the risks, but it will not make the decision. Professional marketing depends partially on sound judgement and reliable information, but it also needs flair and creativity.

2.2   Stage 2: Determine the objectives of the research

The objectives should set out the precise information needed, as clearly as possible: it is very wasteful of time and money to collect answers to questions that did not need to be asked. Ideally objectives should be SMART (specific, measurable, actionable, reasonable, timescaled). The objectives should relate only to the problem or opportunity.

Marketing research can sometimes be a waste of effort and resources:

- The research undertaken may be designed without reference to the decisions that will depend on, or be strongly influenced by, the results of the research

- The research results may be ignored, misused, misunderstood, or misinterpreted. Sometimes this happens accidentally; more often it is deliberate because the results do not fit in with established beliefs

- The research is poorly designed or carried out

The Chartered Institute of Marketing

- The results of the research are themselves inconclusive, giving rise to different opinions about what the research signifies.

With issues like this in mind Wilson (2012) suggests **early consultation and involvement** of all the parties that will be involved in putting into action the decisions taken as a result of the proposed research, for example by setting up a project team. This has the advantage that those closest to the project will probably have the best idea of what **knowledge** the organisation **already possesses**, and does not need to be researched. It also means that the questions that **need** to be answered are more likely to get asked.

Establishing clear research objectives is actually the key to a good piece of research.

Other matters that would be considered at this stage would be the available **budget** and the **timescale** for the work, and perhaps there would be outline thoughts about the **methods** to be used (for instance the scale of the research and the segments of the market to be included). All of this information, together with the requirements for the final **report**, would be included in the **research brief** if the work was now to be put out to tender.

ACTIVITY 3.2

Your company manufactures cruelty-free bath products for a number of supermarket chains. You have been given responsibility for finding out about the market for a new line of cruelty-free cosmetics. List the likely research objectives.

2.3 Stage 3: Design the research and the methods to be used

The **category** of research must first be decided upon: the methods used will depend on that. Research may be **exploratory**, **descriptive** or **causal**.

2.3.1 Exploratory research

As the name suggests, **exploratory** research tends to **break new ground**. For instance, if your organisation has a **completely new idea** for a product or service which consumers have never been offered before, then exploratory research will be most appropriate in the first instance.

- Potential consumers may be totally uninterested, in which case exploratory research will quickly show that it is best to **abandon the idea** before any more money is spent on developing it

- Consumers **may not understand** how the offer could benefit them, in which case exploratory research would show that it may be worth simplifying the product and introducing it to them in a different way, with different promotional techniques and messages

- Consumers may not have responded because the **research methods used** were not appropriate, or because the wrong consumer group was chosen: exploratory research can help to define how more detailed research should be carried out.

Exploratory research may therefore be a **preliminary** to more detailed development of marketing ideas or a more detailed research project. It may even lead to abandonment of a product idea.

Research **methods** should involve as **little cost** and take as **little time** as possible. If use can be made of **existing research** by others then that is certainly desirable, as are methods that are not too labour-and cost-intensive such as **telephone** research or limited **internet surveys**.

2.3.2 Descriptive research

Descriptive research aims to describe what is happening now (a single snapshot) or what has happened over a limited period of time (several snapshots).

- Now (a **'cross-sectional study'**): 'At present 45% of the target market are aware of our product whereas 95% are aware of Competitor A's product'.

- Over time (a **'longitudinal study'**): 'During the period of the in-store promotion (February to April) awareness of our product rose from 45% to 73%'.

In other words, descriptive research is useful for answering 'where are we now?' questions, and it can also be used to summarise how things have changed over a period of time. Published market research reports are examples of descriptive research: if you subscribe today you will find out 'where you were' when the report was last published, and if you wait a while for the next edition you will find out how you have progressed.

The main problem (for researchers) with longitudinal descriptive research is to ensure that their respondents are either the same people each time or, if that is not possible, that answers from very similar respondents are aggregated. Research **methods** are likely to include **telephone** research, with the consumer's agreement, and specially invited **panels** of respondents.

2.3.3 Causal research

Although descriptive research is very common and is much used, it may not really tell us the **cause** of the event or behaviour it describes. To paraphrase Wilson, virtually all marketing research projects fall somewhere along a continuum between purely **descriptive** and purely **causal**.

For example, the descriptive result *'During the period of the in-store promotion (February to April) awareness of our product rose from 45% to 73%'* appears to suggest a reason for the change, but the only thing we know for certain is that two to three months have gone by. The change may be little or nothing to do with the in-store promotion. It may be due to a completely random factor such as temporary unavailability of a competitor's product, or uncontrolled and unmeasured actions taken by in-store staff, or to other promotional efforts such as TV ads.

The relationship between variables like this is not formally taken into account in descriptive research. **Causal** research attempts to identify and establish the relationship between all the variables, and determine whether one variable influences the value of others. **Experimental** research can be carried out, where one variable is deliberately changed to see the effect, if any, on other variables. The most obvious example is to see if lowering the price causes sales to rise.

Research **methods** might be similar to those for longitudinal descriptive research (panels of consumers for instance), but the information they are asked to provide will be more extensive and the time span may be longer. In particular, the researcher will need to consider the **sampling** method and parameters (how many people and of what type), where the people can be found, and the means of obtaining information (**interviews**, **questionnaires** etc).

2.4   Stage 4: Collect the data

Data can be collected from either primary or secondary data sources. We will examine at data collection in much more detail later in this study text.

- **Secondary data** is data collected for another purpose not specifically related to the proposed research; for instance, all the **internal** information in the company's marketing information systems and databases, or information such as **published research** reports, **government** information, **newspapers** and trade journals.

- **Primary data** is information **collected specifically for the study** under consideration. Primary data may be **quantitative** (statistics), **qualitative** (attitudes etc) or **observational** videos of people browsing in a store, for instance).

2.5   Stage 5: Analyse the data

This stage will involve getting the data into analysable form by entering it into a computer and using statistics (for quantitative data) and other means of analysis and summary (qualitative data) to find out what it reveals.

2.6 Stage 6: Report on the findings

The final report is likely to take the form of a PowerPoint-type **presentation** given to an audience of interested parties and a detailed **written report** explaining and summarising the findings, with appendices of figures and tables. Reporting data is covered later in this book.

3 Selecting a market research supplier

Selecting an agency will involve considerations such as the agency's **previous experience** and **expertise** in the area of research, and the **geographical area** to be covered.

Very few organisations can shoulder the cost of a large full-time staff of marketing research workers, especially a 'field force' of researchers spread around the country, or around every country in which the organisation does business.

Choosing the right agency or consultant to work with is a key element in a successful working relationship. The external expert must become a trusted part of the team.

It is equally important that the market researcher has the specialist knowledge and research service capabilities needed by the organisation. In the UK you would expect a research organisation to be associated to the professional body, the Market Research Society, and for those working on the account to have relevant qualifications.

It helps if the agency has some knowledge of the market or business in which the company operates. Therefore, it may be worthwhile to develop a long-standing relationship with the research organisation, because their understanding of the company's business and the marketplace will develop over time.

3.1 Tenders and 'beauty parades'

The selection process will generally involve the organisation sending out its research brief to a number of agencies and inviting each to submit a research proposal (see the next chapter). It is common for the agencies to give an oral presentation of their case: this part of the procedure is known as a 'beauty parade'.

3.2 The final selection of an agency

The MRS (2008) suggests that the following questions are used when deciding between research agencies:

- Which company seems to have understood what you need?
- Which company has perhaps added to your thinking by coming up with ideas of its own?
- Does the proposed research design seem to match your expectations and, if not, are convincing alternatives presented and explained?
- Does the company have relevant experience, either in terms of methodology and/or the subject of your project?
- Assuming that it has understood your needs, does it seem to be offering value for money?
- Which company's work 'feels right'? From your contacts with the agency and from the documents it has produced for you, do you think you trust the organisation and can work with its staff?

Most firms retain an agency after a careful selection process. It is useful to have a list of selection criteria.

- **Size**. Is the agency's size/status comparable to the client organisation?
- **Service levels**. Can the agency source all the client's needs?
- **Experience**. Does it have suitable experience, both as an agency and the individual staff?
- **Confidentiality**. What if it undertakes research projects for competitors?
- **Location/logistics**. Is it nearby / easily contactable?
- **Administrative arrangements**. Are they to the client's satisfaction?

4 Managing the agency relationship

On a day-to-day basis there are a number of issues that can be agreed in order to help to ensure that working relationships remain healthy:

- Implement a Service Level Agreement which outlines the roles and responsibilities of the client and the agency, reporting procedures and expectations of both parties, eg if the client would like a weekly update then this should be stipulated in the agreement, or if the agency would like feedback on research design issues within a certain period.

- The use of periodic reviews of the research process and interim results in order to amend the research design, agree alternative courses of action or abort the project where necessary.

- Ensure that there is one key contact within both the agency and the client so that parties are not inundated by many individuals communicating different messages.

- If any part of the project is to be outsourced, eg data collection, this should be clear at the research tender stage.

- Clarity over any changes in the research design as the project progresses should be formally agreed by both parties, to avoid any surprises once the final research findings are presented (periodic reviews will avoid this issue).

Baker & Mouncey (2003) suggest that good researchers should follow the following rules to enhance the relationship with their clients:

- Get very involved with the marketing team and understand their problems

- Anticipate research opportunities

- Constantly develop research tools which relate to the commercial issues your company and its clients face

- Deliver your research more effectively and more efficiently

- Investigate opportunities to deliver research 'online', especially continuous research

- Encourage informal contact with users

- Take all opportunities to 'educate' senior management on the actual and potential value of research to the business

- Be intellectually attuned to your key clients' needs

- Be sensitive to broad user needs, including the political aspect of commissioning of research and applications in decision making

- Create a trusting and open relationship with users

- Be self-critical, reflective; but value your contribution

It goes without saying that this is the type of relationship that clients should be looking for in a research company. The recruitment of any agency needs to be based on sound relationships at both the business and personal level. Mutual respect, concern and understanding are the cornerstones of good agency-client relations and the best people will go out of their way to ensure that the job is done to the client's specifications. Relationships based solely on power games or solely on price and the budget are unlikely to live for a long time. Remember both parties in any deal have to make money.

Recruiting international agencies is today straightforward, but there are a range of additional complexities involved.

The Chartered Institute of Marketing

5 The research brief and research proposal

5.1 The research brief

The key to good research information, whether collected by an in-house section or an external agency, lies in the quality of the research brief. A research brief is **prepared by the organisation commissioning the research**.

Hague *et al* (2004) suggest using a series of questions as a framework in order to make sure a thorough brief is written. These are:

- Why do this research? What action will be taken when the research is completed?

- What has caused this problem or led to this opportunity?

- What is known about the area of research already? Is there any research that the organisation has already conducted or are there any known secondary sources?

- Who are the target groups for the research?

- What specific information is needed from the research (eg market size, trends, buying behaviour, customer needs, segmentation)?

- What is the proposed budget?

- Are there any initial ideas for the research method?

- Are there any reporting requirements?

- When are the findings required?

The research brief will normally include the following sections.

- **Background.** This covers relevant information about the company, its products and services, its market place.

- **Rationale.** How the need for information arose and what the users intend to do with the information when they have it (what decisions will be taken).

- **Budget.** In general the benefits of collecting information should be greater than the costs of collecting it, but benefits in particular are not always easy to quantify. In any case the budget may be limited by other organisational factors such as availability of cash or a head office allocation of, say, £5,000 per annum for marketing research purposes. Clearly this will affect the scale and type of information search that can be carried out. This item will probably not be revealed to external suppliers, however: see below.

- **Timescale.** Quite obviously, if the decisions have to be made by May then the information needs to be collected and analysed before then. Once again this will have an impact on the scale and type of information search that can be carried out.

- **Objectives.** The precise information needed, set out as clearly as possible. For instance 'To determine customer response to a price reduction of £250 in terms of repeat purchasing, word-of-mouth recommendations and willingness to purchase our other products and services'. The objectives should relate **only** to the rationale: it might be 'nice to know' what type of car customers drive, but if this will make no difference to the decisions that will be taken once the information has been collected, there is no need to know about customers' cars in the first place.

- **Methods.** This need only be an outline, setting out, for instance, the scale of the search, the mix of quantitative and qualitative information needed, the segments of the market to be included.

- **Reports.** How the final information should be presented. Considerations here might include style of reports, degree of summarisation, use of charts and other graphics, format for quantitative information (eg in Excel spreadsheets, for ease of further analysis).

According to Wilson (2012) 'The **budget** available is rarely included within the brief' and that is most probably true of briefs that are **sent out to marketing research suppliers**, who will hopefully return research proposals that meet the organisation's needs, not just as how much research they are prepared to do for the price. However, the organisation obviously needs to have a clear idea of how much it is willing to spend on research. Hague *et al* (2004), for example, argues that many comprehensive plans are sent back to the drawing board because they are too expensive, when agencies have no budget boundaries.

▶ **Assessment tip**

Your assignment will assume that a brief has already been prepared by someone else within your organisation. It is, however, still important that you appreciate what is included.

5.2 The research proposal

▶ **Key term**

Research proposals are prepared by research agencies who have been sent the brief and asked to put in a bid to do the job.

In structure a research proposal is similar to the research brief, but it will be much more detailed in certain parts.

- **Background** and **rationale**. This sets out the agency's understanding of the client company, its products and services and its market place, an understanding of why the research is required and what decisions need to be made. (If they've misunderstood the situation it will be clear to the client at the outset!)

- **Objectives**. These will probably be much the same as those in the brief, although the agency's understanding of research techniques may have helped to define them more precisely still. We will look at these in more detail in the next section of this chapter.

- **Approach and Method**. How the agency proposes to carry out the research, what methods will be used, where the sample will be taken from.

- **Reports**. How the final information will be presented and whether interim reports will be made. Reporting is covered in Chapter 11.

- **Timing**: how long the research will take and how it will be broken down into separate stages if appropriate.

- **Fees and expenses**: this is self-explanatory.

- **Personal CVs** of the main agency personnel who will be involved in the project.

- **Relevant experience/references:** the agency will wish to assure the client that it is capable of carrying out the research, so it will include information about similar projects undertaken in the past, and possibly reference details (previous clients who are willing to testify to the competency of the agency).

- **Contractual details** will set out the agency's terms of trade and clarify matters about ownership of the data collected. See the relevant parts of the ESOMAR code of practice in section 6.3 for an indication of likely contents of this section.

▶ **Assessment tip**

One of the key elements of your assignment will be to prepare a research proposal. You should therefore be fully prepared and ensure that you are highly familiar with the elements. You will need to come back to this part of the text on several occasions as you learn more about the process of research.

5.2.1 Background

The background is an important section because here, as a supplier of research, the agency needs to demonstrate to the client that they have understood the company and their markets. Often, agencies will conduct some secondary research into the market to demonstrate that they are aware of the broader issues and have taken the time to research their potential client.

5.2.2 Objectives

Setting research objectives is one of the most critical stages in the entire research programme. Research which is based on flawed objectives often merely leads to a finding that more research is required in order to address an underlying problem or issue.

Drayton Bird, an established direct marketing expert, has criticised market research as creating a 'blind alley' because he believes that a large proportion of research is fundamentally flawed because researchers fail to address the right questions (Young, 2008). By asking the wrong question Bird was not simply referring to questions within a survey but the fundamental objectives of the research. For example a company may commission research to find out whether customers would buy a new product. The issue that the company should have really investigated is whether customers would replace what they already buy with the new product. In other words, do they like the new product enough to change their behaviour.

Objectives are usually refined through a series of discussions between the research agency and the client. Rarely are the objectives that the client included in their brief the final objectives used to direct the research design (Dillon *et al*, 1994).

Malhotra (2004) observed that, frequently, objectives are too broad (not providing sufficient direction) or too narrow (precluding consideration of other courses of action).

- Overly broad objectives could be stated as: (1) developing a marketing strategy – this project could be endless; (2) improving the competitive position of the firm – from which basis?; (3) improving the company image – amongst whom, any ideas how?

- Too narrow objectives could be stated as: (1) decrease the price of the brand to match competitor's price cut – is this really the central issues?; (2) to specify whether blue or green should be used for new product packaging – are other colours also appropriate?; (3) to outline why customers will buy this product – could it also be that they won't and so wouldn't it be better to take Drayton Bird's view and ask what would lead them to switch.

In order to ensure that your objectives are clear, and neither too broad or narrow, it is good practice to use **research questions** (Dillon *et al*, 1994; Malhotra, 2004) which follow directly from the objective. The research objectives should flow directly from the overall research aim or rationale; research questions then flow from the objectives.

Research questions should not be confused with fieldwork questions, which are used within surveys and interviews. Research questions are not normally phrased in a way such that they could be used directly with respondents.

The diagram below outlines the relationship between the different levels of defining the research problem. Please note that, to be able to show the relationship more clearly, only the research questions and fieldwork questions for objective 1 are shown. In reality, the diagram would look like a pyramid with one aim at the top which then cascades down to several objectives, each of which has several research questions. Each research question will then have several fieldwork questions which may or may not be used within the same data collection tool, eg survey, focus group etc.

Example: research objectives for Anderson Farmhouse Cheeses

Anderson Farmhouse Cheeses, a successful company in Ireland, wants to explore the opportunity to expand their business by exporting to the United States.

The aim of the research is to find out if the market for their cheese is big enough to justify an export sales programme; if there are enough customers in this market segment; and if the sort of cheese produced by the family will sell to this group in sufficient quantities to make a return on investment.

More specifically, the client wants to know the following:

- Who buys imported gourmet cheese?
- Why do they buy it?
- Where do they buy these cheeses?
- What sort of cheese appeals to them?
- What are their perceptions of gourmet cheeses in general, and gourmet cheese from Ireland in particular?

Figure 3.2   Defining a research brief

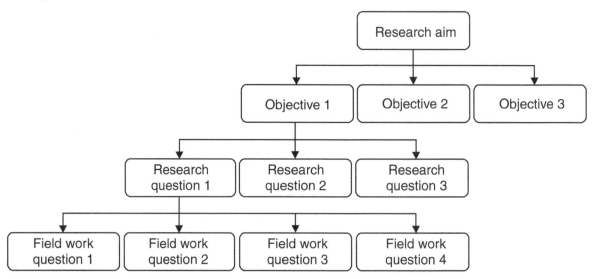

5.2.3 Approach and method

The approach and method is the most comprehensive section of the proposal and it is here that the agency outlines their overall research design. There are many ways to conduct research and there often isn't one best approach (Dillon *et al*, 1994). The researcher at this stage should evaluate alternative courses of action and decide upon the most suitable. Decisions will be based upon:

- The **value of the information** gained by using a particular approach
- The **cost and time** implications
- **Practical issues**, eg the ability to easily gather respondent views, ease of data collection
- Requirements of the **research objectives** and **research questions**.

The next chapter will cover this in more detail, it is important that whatever research methods are used, the objectives of the research are fully covered.

Several issues need to be included in this section of the proposal, including:

- **Phases of research**, eg will data collection be split into a number of phases which will help in refining later data collection tools (Malhotra, 2004). For example phase one may involve secondary research, phase two a qualitative focus group before a final phase three using a quantitative online survey.

- **A justification** outlining why this is an appropriate research design.
- The **overall sampling plan**, eg who will be selected to participate in the various research phases, how will they be selected, how many will need to be approached to participate, what can be done to encourage them to respond.
- The **data collection** fieldwork methods, eg focus groups, questionnaires, online panel etc.
- Any **limitations** of the proposed approach.

5.2.4 Reports

Typically a very brief research report, cross-tabulated data (for quantitative studies), verbatim comments (for qualitative studies) and a research presentation are used.

It is important to clarify the reporting requirements because these can have a deep financial impact on the agency. There will be a huge difference, for example, in the cost of the overall project if an in-depth report is required because of the time needed to write it. Likewise 800 printed copies of a research presentation for use in a large internal training session will place very different financial demands on the overall cost of the research.

5.2.5 Timing

Within this section the researcher will break down all timings within the overall project. Timings are usually broken down into weekly or sometimes daily time periods. Tables or Gantt charts are the most common methods of presenting timings. The researcher should be very specific here and also include timescales for clients to review data collection tools or provide supporting information.

5.2.6 Fees and expenses

Fees should be broken down as much as possible so that the client can see exactly how much the entire project will cost; but also have the flexibility to pick out elements of the research design to cover at a later date, if budgets do not allow the entire project to be completed at one time.

Typically, fees are broken down into:

- Individual research methods, eg survey, focus group
- Expenses to be incurred, eg incentives for respondents, materials as research prompts, any significant travel
- Use of third party, eg focus group viewing facilities, database purchase.

5.2.7 Personal CVs, experiences, references and contract details

These sections are fairly self-explanatory and so we do not need to elaborate much here; however, you should not underestimate their importance. Remember the research proposal is effectively a 'sales pitch' and therefore flagging up the agency's credentials and experience is essential. Clients also like to know a little more about the team who will be addressing their problem and so clarity here helps agency-client relationships enormously. Including references helps to build the credibility of the agency.

It is important that agencies identify who the main day-to-day contact will be.

> ▶ Assessment tip
>
> Within your assignment you are expected to include these sections. Clearly they will be hypothetical, however in order to present your work professionally you will need to include them.

6 Ethical and social responsibilities

6.1 Ethical issues

Ethical issues relating to working relationships between clients and agencies because there is an inherent need for:

- **Goodwill** – on the part of the respondents volunteering information to the agency and client

- **Trust** – on the part of the client trusting the agency to conduct itself professionally and provide accurate information; and the agency trusting the client to be open and provide sufficient background and supporting information

- **Professionalism** – on the part of both the agency and the client; should be maintained at all times in order to maintain credibility

- **Confidentiality** – investigating sensitive information about markets and competitive environments will require confidentiality agreements on the part of agencies. Agencies which disclose information to third parties without the prior consent of their clients risk losing valuable future business.

▶ **Assessment tip**

Ethical topics arose in the December 2008 / March 2009 assignment – the ethics of marketing research and code of conduct issues.

6.2 The Market Research Society (MRS) professional standards

The MRS professional standards are:

- **The MRS Code of Conduct:** This is designed to support all those engaged in market, social or opinion research in maintaining professional standards. The Code is also intended to reassure the general public and other interested parties that research is carried out in a professional and ethical manner

- **MRS Regulations and binding Guidelines:** These expand in more detail on specific ethical issues within the Code, for example a regulation applying to the use of incentives and prize draws and a guideline for members on the 1998 Data Protection Act

- **MRS Guidelines:** These supplement the Code and Regulations, providing interpretation and best practice advice. For example, there are guidelines on such issues as: business-to-business research, conducting research with children and conducting research with employees

The MRS regularly updates and amends these professional standards, so it is important to keep up to date.

These are the principles of the MRS Code of Conduct:

- Researchers shall ensure that participation in their activities is based on voluntary informed consent.

- Researchers shall be straightforward and honest in all their professional and business relationships.

- Researchers shall be transparent as to the subject and purpose of data collection.

- Researchers shall respect the confidentiality of information collected in their professional activities.

- Researchers shall respect the rights and well-being of all individuals.

- Researchers shall ensure that respondents are not harmed or adversely affected by their professional activities.

- Researchers shall balance the needs of individuals, clients and their professional activities.

- Researchers shall exercise independent professional judgement in the design, conduct and reporting of their professional activities.

The Chartered Institute of Marketing

- Researchers shall ensure that their professional activities are conducted by persons with appropriate training, qualifications and experience.

- Researchers shall protect the reputation and integrity of the profession.

6.3 ICC/ESOMAR International Code of Conduct

ESOMAR is the world association for market and opinion research professionals and was founded in 1948 as the European Society for Opinion and Marketing Research. It has members in over 120 countries.

The ICC/ESOMAR Code on Market and Social Research was developed jointly with the International Chamber of Commerce (ICC) to enhance the public's confidence in market research by emphasising the rights and safeguards to which they are entitled under this Code.

The Code sets out the professional and ethical rules which market and social researchers follow and has been adopted by 50 national market research associations worldwide, including the MRS in the UK.

ESOMAR also publishes Guidelines for researchers on relevant issues such as: Online Research, Mystery Shopping and Interviewing Children.

Details and downloads of the ICC/ESOMAR Code and Guidelines can be obtained free from the ESOMAR website: http://www.esomar.org/index.php/codes-guidelines.html

This Code is designed primarily as a framework for self-regulation. With this in mind, ICC/ESOMAR recommend the worldwide use of the Code, which intends to fulfil the following objectives:

- To set out the ethical rules which market researchers shall follow

- To enhance the public's confidence in market research by emphasising the rights and safeguards to which they are entitled under this Code

- To emphasise the need for a special responsibility when seeking the opinions of children and young people

- To safeguard freedom for market researchers to seek, receive and impart information (as embodied in article 19 of the United Nations International Covenant of Civil and Political Rights)

- To minimise the need for governmental and/or intergovernmental legislation or regulation.

The Code is based on these key fundamentals:

- Market researchers shall conform to all relevant national and international laws.

- Market researchers shall behave ethically and shall not do anything which might damage the reputation of market research.

- Market researchers shall take special care when carrying out research among children and young people.

- Respondents' co-operation is voluntary and must be based on adequate, and not misleading, information about the general purpose and nature of the project when their agreement to participate is being obtained and all such statements shall be honoured.

- The rights of respondents as private individuals shall be respected by market researchers and they shall not be harmed or adversely affected as the direct result of co-operating in a market research project.

- Market researchers shall never allow personal data they collect in a market research project to be used for any purpose other than market research.

- Market researchers shall ensure that projects and activities are designed, carried out, reported and documented accurately, transparently and objectively.

- Market researchers shall conform to the accepted principles of fair competition.

Table 3.2   6.3.1 ICC/ESOMAR code of marketing and social research practice

General	
B1	Marketing research must always be carried out objectively and in accordance with established scientific principles.
B2	Marketing research must always conform to the national and international legislation which applies in those countries involved in a given research project.

The Rights of Respondents	
B3	Respondents' co-operation in a marketing research project is entirely voluntary at all stages. They must not be misled when being asked for co-operation.
B4	Respondents' anonymity must be strictly preserved. If the respondent on request from the Researcher has given permission for data to be passed on in a form which allows that respondent to be identified personally: (a) The Respondent must first have been told to whom the information would be supplied and the purposes for which it will be used, and also (b) The Researcher must ensure that the information will not be used for any non-research purpose and that the recipient of the information has agreed to conform to the requirements of the Code.
B5	The Researcher must take all reasonable precautions to ensure that Respondents are in no way directly harmed or adversely affected as a result of their participation in a marketing research project.
B6	The Researcher must take special care when interviewing children and young people. The informed consent of the parent or responsible adult must first be obtained for interviews with children.
B7	Respondents must be told (normally at the beginning of the interview) if observation techniques or recording equipment are used, except where these are used in a public place. If a respondent so wishes, the record or relevant section of it must be destroyed or deleted. Respondents' anonymity must not be infringed by the use of such methods.
B8	Respondents must be enabled to check without difficulty the identity and bona fides of the Researcher.

The Professional Responsibilities of Researchers	
B9	Researchers must not, whether knowingly or negligently, act in any way which could bring discredit on the marketing research profession or lead to a loss of public confidence in it.
B10	Researchers must not make false claims about their skills and experience or about those of their organisation.
B11	Researchers must not unjustifiably criticise or disparage other Researchers.
B12	Researchers must always strive to design research which is cost-efficient and of adequate quality, and then to carry this out to the specification agreed with the Client.
B13	Researchers must ensure the security of all research records in their possession.
B14	Researchers must not knowingly allow the dissemination of conclusions from a marketing research project which are not adequately supported by the data. They must always be prepared to make available the technical information necessary to assess the validity of any published findings.
B15	When acting in their capacity as Researchers the latter must not undertake any non-research activities, for example database marketing involving data about individuals which will be used for direct marketing and promotional activities. Any such non-research activities must always, in the way they are organised and carried out, be clearly differentiated from marketing research activities.

Mutual Rights and Responsibilities of Researchers and Clients	
B16	These rights and responsibilities will normally be governed by a written Contract between the Researcher and the Client. The parties may amend the provisions of rules B19–B23 below if they have agreed this in writing beforehand; but the other requirements of this Code may not be altered in this way. Marketing research must also always be conducted according to the principles of fair competition, as generally understood and accepted.
B17	The Researcher must inform the Client if the work to be carried out for that Client is to be combined or syndicated in the same project with work for other Clients but must not disclose the identity of such clients without their permission.
B18	The Researcher must inform the Client as soon as possible in advance when any part of the work for that Client is to be subcontracted outside the Researcher's own organisation (including the use of any outside consultants). On

request the Client must be told the identity of any such subcontractor.

B19	The Client does not have the right, without prior agreement between the parties involved, to exclusive use of the Researcher's services or those of his organisation, whether in whole or in part. In carrying out work for different clients, however, the Researcher must endeavour to avoid possible clashes of interest between the services provided to those clients.
B20	The following Records remain the property of the Client and must not be disclosed by the Researcher to any third party without the Client's permission: (a) marketing research briefs, specifications and other information provided by the Client; (b) research data and findings from a marketing research project (except in the case of syndicated or multi-client projects or services where the same data are available to more than one client). The Client has, however, no right to know the names or addresses of Respondents unless the latter's explicit permission for this has first been obtained by the Researcher (this particular requirement cannot be altered under Rule B16).
B21	Unless it is specifically agreed to the contrary, the following Records remain the property of the Researcher: (a) marketing research proposals and cost quotations (unless these have been paid for by the Client). They must not be disclosed by the Client to any third party, other than to a consultant working for the Client on that project (with the exception of any consultant working also for a competitor of the Researcher). In particular, they must not be used by the Client to influence research proposals or cost quotations from other Researchers. (b) the contents of a report in the case of syndicated research and/or multi-client projects or services where the same data are available to more than one client and where it is clearly understood that the resulting reports are available for general purchase or subscription. The Client may not disclose the findings of such research to any third party (other than his own consultants and advisors for use in connection with his business) without the permission of the Researcher. (c) all other research Records prepared by the Researcher (with the exception in the case of non-syndicated projects of the report to the Client, and also the research design and questionnaire where the costs of developing these are covered by the charges paid by the Client)..
B22	The Researcher must conform to current agreed professional practice relating to the keeping of such records for an appropriate period of time after the end of the project. On request the Researcher must supply the Client with duplicate copies of such records provided that such duplicates do not breach anonymity and confidentiality requirements (Rule B4); that the request is made within the agreed time limit for keeping the Records; and that the Client pays the reasonable costs of providing the duplicates.
B23	The Researcher must not disclose the identity of the Client (provided there is no legal obligation to do so) or any confidential information about the latter's business, to any third party without the Client's permission.
B24	The Researcher must, on request, allow the Client to arrange for checks on the quality of fieldwork and data preparation provided that the Client pays any additional costs involved in this. Any such checks must conform to the requirements of Rule B4.
B25	The Researcher must provide the Client with all appropriate technical details of any research project carried out for that Client.
B26	When reporting on the results of a marketing research project the Researcher must make a clear distinction between the findings as such, the Researcher's interpretation of these and any recommendations based on them.
B27	Where any of the findings of a research project are published by the Client, the latter has a responsibility to ensure that these are not misleading. The Researcher must be consulted and agree in advance the form and content of publication, and must take action to correct any misleading statements about the research and its findings.
B28	Researchers must not allow their names to be used in connection with any research project as an assurance that the latter has been carried out in conformity with this Code unless they are confident that the project has in all respects met the Code's requirements.
B29	Researchers must ensure that Clients are aware of the existence of this Code and of the need to comply with its requirements.

ACTIVITY 3.3

As the Research Manager for a UK-based online retailer, you need to select a marketing research firm that specialises in researching consumers' shopping on the internet. Make a list of five such firms. Which one will you select and why?

- The information industry has changed dramatically over the last 20 years in line with changes in business generally.

- Some larger organisations have their own marketing research (or 'customer insight') departments, but for most this would be too expensive.

- Agencies include specialist agencies of various kinds (field agencies, data analysis agencies and so on), syndicated research agencies, list brokers, profilers, full service agencies and independent consultants.

- The main professional bodies are the Marketing Research Society and ESOMAR.

- The marketing research process generally involves the following stages:

    - Definition: identify and define the opportunity or threat
    - Objectives: determine precisely what you need to know to deal with the opportunity or threat
    - Design the research and the methods to be used (exploratory, descriptive, causal)
    - Collect the data
    - Analyse the data
    - Report on the findings

- A research brief is a document prepared by an organisation commissioning research. Typically it contains the following sections: Background, Rationale, Budget, Timescale, Objectives, Methods and Reports. The budget would typically not be revealed to agencies.

- Research proposals are prepared and submitted to the client by agencies who receive the brief. Typical contents are as follows: Background, Objectives, Approach and Method, Reports, Timing, Fees and expenses, Personal CVs, Relevant experience, Contractual details.

- Setting and refining objectives is key to effective research.

- The ICC/ESOMAR have issued a code of practice for marketing research professionals. Broadly, this covers The Rights of Respondents, The Professional Responsibilities of Researchers, and Mutual Rights and Responsibilities of Researchers and Clients.

FURTHER READING

Chapters 1 and 2 of the following:

Bradley, N. (2010) *Marketing research: Tools & techniques*. 2nd edition. Oxford, Oxford University Press.

Wilson, A. (2012) *Marketing research: An integrated approach*. 3rd edition. Harlow, Financial Times Prentice Hall.

Bain, R. (2011) Global MR industry grew 2.8% in 2010, says Esomar. *Research*, http://www.research-live.com/news/financial/global-mr-industry-grew-28-in-2010-says-esomar/4005985.article [Accessed 02 July 2012].

Baker, S. and Mouncey, P. (2003) The market researcher's manifesto. *International Journal of Marketing Research* 45(4).

CATALYST (2012) Think Tank Overview. http://www.catalyst-project.eu/05tt.html [Accessed 02 July 2012].

Dillon, W., Madden, T. and Firtle, N. (1994) *Marketing research in a marketing environment*. 3rd edition. Illinois: Irwin.

ESOMAR (2012) Global Market Research. http://www.esomar.org/web/research_papers/book.php?id=2253 [Accessed 02 July 2012].

Hague, P., Hague, M. and Morgan, C. (2004) *Market research in practice: A guide to the basics.* London. Kogan Page.

Malhotra, N. (2004). *Marketing research: An applied orientation,* 4th edition. Upper Saddle River, NJ: Prentice Hall.

MRS (2012) http://www.mrs.org [Accessed 02 July 2012].

Research, (2003) Think tank Catalyst sets up research pool. http://www.research-live.com/news/think-tank-catalyst-set-up-research-pool/2001133.article [Accessed May 2012].

Wilson, A. (2012) *Marketing research: An integrated approach*, 3rd edition, Harlow. Financial Times Prentice Hall.

QUICK QUIZ

1   What are the benefits of using external agencies for market research?
2   What are list brokers?
3   Which are the main professional bodies in the market research industry?
4   Outline the stages of the market research process.
5   What are the factors that companies consider in selecting a market research agency?
6   What is a research brief?
7   What are the main contents of a research proposal?
8   What are the main aspects of the MRS professional standards?

Activity 3.1

Food and drink

- Added Value
- Consumer Insight
- Millward Brown
- Mintel
- Engage Research Limited
- Ipsos MORI

Transportation

- Alchemy Research Associates
- BMG Research Limited
- Explain Market Research Limited
- Ipsos Observer
- Millward Brown
- Quadrangle

Non-profit

- Beehive Research Limited
- Chrysalis Research
- Consensus Research
- Mango Research Limited
- Space Doctors
- The Analytics Hub

Activity 3.2

We've not given you enough information to enable you to be too precise. You would have much more information in real life of course.

To collect information about the market for a new line of cruelty-free cosmetics (lipsticks, eyeshadow and so on) with a view to drawing up and implementing a marketing plan you would need information on the following:

(a) The size of market, value, number of items sold, number of customers

(b) The leading companies and their respective market share

(c) The breakdown of market by type of cosmetic (lipstick, eyeshadow etc)

(d) Current consumer trends in buying cruelty-free cosmetics (price, colour and so on)

(e) Consumer preferences in terms of packaging/presentation

(f) The importance to consumers of having a choice of colours within the range

(g) The influence on consumers of advertising and promotion that emphasises the cruelty-free nature of products.

Remember that objectives need to be SMART.

Table 3.2   Examples of research objectives

Research objectives	Discover re Action Programme above:
Specific	Size of market for *cruelty-free* cosmetics not cosmetics in general
Measurable	Respective market share in percentage terms of leading players
Actionable	Price range within which consumers will buy
Reasonable	A defined number of preferred colours
Timescaled	Information within 3 months so product can be marketed for Christmas

Table 3.3   Application of research objectives

Type	Application
Product research (Product)	Likely acceptance of new products
Analysis of substitute products Comparison of competition products Test marketing Product extension Brand name generation and testing Product testing of existing products Packaging design studies	
Price research (Price)	Competitor prices (analysis)
Cost analysis Profit analysis Market potential Sales potential Sales forecast (volume) Customer perception of price Effect of price change on demand (elasticity of demand) Discounting Credit terms	
Distribution research (Place)	Planning channel decisions
Design and location of distribution centres In-house versus outsource logistics Export/international studies Channel coverage studies	
Advertising and communications research (Promotion)	Brand preferences
Product satisfaction Brand awareness studies Segmentation studies Buying intentions Monitor and evaluate buyer behaviour Buying habit/pattern studies	Brand attitude

Activity 3.3

A list of possible firms may include:

1. eDigital Research
2. Fieldwork UK
3. New experience
4. RS consulting
5. Mintel

These firms have been chosen because they all research consumer shopping on the internet.

1   Trained and experienced staff, objectivity, security and cost-effectiveness.

2   List brokers create or acquire lists of potential customers for the purpose of selling them on to companies who are interested.

3   Marketing Research Society and ESOMAR

4   Definition, objectives, design the research, collect the data, analyse the data and report the findings.

5   Size, service levels, experience, confidentiality, location/logistics and administrative arrangements.

6   It is a document prepared by an organisation commissioning research.

7   Background, objectives, approach and method, reports, timing, fees and expenses, personal CVs, relevant experience and contractual details.

8   The MRS Code of Conduct, MRS Regulations and Binding Guidelines and MRS Guidelines.

CHAPTER 4

Secondary data

Introduction

In most cases the data collection stage of the market research process starts with the identification and collection of information that already exists about the research problem. This chapter evaluates the uses, benefits and limitations of secondary data in market research. The first section defines the concept of secondary data and explains the principles behind its collection.

The second section discusses the various ways in which secondary data is used today. The third section discusses the benefits and limitations of secondary research. The fourth section outlines and explains the various sources of secondary research data. The fifth section discusses the use of panels and indexes in market research.

The final section explores strategies for finding the information you need on the internet, which has become the most important source of information for modern market researchers.

Topic list

4.1	Evaluate the uses, benefits and limitations of secondary data:
	■ Benefits
	■ Limitations
	■ Sources of secondary data
	■ Internet search strategies
	■ Integrating secondary data with primary data

1 What is secondary data?

> ▶ Key term
>
> **Secondary data** is 'data that has already been published by someone else, at some other time period, usually for some other reason than the present researcher has in mind'. (Crouch & Housden, 2003)

Secondary data is data that already exists in some form. Collection of secondary data is known as 'desk research'. Originally this was to distinguish it from research that involves getting out and about in the world, talking to people and watching them. In fact a great deal of research can now be **done from your desk** in a literal sense, using your computer and the internet.

Secondary data is data (including internal data) not created specifically for the purpose at hand but used and analysed to provide marketing information where primary data is not (yet) available or not sufficient.

It may seem odd that we deal with 'secondary' data **before we look at primary data**, but it would very silly to embark on substantial amounts of **primary** research without seeing what secondary data already exists. **Checking what is known already** is also likely to give insights into how and what to investigate further.

Desk research includes using library sources, the organisation's information system, databases and internal reports.

As consumers ourselves (as well as marketers) we are continually using secondary data for our own purchasing decisions. If a movie is recommended by a friend you may well go and see it, too, even though your friend did not see it for your benefit. Secondary data is **data neither collected by, nor specifically for, the user**, and is often collected under conditions not known by the user.

Secondary data **cannot replace the experience itself** nor the more rigorous enquiries we might decide to make ourselves. If you know that your friend usually likes the same sort of movies as you there is a good chance that you will like your friend's latest recommendation. But the movie may contain violent scenes that you cannot stomach, or you may hate musicals because they are unreal, or whatever. Likewise you might see a dress or suit that is recommended in a fashion magazine: you would still go out and look at the garment 'in the flesh', feel it, try it on and so forth, before you decided to buy it.

Desk research typically involves **knowing where and how to look for** existing information. That is not necessarily as easy as it sounds, but there are clear principles. Here are some typical activities.

- Accessing the organisation's own information systems records and databases. As we've seen, internal information gathered by other departments, for a different purpose to the research in hand, would include:
  - Production data about quantities produced, materials and labour used etc
  - Data about inventory/stock
  - Data from the sales system about sales volumes, analysed by sales area, salesperson, quantity, profitability, distribution outlet, customer etc

    – Data about marketing itself – promotion and brand data, current marketing plans, previous marketing audits.

- Tapping into the **internet** and subscription-based **on-line databases**

- Making use of **library sources**, such as journals, periodicals, recent academic books etc

- **Buying in data and reports** prepared externally, either as secondary data likely to be of interest to many users or as primary data collected for another organisation but then syndicated.

2 The uses of secondary data

Secondary information is now **available** in every form and on a **huge scale**. The problem is how to decide what information is required. The use of secondary data will generally come **early** in the process of **marketing research**. In some cases, secondary data may be sufficient in itself, but not always.

Secondary data:

- Can provide a backdrop to primary research
- Can act as a substitute for field research
- Can be used as a technique in itself.

2.1 Backdrop to primary research

In **unfamiliar territory**, it is natural that the marketer will carry out some **basic research** in the area, using journals, existing market reports, the press and any contacts with relevant knowledge. Such investigations will aid the marketer by providing guidance on a number of areas:

- Possible data sources
- Methods of data collection (relevant populations, sampling methods)
- The general state of the market (demand, competition and the like).

2.2 Substitute for primary research

The often substantial **cost** of primary research **might be avoided** if existing secondary data is sufficient. This data might not be perfect for the needs of the business, though, and to judge whether it *is* enough, or whether primary research ought to be undertaken, a cost-benefit analysis should be implemented, weighing up the advantages of each method.

There are some situations in which secondary data is bound to be **insufficient**. For instance, if your brand new version of an existing product is hugely superior to your competitors' versions because of your unique use of new technology, you have changed the entire market. Primary research will be a necessity to find out the impact of your product.

2.3 A technique in itself

Some types of information **can only be acquired** by examining secondary data, in particular **trends over time**. Historical data cannot realistically be replaced by a one-off study and an organisation's internal data would only give a limited picture (Dillon *et al*, 1994).

3 Benefits and limitations of secondary research

Secondary sources of data are of **limited use** because of the **scope for compounding errors** arising from why and how the data was collected in the first place, who collected it and how long ago.

When considering the quality of the secondary data it is a good idea to consider the following characteristics:

- The **producers** of the data (they may have an axe to grind; trade associations may not include data which runs counter to the interest of its members).

- The **reason for the data** being collected in the first place.

- The **collection method** (random samples with a poor response rate are particularly questionable).

- How **old** the data is (government statistics and information based on them are often relatively dated, though information technology has speeded up the process).

- **How parameters were defined**. For instance, the definition of ' family' used by some researchers could be different to that used by others.

(Malhotra, 2004; Dillon *et al*, 1994)

3.1 Advantages and disadvantages of secondary data

The **advantages** arising from the use of secondary data include the following.

- Secondary data may solve the problem without the need for any primary research: **time and money is thereby saved**.

- Cost savings can be substantial because secondary data sources are a great deal **cheaper** than those for primary research.

- Secondary data, while not necessarily fulfilling all the needs of the business, can be of great use by:

    - **Setting the parameters**, defining a hypothesis, highlighting variables; in other words, helping to focus on the central problem.

    - **Providing guidance**, by showing past methods of research, for primary data collection.

    - **Helping to assimilate the primary research** with past research, highlighting trends and the like.

    - **Defining sampling parameter**, (target populations, variables).

There are, of course, plenty of **disadvantages** to the use of secondary data.

- **Relevance**. The data may not be relevant to the research objectives in terms of the data content itself, classifications used or units of measurement.

- **Cost**. Although secondary data is usually cheaper than primary data, some specialist reports can cost large amounts of money. A cost-benefit analysis will determine whether such secondary data should be used or whether primary research would be more economical.

- **Availability**. Secondary data may not exist in the specific product or market area.

- **Bias**. The secondary data may be biased, depending on who originally obtained it and for what purpose. Attempts should be made to obtain the most original source of the data, to assess it for such bias.

- **Accuracy**. The accuracy of the data should be questioned. Here is a possible checklist.

    - Was the sample representative?

    - Was the questionnaire or other measurement instrument(s) properly constructed?

    - Were possible biases in response or in non-response corrected and accounted for?

    - Was the data properly analysed using appropriate statistical techniques?

The Chartered Institute of Marketing

– Was a sufficiently large sample used?

– Does the report include the raw data?

– To what degree were the field-workers supervised?

In addition, was any raw data omitted from the final report, and why?

- **Sufficiency**. Even after fulfilling all the above criteria, the secondary data may be insufficient and primary research would therefore be necessary.

The golden rule when using secondary data is **only use meaningful data**. It is obviously sensible to begin with internal sources and a firm with a good management information system should be able to provide a great deal of data. External information should be consulted in order of ease and speed of access: directories, catalogues and indexes, before books, abstracts and periodicals. A good librarian should be a great help (Hague, 2004).

4 Sources of secondary data

There are many varied secondary sources and it can be quite complex to classify them in specific ways. The diagram that follows shows a basic overview.

Figure 4.1   Sources of secondary data

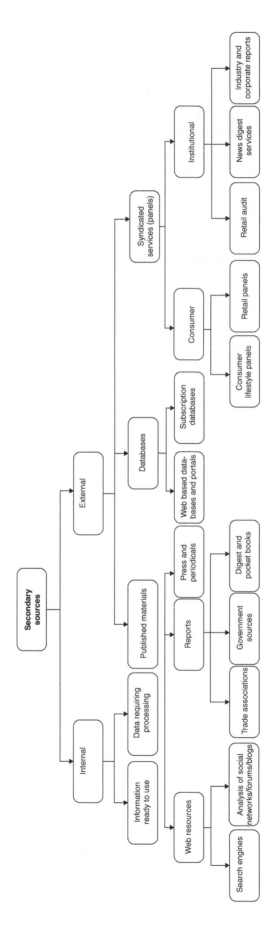

4.1 Directories

Directories can make a good starting point for research. The information provided is usually on industries and markets, manufacturers (size, location), products, sales and profits. Examples of business directories include Kompass Register (Kompass), Who owns Whom (Dun & Bradstreet) and Key British Enterprises (Dun & Bradstreet).

4.2 Computerised databases

These include the following.

- ACORN (consumption indices by class of neighbourhood) (http://www.caci.co.uk)
- Marketing Surveys Index (CIM) (http://www.cim.co.uk)
- MRS Yearbook (Market Research Agencies and their specialisms) (http://www.mrs.org.uk)
- TGI and other syndicated omnibus surveys (http://www.tgisurveys.com)
- Kompass Online (http://www.kompass.co.uk)
- Financial Times Company Information (http://www.ft.com) and many other newspapers
- Hoppenstedt Austria/Germany/Netherlands (http://www.hoppenstedt.de)
- Jordanwatch (http://www.jordans.co.uk)
- Reuters (http://www.reuters.com)
- LexisNexis (http://www.lexisnexis.com)

Such databases are generally **subscription-based**. Subscriptions are not cheap, but it is usually much less expensive than collecting the information oneself. A trained operator should be used to begin with, to avoid expensive waste of the resources.

4.3 Associations

There are associations in almost every field of business and leisure activity. All these bodies collect and publish data for their members, which can be of great interest to other users. Examples of such bodies include the Road Haulage Association (RHA), the British Association of Ski Instructors and … you name it, there will almost certainly be an association for it.

4.4 Government agencies

There is a wealth of published statistics which can be used in marketing research. There are two prime sources – government and non-government.

Governments are a major source of economic information and information about industry and population trends. To find material from the UK on the web, the best place to start is http://www.statistics.gov.uk. Other countries have similar government sites.

Official statistics are also published by other government bodies such as the European Union, the United Nations and local authorities.

4.5 Non-government sources of information

There are numerous other sources.

- Companies and other organisations specialising in the provision of economic and financial data (eg the Financial Times Business Information Service, the Data Research Institute, LexisNexis, Reuters, the Extel Group).

- Directories and yearbooks, such as Kompass or Kelly's Directory (online as http://www.kellysearch.com)

- Professional institutions (eg Chartered Institute of Marketing, Industrial Marketing Research Association, Chartered Management Institute, Institute of Practitioners in Advertising)

- Specialist libraries, such as the City Business Library in London, collect published information from a wide variety of sources

- Trade associations, trade unions and Chambers of Commerce

- Trade journals

- Commercial organisations such as banks and TV networks

- Market research agencies.

4.6 Environmental scanning

Environmental scanning means **keeping your eyes and ears open to** what is going on generally in **the market place**, especially with respect to competitors, and more widely in the technological, social, economic and political environment. Much of the data will be qualitative but could be systematically logged and backed up by quantitative data if possible.

The result of environmental scanning is **market intelligence**. Excellent sources are as follows:

- Business and financial newspapers, especially the *Financial Times* and the *Wall Street Journal*

- General business magazines, such as the *Economist*, *Business Week* and *The Marketer* (published by The Chartered Institute of Marketing (CIM) and sent to CIM students)

- Trade journals, such as *Research*, for marketing research or *The Grocer* for retailers or a huge host of others for all sorts of businesses

- Academic journals, such as *Harvard Business Review*

- Attending conferences, exhibitions, courses and trade fairs

- Making use of salesforce feedback

- Developing and making use of a network of personal contacts in the trade

- Watching competitors (extremely important).

With regard to watching competitors, a **competitor intelligence system** needs to be set up to cope with a vast amount of data from:

- Financial statements
- Common customers and suppliers
- Inspection of a competitor's products
- The competitor's former employees
- Job advertisements.

In other words, there is a combination of published data and 'field data', which need to be compiled (eg clipping services on- or offline, standard monthly reports on competitors' activities), catalogued, and analysed (summarised, ranked by reliability, extrapolated data from financial reports).

The object of what is usually an informal but constant process is to ensure that the organisation is not caught by surprise by developments which could have and should have been picked up. The organisation needs to be able to adapt to changing circumstances.

The Chartered Institute of Marketing

4.7 Other published sources

This group includes all other publications.

- Some important **periodicals** (often available in the public libraries)

  - *Economist* (general) (http://www.economist.com)
  - *Campaign* (advertising) (http://www.campaignlive.com)
  - World Advertising Research Center (http://www.warc.com), publishers of ADMAP (advertising)
  - Mintel (consumer market reports) (http://www.mintel.com)
  - BRAD (all media selling advertising space in the UK including TV, radio, newspapers and magazines) (http://www.intellagencia.com)

> ▶ **Assessment tip**
>
> A strong awareness of the different sources of secondary data is essential for marketing managers. The examiner will definitely not be impressed if you propose methods for collecting primary data that could be easily obtained from the library!

4.8 Web 2.0

Web 2.0 refers to the generation of tools and services that allow **private individuals to publish** and collaborate in ways previously available only to corporations with serious budgets, or to dedicated enthusiasts and semi-professional web builders (Cooke & Buckley, 2008).

Blogs, online forums and social networks are increasingly being used as a means of gathering insights into consumers and organisations because they are viewed in the course of their natural behaviours. It also means that there is a wealth of new information available. The availability of this technology is also being used extensively by research agencies who specialise in research panels, because of the ability to maintain fast contact with respondents who have agreed to remain on panels as frequent participants. Panels are discussed in the next section and certainly are a key growth area for researchers.

Many consumers, particularly, are increasingly choosing to join a wide range of research panels.

4.9 Web 3.0

Web 3.0 is the next generation of the internet which is referred to as the semantic web. The semantic web is a place where machines can read webpages in the same way as humans and where search engines and software can easily trawl the internet to find what we are looking for. Many internet experts believe that Web 3.0 will make the task of searching for information faster and easier. Instead of multiple searches, you should be able to type a complex sentence or two in your Web 3.0 browser, and the Web will do the rest of the work for you. Not only will your web browser do all the searching for you, it will also organise the results. It is also believed that the Web 3.0 browser will act like a personal assistant by learning about you and your interests as you use the web on a daily basis. The more it understands you, the less specific you will need to be with your questions.

Web 3.0 will significantly increase the amount of data that is available to market researchers and should facilitate a much deeper understanding of consumer behaviour.

5 Panels and indexes

The sources of secondary data we have looked at so far have generally been **free** because they are **in the public domain**. Inexpensiveness is an advantage which can be offset by the fact that the information is non-specific and needs considerable analysis before being useable.

A middle step between adapting secondary data and commissioning primary research is the **purchase of data collected by market research companies** or business publishing houses. The data tends to be expensive but less costly than primary research.

There are plenty of commercial sources of secondary data; a number of guides to these sources are available.

- *The Source Book*, Key Note Publications
- *Guide to Official Statistics*, HMSO
- *Published Data of European Markets*, Industrial Aids Ltd
- *Compendium of Marketing Information Sources*, Euromonitor
- *Market-Search*, British Overseas Trade Board

Commonly used sources of data on particular industries and markets are:

- Key Note Publications
- *Retail Business*, Economist Intelligence Unit
- Mintel publications
- *Market Research GB*, Euromonitor

5.1 Consumer panels

▶ **Key term**

A form of continuous research which results in secondary data is that generated by **consumer panels**. These constitute a representative sample of individuals and households whose buying activity in a defined area is monitored either continuously (every day, with results aggregated) or at regular intervals, over a period of time. There are panels set up to monitor purchases of groceries, consumer durables, cars, baby products and many others.

Most consumer panels consist of a **representative cross-section of consumers** who have agreed to give information about their attitudes or buying habits (through personal visits or postal questionnaires) at regular intervals. Consumer panels with personal visits are called **home audit panels**.

THE REAL WORLD

Valued Opinions

Valued Opinions is an internet-based survey site with (May 2012) over 400,000 members worldwide. The company is a member of MRS, ESOMAR and the MRA; the holding company, Research Now, is a subsidiary of the American company e-Rewards inc, which has been conducting research in a variety of ways since 1999.

Valued Opinions has a simple premise: attract and retain a panel of internet-based members of the community, and offer their services to their clients. Respondents initially submit their profile, which helps to filter research requests to those most apparently suitable. Each internet-based questionnaire, created either by Valued Opinions or, directly, by their clients, is then forwarded to those most likely to be suitable. Initial survey questions are then used to ensure that only relevant respondents are selected: that they are of the correct gender/ age/ educational background/ family/ income/ location – whatever is deemed appropriate for inclusion in the current sample frame.

Participants receive an incentive of, typically, between 50p and £2 for completing a survey, although this can be considerably more in certain cases. The incentive is set by the client, and is based on the survey length and the degree of 'specialism' and 'rarity' of the respondent. The incentives are 'banked' and when the value accrued is at least £10, respondents can withdraw their reward in the form of £10 vouchers from many of the UK's major high street stores, including Sainsbury's, Tesco and M&S; Amazon, iTunes and other electronic retailers are also included, and the vouchers can also be used as charitable donations to, currently, WWF, British Red Cross or Charitable Vision.

Valued Opinion's clients range from major broadcasters to regional tourist boards; from manufacturers of electronic equipment to some of the major supermarkets; financial products and services, beverages, automobiles, technology, travel – the list of survey topics is almost endless.

For more information visit https://www.valuedopinions.co.uk/ or http://www.researchnow.com

5.2 Retail panels

A research firm sends 'auditors' to selected outlets at regular intervals to count stock and deliveries, thus enabling an estimate of throughput to be made. Sometimes it is possible to do a universal audit of all retail outlets.

EPOS makes the process easier (Wilson, 2012). The audits provide details of the following.

- **Retail sales** for selected products and brands, sales by different types of retail outlet, market shares and brand shares

- **Retail stocks** of products and brands (enabling a firm subscribing to the audit to compare stocks of its own goods with those of competitors)

- **Selling prices** in retail outlets, including information about discounts.

5.3 Kantor Worldpanel

Kantar Worldpanel is a world leader in consumer knowledge and insights based on continuous consumer panels. Combining market monitoring, analytics and market research solutions they source and deliver macro and micro detail to their clients. Their information about what people buy or use – and why – is clearly of significant value for brand owners and retailers.

They have been operating in various guises for over 60 years, have a staff of over 3,000 and operate in more than 50 countries directly or through partners. Areas they cover include FMCG, impulse products, fashion, baby, telecommunications and entertainment. In the UK they regularly monitor over 30,000 households using a variety of approaches including in-home barcode scanning, till receipt harvesting, SMS and web-based methods.

5.4 Omnibus surveys

TNS Research International (http://www.tns-ri.co.uk) and GfK (http://www.gfknop.com) are two of the major providers of omnibus surveys; as already explained, these are 'composite' general surveys taking place regularly (just like a bus service) onto which different companies can pay to have their own specific questions included (just as you pay to jump on a bus to share in part of the journey).

Costs, naturally, vary according to the type of question asked ('yes/no' questions are clearly easier to pose, respond to and assess than completely open questions) and the number of questions per section of the survey and the frequency of use of the omnibus surveys. The surveys can be excellent value for money in allowing companies to access minority groups, measure awareness, provide penetration or profile data, especially for the smaller organisation. The surveys are typically carried out online or by telephone with (usually) a regular panel of participants; or face-to-face with random participants. By asking questions on an omnibus it is easily possible to track movements in attitudes, behaviour and awareness over time.

5.5　Target Group Index (TGI)

TGI is owned by Kantar Media but has its own website (http://www.tgisurveys.com). The purpose of TGI is to increase the efficiency of marketing operations by identifying and describing **target groups** of consumers and their **exposure to the media** (newspapers, magazines, television and radio) and the extent to which they see or hear other media.

In design, TGI is a regular interval survey and is also 'single source', in that it covers both **product usage data** and **media exposure data**.

Respondents are questioned on a number of areas; **purchase behaviour and media use are cross-tabulated** to enable more accurate media audience targeting.

Questions to respondents cover:

- Their use of 400 different products covering 3,500 brands
- Their readership of over 170 magazines and newspapers
- Cinema attendance
- ITV television watching
- Listening patterns for commercial radio stations
- Their lifestyles, based on nearly 200 attitude questions.

The major **product fields** covered are foods, household goods, medicaments, toiletries and cosmetics, drink, confectionery, tobacco, motoring, clothing, leisure, holidays, financial services and consumer durables. It is worth noting that respondents are only asked about the use, ownership and consumption of the products identified, not about purchases made or prices paid.

6　Internet search strategies

The **internet** is the richest secondary source of information of all, on practically any subject you can think of. Not all of it is good information, however, and although in theory it is easy to search the internet, in practice it often takes longer to find exactly what you want than another method would have taken. Knowing which search tool to use and how to use it is a key skill for a researcher.

There are a number of ways to access information on the internet.

- Go directly to a site, if you have the address
- Browse or surf
- Explore a subject directory or portal
- Conduct a search using a search engine
- Explore information stored in live databases on the web, known as the 'invisible web or the 'deep web'.

The distinctions between directories, search engines and so on are becoming increasingly blurred, as each type of search tool picks up and adopts ideas from its competitors.

THE REAL WORLD

Search engines

Modern search engines such as Google (http://www.google.com), Bing (http://www.bing.com) or others order search results by links or popularity, by concept, by keyword, or by type of site.

The algorithms used to find and prioritise the results are closely guarded secrets - and also ever-changing. In general, the number of 'hits' a site receives, the links others make to it, the apparent importance of the site and its impartiality, coupled with the relevance to the search term(s) in question, are all combined to 'rank' the results into the order we see on screen. Google and others accept payments from some companies in order to secure separate priority listings on the first page (just as advertisers pay for back page or inside front cover magazine spots, for example).

A growing market in search engine optimisation (SEO) has grown up over the past few years, especially for sites for smaller companies; there is an 'ongoing battle' between these people and the search engines; and also between artificially making the

---

The Chartered Institute of Marketing

content more relevant for the search engines – or making the content read naturally and correctly for its users. An interesting activity lies in trying different search engines for the same term and comparing the results for relevance, importance and accuracy.

At time of writing, May 2012, Google have just announced a major change, called Penguin, to the algorithm they use to rank websites, and this appears to be causing a large number of sites to move down the ratings table.

Based on initial analyses and reports, sites affected by this new update tend to show the following patterns:

- Websites that possess high traffic, keyword matching domains
- Websites that have a high proportion of links with the same anchor text
- Websites with 'empty' pages ('copy coming soon' for example)
- Websites that generally have higher keyword density throughout the site
- Websites that have the majority of their back links to one page.

Dead links, long website addresses, longer load times – these also appear to be considered within the algorithm.

The basic requirement, from initial analysis of 'successful' sites, is that Google appears to be giving much greater prominence to sites that have a better visitor interaction and experience. For more information, use a search engine and look for 'penguin' and 'google'.

The battle between site owners, SEO advisers, and Google is about to get more intense!

6.1 Going directly to an internet address

You may know the precise address of an internet site that you wish to visit. TV and radio programs and advertisements frequently give you a web address to visit to find more information. You will also see addresses in newspapers, magazines and books. You may be sent a link in an e-mail.

Typically the format is something like 'www.bbc.co.uk'. This is also known as a **uniform resource locator** or **url** for short.

All you need to do is type the url into the address box of your browser.

ACTIVITY 4.2

Up-to-date versions of Microsoft Internet Explorer and Netscape Navigator can sometimes find the precise site you are looking for if you just type a guess directly in the address box.

Try this with four or five well-known organisations and see what results you get. Can you see any drawbacks to this method of finding sites?

6.2 Browsing or surfing

Random browsing of pages on the Web is another haphazard way of collecting information, although it can be very interesting if you are not pressed for time.

For instance, you may visit a particular news site regularly and find that an article contains links to other pages, either within that site or on an external site that contains more information about the topic. To see this in action, find an article of interest to you at http://www.bbc.co.uk and follow up some of the external links.

6.3 Directories and portals

A **directory** is a service that offers links to web pages organised into subject categories. Directory services supposedly contain links only to pages that have been evaluated by human beings, using various selection criteria, though the selectivity varies among services.

The best known example of a directory is Yahoo! (http://www.yahoo.com), although Yahoo! does not evaluate sites as carefully as some other directories and it is aimed more at the leisure interests of home computer users than at the serious academic or business researcher.

Most directories also include some kind of search facility, which either searches the directory only or (confusingly) searches the web in general, perhaps using another type of search tool. Yahoo searches, for instance, are powered by the Google search engine (described below), so Yahoo is actually a mixture between a directory and a search engine.

The best subject directories include notes about sites written by independent reviewers, describing and evaluating site content.

A **portal** is similar to a directory (and the terms are often used interchangeably) but many portals are much narrower in scope, restricting their links to specific subjects. Examples include http://www.thisislondon.co.uk and http://www.fool.com (for investors) or, more generally, the home pages of most of the leading ISPs.

Yet another term you may see used is **vortal** (vertical industry portal) which is a portal providing information and resources for a particular industry. Examples include http://www.accountingweb.co.uk and http://www.privatehealth.co.uk amongst thousands of others.

Typical services offered by portal or vortal sites include a directory of related websites, a facility to search for other sites, news, and community services such as discussion boards and suppliers' directories.

6.4   Search engines

Search engines such as Bing or Google retrieve links to, and brief descriptions of, websites containing a word or phrase entered by the user. The descriptions are derived from the webpage itself: there is no human judgement involved other than the judgement of the original author of the page.

Search engines are fairly indiscriminate. Some of the results they give may come from reputable sources and provide you with valuable up-to-date information, but others may be out of date, inaccurate or incomplete.

With a **'first generation'** search engine such as the original **AltaVista** (http://www.altavista.com) the results of a search are usually presented in 'term-ranked' order. This means that a document appears higher in the list of results if your search terms occur very frequently in the document, or in the document title, or near the beginning of the document, or close together in the document.

Many, if not all, first generation search engines have transformed themselves into portals and/or have some 'second-generation' features, because basic term-ranked searching is indiscriminate and gives far too many results.

'Second generation' search engines such as **Google** (http://www.google.com) order search results by links or popularity, by concept, by keyword, or by type of site. These search engines generally give better quality results because there is at least some human element in determining what is relevant.

For example, one of the ways that **Google** ranks pages is according to the number of other pages that link to it. The more web authors there are who have decided that it is worth including a link to a page, the more likely it is that the page is useful and relevant to the topic you are searching for.

Can you trust the internet?

There are lies, damned lies, and the internet! We know that statistics may not present the complete truth, and that we shouldn't believe everything we read in the newspapers; equally, we should be diligent about our use of the internet. In general, a simple rule is always to check your sources, and ensure you find independent verifications of any 'fact' before you act on it. Even the most authoritative source can make a genuine error, but there are a few things you can do to lessen the likelihood of your passing off *rubbish* as *fact*!

First of all, check the website url – especially the last few letters, which give a good indication of the type of site. **.edu** or **.ac** usually indicate an official educational institution; **.gov** is usually national or local government. These sites, although they may have some political bias, are usually accurate in terms of data and general information and should be able to be relied on. Sites with **.org** are usually, but not always, not-for-profit organisations and, unless they have clear affiliations in favour or against any topic, will also generally have valid data.

Commercial sites ending in **.co.uk**, **.com** or **.tv** etc can be set up by any commercial organisation; you should take notice of the country of registration for more general relevance to your needs; **.com** can be based anywhere, but national registrations (for example, **.fr**, **.de**, **.es**, **.be** etc) usually represent organisations based in those countries (France, Germany, Spain or Belgium, in the examples shown). However, anyone (for example) in England can register a website with any of these names, so the sites aren't guaranteed to be resident in those countries. Check for general information about the owners of a site by looking at the 'about us' or 'legal' links, which are usually to be found on each site; if you can't find them, maybe that should ringing a warning bell or two.

Journals, magazines, publishers and broadcasters invariably have an online presence and should be a good source of authoritative data.

Conference proceedings can look authoritative, but the data is only as good as the presenter. What were his or her *bona fides*? How much else has he or she published?

Beyond this, the simple rule of 'triangulating' your data – making sure that three different sources all agree – is the sensible watchword to keep your reputation intact. The internet makes it easy to find, and also to be fooled – but it also makes it very easy to check, so there is little excuse for being caught unawares.

6.5 Internet databases

Many websites consist of pages that are generated 'dynamically' using content stored in a database. In other words the contents that you see are only assembled – and put into a web page that your browser can read – on request. The page does not actually exist in the form of a saved file and therefore it can't be found by a search engine or listed in a directory.

Typical sites that use databases will be those that have often-changing data such as airline information sites, and news-related sites with up-to-the-minute current stories and archived stories and articles going back several years.

Such content is called the 'invisible' web or the 'deep' web and estimates suggest that there is now at least 500 times more material in this form than there is on the conventional web. The reason is because it is more efficient to store data in this way. Most web pages consist of standard elements like logos and navigation menus and tables defining layout, so it is more efficient to create a single template for all the elements that do not change and simply 'plug' the required information into a space in the template.

Clearly you cannot afford to ignore such a large source of information, but how do you find it? The only way you can do so is to search the database itself. This is not as complicated as it sounds: from the point of view of the user you either just click on what appears to be an ordinary link or you type a few words in the 'Search' box on the site itself.

For example if you were using http://www.dictionary.com and wanted to find definitions for the term 'dynamic' you would simply type 'dynamic' into the search box and click on the 'Look it up' button. This takes you to the URL dictionary.reference.com/search?q=dynamic: the part of the URL after the question mark is actually an instruction to extract relevant material from the site's database about the term 'dynamic' and present it in a web page.

6.6 Refining a search

Many people – especially new users – find searching the web extremely frustrating because they cannot find what they are looking for quickly enough. In this section we describe some of the things you can do to make your searches more productive.

6.6.1 Use your initial search proactively

If you are researching a new topic the chances are that you will not be very familiar with the concepts and terminology of that subject.

In this case, when you do an initial search spend a few moments skim-reading the first few results pages. They probably won't tell you what you want to know, but they may well include words and phrases that you could add to your search terms to give more useful results, or words and phrases that you could exclude from your search (we'll explain how to do this in a moment).

Some search engines display words such as More Like This or Similar Pages next to each entry. For instance if you searched for 'management tips' you would find that one of the first few results was to do with time management. If time management happened to be your specific interest you could get a new list of sites specifically on that subject simply by clicking on the Similar Pages or More Like This link.

6.6.2 Restrict the search area

Some search engines have options to restrict the number of sites searched, for instance to UK sites only, or to English language sites only. Even if that option is not available you will generally find that if you simply add UK to your search term the results will be closer to the ones you need.

6.6.3 Advanced search techniques

On many (though not all) sites the search facility allows you to use **symbols** and/or what are known as **Boolean operators** to help refine what should and should not be searched for. These so-called 'advanced' searching techniques are extremely useful.

Different search engines have slightly different rules for formulating queries, so it is always a good idea to **read the help files** at the site before you start a search.

- **Plus signs (+).** If you put a plus sign (+) directly in front of a word (with no space) this tells the search engine that the word **must** be present in all the pages that are found. So if you type **+management +tips**, you will only get pages that contain both words (though not necessarily together or in the order you specify).

- **Minus signs (–).** As you might expect, the – sign works in the opposite way to +. If you put a minus sign directly in front of a word the search engine will **ignore** any documents that contain that word. So, if you type **+management +tips –racing** you will avoid pages that have tips on the horses! However intuitive you are at using the minus sign, you are still likely to get links that you are not interested in. You probably would not think of typing, say, **+management +tips –pest,** for example, because the idea of pest management in gardening would probably not occur to you when you were thinking about managing your workteam.

- **Quotation marks (").** To find **only** pages that contain the phrase **management tips,** with the words together in that order, you enclose them in double quotation marks: **"management tips"**. This is very useful so long as your phrase is only two or three words long or if you know exactly how the phrase should be worded (because it is a famous quotation, say).

The Chartered Institute of Marketing

- **OR.** There is a good chance that some of the pages relevant to your search will use alternative words to the ones you first think of. If you can guess what the alternatives might be you can use OR to make the search engine look for pages that contain at least one of them: for instance **management +tips OR hints OR advice**.

ACTIVITY 4.3

Try all of these techniques in a search engine such as Google and observe the different results that you get. You can either use our example 'management tips' or some other phrase of your own, if you prefer.

CHAPTER ROUNDUP

- The collection of secondary data is often referred to as desk research. Desk research includes using library sources, the organisation's information system, databases and internal reports.

- The internet is the richest secondary source of information of all.

- Many useful reports and statistics are published by government and non-government sources.

- Environmental scanning is an informal process resulting in the possession of market intelligence. Sources include newspapers, journals and attending conferences.

- Data and reports can be bought in from marketing research organisations. Often these are the result of continuous research using consumer and retail panels.

- Secondary sources of data are of limited use because of the scope for compounding errors arising from why and how the data were collected in the first place, who collected them and how long ago.

- Secondary data can be immensely cost-effective, but must be used with care.

FURTHER READING

Chapter 3 of the following:

Bradley, N. (2010) *Marketing research: Tools & techniques*. 2nd edition. Oxford, Oxford University Press.

Wilson, A. (2012) *Marketing research: An integrated approach*. 3rd edition. Harlow, Financial Times Prentice Hall.

REFERENCES

Cooke, N. and Buckley, N. (2008) Web 2.0, social networks and the future of market research. *International Journal of Market Research,* 50(2) p267–292.

Crouch, S. and Housden, M. (2003) *Marketing research for managers*, 3rd edition. Oxford. Butterworth Heinemann.

Dillon, W., Madden, T. and Firtle, N. (1994) *Marketing research in a marketing environment*, 3rd edition. Illinois, Irwin.

Hague, P., Hague, M. and Morgan, C. (2004) *Market research in practice: A guide to the basics*. London. Kogan Page.

Malhotra, N. (2004) *Marketing research: An applied orientation*. 4th edition. Upper Saddle River, NJ, Prentice Hall.

Metz, C. (2007) Web 3.0. *PC Mag*, http://www.pcmag.com/artice2/0.2817,2102852,00.asp [Accessed 12 June 2012].

Strickland, J. (2011) How web 3.0 will work. How stuff works, http://computer.howstuffworks.com/web.30.htm [Accessed 12 June 2012].

Wilson, A (2012) *Marketing Research: An integrated approach,* 3rd edition. Harlow, Financial Times Prentice Hall.

The Chartered Institute of Marketing

1   What is secondary data?
2   What are the main uses of secondary data?
3   What are the disadvantages of secondary data?
4   Outline five sources of secondary data.
5   Identify four ways of searching for information on the internet.
6   What are consumer panels?
7   What is environmental scanning?

ACTIVITY DEBRIEFS

Activity 4.1

The limitations of desk research are:

(a)   The data gathered is, by definition, not specific to the matter under analysis. It was gathered and prepared for another purpose and so is unlikely to be ideal.

(b)   Because it was gathered for another purpose, the data is likely to require a fair amount of adaptation and analysis before it can be used.

(c)   The data gathered is historical and may be out of date.

Activity 4.2

This approach is too haphazard, as you have probably discovered, having tried this activity. The main drawback is that you usually need to guess the second part of the address (.com, .co.uk, .org, .net): it may take several goes before you get it right, in which case it would have been quicker to use a proper search tool.

Activity 4.3

This is a 'hands-on' exercise.

1   Secondary data is data that already exists in some form.

2   It can provide a backdrop to primary research, act as a substitute for field research and be used as a technique in itself.

3   They are relevance, cost, availability, bias, accuracy and sufficiency.

4   Directories, computerised databases, associations, government agencies and non-government sources of information.

5   Going directly to the URL, browsing or surfing, directories and portals and search engines.

6   They constitute a representative sample of individuals and households whose buying activity in a defined area is monitored either continuously or at regular intervals, over a period of time.

7   It is an informal process resulting in the possession of market intelligence; usually from sources such as newspapers, journals and attending conferences.

CHAPTER 5

Observation and experimentation

Introduction

After collecting and analysing the information that is already available on the research problem, the researcher will decide on the most effective and efficient method for gathering primary data. This chapter identifies and evaluates the various techniques used for observing behaviour and undertaking experimentation. The first section defines the concept of observation and explores the various categories of observation used in marketing research.

The second section discusses the advantages and disadvantages of observation as a research method. The third section explores the different methods used by researchers to observe behaviour, including audits and scanner-based research, television viewing measurement, internet monitoring and mystery shopping.

The final section identifies and evaluates the various techniques for undertaking experimentation, including hall tests, placement tests and simulated test markets.

Topic list

What is observation?   ①

Advantages and disadvantages of observation   ②

Observation techniques   ③

Experimentation   ④

4.2	Evaluate the various procedures used for observing behaviour:
	■ Categories of observation (natural v contrived, visible v hidden, structured v unstructured, mechanised v human, participant v non-participant)
	■ Audits and scanner-based research
	■ Television viewing measurement
	■ Internet monitoring
	■ Mystery shopping
4.5	Identify and evaluate the various techniques for undertaking experimentation:
	■ Hall tests
	■ Placement tests
	■ Simulated test markets

1 What is observation?

▶ **Key term**

Observation is 'a non-verbal means of obtaining primary data as an alternative or complement to questioning' (MRS, 2010).

Observation takes various forms: home audit, direct observation, and the use of physical and technological recording devices.

Interviews and questionnaires depend on respondents answering questions on behaviour and attitudes truthfully. Sometimes it is necessary to **observe behaviour,** not only because respondents are unwilling to answer questions but because such questions do not record behaviour and are therefore unable to provide the researcher with answers (Hague *et al*, 2006).

There are a number of decisions to make with regard to observations as outlined in the table below.

Table 5.1   Categories of observation

Categories of observation	
Natural In setting natural to the consumer / market setting, eg a consumer using the new food to prepare a meal at home with a researcher present	**Contrived** Created specifically for the purposes of the observation, eg a test kitchen to observe how consumers eat a new food product
Visible Respondents aware they are being observed	**Hidden** Respondent unaware that they are being observed
Structured There are pre-defined ideas about what the researcher is looking for	**Unstructured** The researcher observes respondents with no pre-defined ideas about what they are looking for
Mechanised Uses measuring and recording devices, eg cameras, counters etc	**Human** The researcher conducts the observation for themselves
Participant The respondent is actively asked to carry out actions, eg use a specific product	**Non-participant** The respondent is not asked to behave in any specific way

1.1 Direct vs indirect observation

- **Indirect observation.** Also termed home audit, this involves the investigation of the respondent's home, office or premises so as to determine the extent of ownership of certain products/brands. (Note that the home audit and diary panels are termed **consumer panel** research.)

- **Direct observation.** This involves, not surprisingly, the direct observation of the behaviour of the respondent by the researcher. An event must meet three criteria to be a fit subject for direct observation.

  - The event being observed must only occupy a **short period** of time

  - It must be **frequently** performed

  - The event must be **visible** (and so feelings, beliefs and attitudes are not suitable topics for this technique).

1.2 Natural vs contrived

In **natural settings** video and movie cameras are used to record behaviour. In such settings there is an increased chance of observing real behaviour but the researcher might have to wait a long time until the behaviour occurs. Rather more prosaically, many retail outlets use **pressure mats** or automatic **sliding doors** to record basic information on number of shoppers.

Laboratory settings (contrived setting) are sometimes criticised on the grounds that consumers sometimes act differently when they are asked to respond within an unfamiliar setting. For some research projects this trait could actually be a positive feature, especially for new product development projects.

1.3 Visible vs hidden

Sometimes the researcher can influence the findings of the research unintentionally, simply by being present. Think about how you may act differently when you realise you are being watched or filmed. The researcher effect can sometimes have direct implications for the research results.

ACTIVITY 5.1

Imagine that you are a researcher and you need to observe the behaviour of a group of business professionals and their response to a new prototype. Should you conduct hidden or visible research and practically how would you observe them?

1.4 Structured vs unstructured

Structured (the researcher must know what is to be observed) or **unstructured** (the situation does not allow for the data requirements to be predetermined). Unstructured observation is more qualitative in nature and therefore more difficult to analyse. It is useful however because there may be behaviours that are discovered that the research had not expected prior to the fieldwork.

1.5 Mechanised vs human

Recording devices record micro behaviour in laboratory settings and macro behaviour in natural settings; they can be used in both direct and indirect forms of observation.

While questionnaires and diaries essentially record answers to direct questions, other devices are used to record **observations**, for instance of the order in which a consumer proceeds around a supermarket.

1.5.1 Manual recording systems

A consumer **diary** allows the consumer to record behaviour on or between different dates or even times of the day. The diary is completed every time a certain behaviour occurs, rather than behaviour being recalled at times specified by the researcher. It is thus an **accurate means of recording repetitive information** for, say, a consumer panel.

Diary-filling **can be very detailed and onerous** and it is rare that a household, even a member of a consumer panel, is asked to complete one for longer than two weeks. The problem is that the data recorded needs to be both accurate and up-to-date, whilst the room for error, with new brands on the market for instance, is vast.

During group discussion, **non-verbal communication** can be observed so as to assess the validity of a respondent's replies. This will rely on a researcher's skill in interpreting behaviour and cannot be mechanised.

1.5.2 Electronic recording systems

An explosion in market research data has been made possible by the development of **electronic recording devices**.

- **EPOS** (electronic point of sale systems) with scanners of barcodes provide fast and accurate records of sales, times and prices.

- **Electronic questionnaires** and diaries, discussed above, allow information to be input directly into a computer system, so results can be reviewed at any time in the survey and range and topical checks applied.

- **Audio and video recording devices** may be used to record interviews, especially depth ones, and camcorders can be used to record consumer behaviour.

A large range of measuring equipment is available such as:

- **Psychogalvanometers** measure a subject's response to, say, an advertisement by measuring the perspiration rate (which tends to increase when the subject is excited).

- **Eye cameras** are used to assess which parts of, for example, an advertisement attract most attention and which parts are neglected.

- **Pupilometric cameras** are used in assessing the visual stimulation derived from an image.

The key point about electronic recording devices is that **information recorded is complete**, so sampling and estimating are not required.

▶ **Assessment tip**

Observation methods that involve electronic devices and monitoring of computer usage have become more popular during the past few years. An understanding of how and when they can be used will enable you to propose creative ideas in your research design.

1.6 Participant vs non-participant

▶ **Key term**

Participant observation is a technique by which a researcher studies an activity or the life of a group by sharing in the activities.

The researcher interacts with the individuals or subjects being observed in order to collect data for the research. Mystery shopping is the most popular type of participant observation.

Non-participant observation is a research technique whereby the researcher watches the subjects of the study, with their knowledge, but without taking an active part in the situation under investigation. Non-participant observation is sometimes criticised on the grounds

that the very fact of their being observed may lead people to behave differently, thus invalidating the research data obtained. Even the video recorders used in recent years for non-participant observation have been known to alter the behaviour of some research subjects.

Non-participant observation is being used more because of the large scale use of observation to see how people behave online.

ACTIVITY 5.2

Is the observation of shoppers in a store and their movements to different sections likely to be natural or contrived and visible or disguised?

2 Advantages and disadvantages of observation

2.1 Advantages of observation

Observation has several advantages:

- It is not dependent on the respondents' memory. It records exactly what has happened, not what the respondent believes has happened

- The potential for bias in research is reduced as the researcher is the witness of behaviour rather than actively asking for information – the way an interviewer asks for information can influence responses

- Mechanical recording of observed behaviour may reduce the incidence of reporting errors

- Observation does not rely on the verbal skills of a respondent to describe the behaviour

- Observation measures what has happened, not what respondents say that they will do in a certain situation

- Observation can counter the high refusal rates in some markets

- Observation can be used to monitor behaviour preceding an action. For example, picking up and looking at competing products before making a final decision

- Observation does not interfere with the respondents' day-to-day life. It is their activity that is of interest. They do not have to fill in diaries or complete questionnaires.

2.2 Disadvantages of observation

- It may not be feasible. You can enjoy watching a customer pick your product, and no other, off the shelf, but you will have no idea why they did so

- It may be labour intensive (one observer can only observe a limited number of things). Timed video and CCTV are obviously of great assistance, and you can have several cameras, but you are unlikely to capture everything, and collating and interpreting the data may be highly time consuming

- Attitudes and feelings cannot be observed. If a customer approaches a store and then turns round and walks away without entering you have no way of knowing why, just by watching.

The use of observation as a data collection method has been stimulated by advances in electronics. **EPOS** systems allow firms to virtually 'observe' stock on hand, inflows, outflows and the speed at which stock items are moving through the store. **CCTV** is useful to combat shoplifting, but arguably much more so because of the behaviours it can reveal.

The role of observation in revealing behaviour is most obvious when dealing with the expression of behaviour that may be viewed as anti-social or revealing a negative view of the individual. In surveys of smoking behaviour, respondents have been shown to under-report the number of cigarettes they smoke by up to 100%. The same applies to alcohol units. Very often GPs will write cigarettes smoked as 10/20; 10 being the reported number, 20 the more likely figure.

3 Observation techniques

3.1 Retail audits

Retail audits are used by organisations to assess consumer demand for their products.

At set intervals **researchers visit a sample of shops**, audit (count) the stock in question and record the details of any deliveries since the last audit. Using the calculation

sales = original stock + deliveries − final stock

they are able to calculate the sales of the product since the last audit.

Shops are segmented according to their type (multiples, independent, department) and by the volume of business. Those shops which sell the largest range of products in which the organisation is interested are usually the ones upon which the auditors concentrate.

Retail audits **investigate product types** and hence the client of the research company can be provided with information on their competitors' products as well as their own.

3.2 Mystery shopping

> ▶ **Key term**
>
> **Mystery shopping** is 'the collection of information from retail outlets, showrooms and so on by people trained to observe, experience, record and measure the customer service process posing as ordinary members of the public' (MRS, 2010).

There is a limit to the amount and type of information that can be captured by most forms of observation, although **mystery shopping** is one form that allows a wide range of marketing variables to be researched.

Mystery shopping may be carried out by researchers themselves or by specially recruited and trained members of the public. As the name suggests it involves a person posing as a genuine customer (not just in a shop, it could be **any sort of customer** for **any sort of business**) and reporting back on whatever aspect of the customer experience the researcher is interested in.

The Chartered Institute of Marketing

Mystery shopping

To retain more customers and maintain a competitive edge, a company's personnel must provide service excellence – time after time, day in and day out. The dealings between frontline staff and customers define the excellence – or otherwise – of a business or brand; in today's competitive world, having a detailed understanding of these interactions has never been more important.

This is where mystery shopping comes into its element, as it offers a window into the way customers and clients experience a company's products and services, revealing how employees are interacting with customers; where, how – and if! – the company's products are recommended; and how well staff comply with prescribed service and training standards. It can also look at product availability and price, and provide reports on store environments and point-of-sale communications – and can compare and benchmark one company's performance against its competitors.

Amber Arch, GfK, JKS and MarketForce are four typical mystery shopping companies; as with the Superpanels mentioned elsewhere, they work with a team of respondents on whom they can call to make test purchases, phone calls and general inspections – without the salesperson knowing they are being 'observed': in short, to act as a real customer.

Once a would-be mystery shopper has passed an initial selection routine, they submit a detailed profile; this enables the mystery shopping company to offer their clients exactly the right blend of customers for a specific assignment – male, aged over 50, needing car insurance, in high risk area, for example; or family in a terraced house seeking change of energy supplier; female needing to obtain an MOT; young person buying mobile phone; the list is endless, and the size of the panel – and the depth and precision of the member profile – allows careful selection of exactly the right 'typical customer'.

Fees are paid to the shopper (typically £5–£15, but varying according to the precise duties required) and test purchases may be made if specified by the client. The mystery shopper has a clear brief from the end client as to exactly what is required, and is required to report back very shortly after the visit.

The Mystery Shoppers Providers Association (MSPA), an international organisation with over 350 members worldwide, represents the industry; it has its own standards and code of ethics and runs training courses and an annual international conference.

Check out companies which offer 'mystery shopping' in an internet search engine, or visit the following for more information on their activities.

http://www.mspa-eu.org/en.html
http://www.amberarch.com/
http://www.gfkmysteryshopping.co.uk/
http://www.jksmysteryshopping.co.uk/
http://uk.marketforce.com/mystery-shopping/

Issues in using mystery shopping as a research technique include the following.

- A **suitable number** of different shoppers must be used because the results may be affected by the **characteristics of the shopper** as well as of the organisation being researched. The shoppers should fit the profiles of consumers in the organisation's genuine target markets.

- Some observations made will inevitably be **subjective** and this must be taken into account.

- **Credibility** is an issue with certain types of purchase: for instance people do not buy several cars a week. Certain types of purchase, particularly in financial services, involve the selling organisation checking the credentials of the customer.

- Mystery shoppers may need to be trained in **data collection skills**: they will not be very 'mysterious' if they fill in a data sheet during a face-to-face encounter with a selling organisation!

Review the MRS guidelines on mystery shopping at http://www.mrs.org.uk

3.3 Accompanied shopping

Researchers sometimes actually visit stores with respondents, go to their workplaces to shadow or even spend time in respondents' homes in order to better appreciate how they behave. Related terms used are shadowing, consumer safaris and consumer buddying.

3.4 In-home scanning

Consumer panel research has traditionally relied on diaries or home audits to collect data. However, both Neilsen and AGB have now launched new panels based on in-home scanning, where each household is equipped with a **hand-held laser scanner** or light pen for reading the barcodes on the products they buy. This has revolutionised the consumer panel process because it obviates the need for diary completion and, plausibly, generates much higher levels of accuracy and comprehensiveness.

All panellists need to do is run the scanner or light-pen over the **barcode** as they unpack their shopping. The barcode instantly records the country of origin, the manufacturer, the product, and the product variant if applicable. Other **information can be keyed in** at the same time using the number keys attached to the scanner, including price, source of purchase, date of purchase, promotions, and who made the purchase.

3.5 Internet monitoring

The monitoring of internet usage happens in several ways, including **visitor counters**, **log files**, **page tagging** and **cookies**. Visitor counters are developed as part of a website to give a count of the number of visits to the page. They are usually displayed on the website and represent a simple way to monitor web page traffic. Log files hold information on every action each web page makes in order to ensure correct functioning. With the aid of purpose-built programs, the information can be analysed to provide useful data. Page tagging uses JavaScript on each web page to notify a third-party server when a page is rendered by a web browser.

The use of cookies allows the website owner to identify repeat visits. A cookie is a text file placed on the browser's computer that allows the browser's computer to be identified on subsequent visits. A cookie may contain the computer's address or the details of a customer registration. This means that when the customer logs on, a personalised greeting can be made or passwords provided. Cookies cannot extract information. Most online retailers use this system; for example, Amazon will drive content to particular customers based on their previous behaviour. Browser behaviour through the site can also be captured and used. This has been used to tailor-make print brochures based on customers' browsing behaviour. We can track where browsers have come from and where they go to after leaving the site.

In recent years marketers have also been able to monitor the user-generated content posted on social media sites (Facebook and LinkedIn), blogs, micro-blogs (Twitter) and video-sharing sites (YouTube, Vimeo and Blip.tv).

Mobext sees insight potential for mobile GPS tracking

Tracking consumer movements using GPS technology in mobile phones holds valuable insight potential for advertisers, according to Mobext, the Havas-owned mobile marketing network. But it warns that getting people to share such data may prove tricky.

Mobext ran a study late last year, in partnership with mobile consumer analytics firm Cadio, which involved a small number of Sprint Wireless subscribers. These opted-in participants agreed to share semi-continuous GPS data with Cadio, meaning their location was logged every 10 minutes.

The 25-54 year-olds who took part were tracked visiting more than 200 places, including shops, airports, hotels, train stations and supermarkets.

Data was analysed and generated findings as follows: panellists who went to Wal-Mart were 60% more likely to dine out than Target customers; but of those Target customers who did dine out, 25% went to a restaurant prior to going to Target while 25% went after.

Mobext sees potential here for using this data to influence retailers to expand their snack food range, say, or to form partnerships with nearby restaurants to drive complementary traffic between stores.

Knowing how often and at what time certain customers like to shop can also help retailers in tailoring their messaging, said Mobext, while analysing travel patterns – the daily commute, for instance – also has benefits for media planning.

(*Research*, 2010)

3.6 Television viewing measurement

This is the procedure used to measure the number of viewers watching a particular television programme. Around 5,100 UK households have electronic meters attached to their television sets to register when the set is turned on and what channel they are watching at different times of the day. The information collected is important to the charging made for advertising slots and the scheduling of programmes.

---

4 Experimentation

> **▶ Key term**
>
> **Testing** is 'research which measures causality and involves the researcher changing one variable (eg price, packaging, shelf display, etc), while observing the effects of those changes on another variable (eg sales) and controlling the extraneous variables'. (Wilson, 2012)

Testing may be carried out on promotional materials and messages and on products (field tests) or on samples of entire markets.

4.1 Laboratory tests

Laboratory experiments are most often used for measuring response to **advertisements**, to **product design** and to **package design**. They can take place before the item being tested is generally released (pre-testing), or after (post-testing).

In theory an **artificial environment** is set up by the researcher in which most of the crucial factors which may affect the outcome of the research are controlled. However, in pre-tests in particular it can be **difficult to design an experiment** which isolates the impact of one factor in a product or package from all the other factors which make up the proposed item, and which are likely to be the subjects of other experiments.

4.2 Hall tests

Generally these involve the prior recruitment of respondents who are then taken to a 'hall'. The hall test is most appropriate for a situation with **test materials** that can be **evaluated** quickly such as a new pack design or advertisement. They are most commonly used for **quantitative research**, but they can include observation and qualitative techniques alongside a structured questionnaire. They may include usage of a product and an interview during which a respondent is asked to give his or her opinions about a product and evaluate it, as well as make a future usage and purchase declaration. An individual test usually lasts about **20 minutes**, although the simplest versions may only involve tasting a product and evaluating it on a scale.

4.3 Field tests

With some products it is difficult for consumers to form an immediate opinion based on a short trial in unfamiliar surroundings. These include products such as domestic appliances, cars and some items of office equipment. These are better **tested over time** in the **place where they will be used**. Some products are only intended to work over a period of time (such as anti-ageing cream). Results are collated by the respondent in a diary or similar format and the results are then sent to the tester, by post or online. While they may be expensive and time consuming to conduct, these surveys have the advantage that extended testing can be carried out in realistic scenarios.

In a field test **a product is tested in realistic surroundings**, that is in the environment in which it will be bought and/or consumed once launched. Whilst the researcher has less control over extraneous variables, field experiments do give a more realistic idea of future behaviour. They are also known as product or **placement tests**.

Field tests are usually carried out for products in what the marketer hopes is their final form. They are therefore **expensive** as the product has to be made and marketed in small quantities, and they are **risky** in that competitors will inevitably get a good look. Laboratory experiments are often preferred but there are some elements of the marketing mix, such as distribution, which do not lend themselves to laboratory tests.

There are **three main types** of field test.

- A sample of consumers **try the product out at home** and report findings, usually by completing a questionnaire. The consumers are often members of a carefully selected **consumer panel**. Such in-home placement tests are often used for toiletry and other personal products.

- **Retail outlets** are used as the site for testing merchandising, packaging and point-of-sale material (**store tests**). There should be a reasonable cross-section of stores, both by size and by region, and ideally a control group. Results are measured primarily by changes in sales by store, but sometimes also by interview surveys of consumers.

- **Test marketing** is an expensive but often vital experiment in which one or more marketing actions (such as a new product) are **tried out in limited areas of the market** in order to predict sales volume, profitability, market share, consumer, retailer and distributor behaviour and regional variances. It is vital that the experiment be properly controlled since the prediction of a new product's success, or a successful change in the marketing mix of an existing product, very often depends on it. For example, the area chosen should be an accurate representation of the country as a whole. Mistakes can be expensive. The major drawback of test marketing is that it gives competitors a chance to see the new product – so it should be a short test!

Placement tests can be used for products that need to be tested over a period of time, such as household appliances or cosmetics.

- Observation is a non-verbal means of obtaining primary data as an alternative or complement to questioning.

- The role of observation in revealing behaviour is most obvious when dealing with the expression of behaviour that may be viewed as anti-social or revealing a negative view of the individual.

- Observation techniques include retail audits, mystery shopping, accompanied shopping, in-home scanning, internet monitoring, and television viewing measurement.

- Experimentation methods include laboratory tests, hall tests and field tests.

FURTHER READING

Chapters 7 and 8 of:

Bradley, N. (2010) *Marketing research: Tools & techniques.* 2nd edition. Oxford, Oxford University Press.

Chapter 4 of:

Wilson, A. (2012) *Marketing research: An integrated approach.* 3rd edition. Harlow, Financial Times Prentice Hall.

REFERENCES

Hague, P., Hague, M. and Morgan, C. (2004) *Market research in practice: A guide to the basics.* London. Kogan Page.

Tarran, B. (2010) Mobext sees insight potential for mobile GPS tracking. *Research,* http://www.research-live.com/news/technology/mobext-sees-insight-potential-for-mobile-gps-tracking/4002583.article [Accessed 02 July 2012].

Wilson, A. (2012) *Marketing research: An integrated approach*, 3rd edition. Harlow, Financial Times Prentice Hall.

QUICK QUIZ

1   What is observation?
2   Identify three electronic recording devices used for observation.
3   What is participant observation?
4   What is mystery shopping?
5   In what ways do companies monitor internet usage?
6   What is experimentation?
7   What are the main types of tests used in experimentation?

Activity 5.1

In this scenario you probably would be fine to remain visible because these respondents are likely to appreciate why you need to consider their reactions. You could openly tell them at the beginning of a prototype launch that you are interested in their initial reactions and would like to record that part of the meeting.

Activity 5.2

This is a natural setting. Ideally this should be hidden because there is the potential for consumers to behave differently if they know that they are being observed. Accompanied shopping however is a strategy used where consumers openly shop with a researcher and discuss their behaviour.

Activity 5.3

This is a 'hands-on' exercise.

1   It is 'a non-verbal means of obtaining primary data as an alternative or complement to questioning'.

2   EPOS, electronic questionnaires and audio and recording devices.

3   A technique by which a researcher studies an activity or the life of a group by sharing in the activities.

4   It is 'the collection of information from retail outlets, showrooms, etc by people trained to observe, experience, record and measure the customer service process posing as ordinary members of the public'.

5   They use visitor counters, log files, page tagging and cookies.

6   This is 'research which measures causality and involves the researcher changing one variable while observing the effects of those changes on another variable and controlling the extraneous variables'.

7   Laboratory tests, hall tests and field tests.

CHAPTER 6

Qualitative research

Introduction

This chapter identifies and evaluates the various techniques for collecting qualitative data. Unlike observation and experimentation, these techniques usually involve a lot more interaction between the researcher and respondents. The first section defines the concept of qualitative research and identifies the different ways in which it is used in marketing research.

The second section discusses the different methods used to collect qualitative data, including unstructured interviews, depth interviews, projective techniques, focus groups and online qualitative research.

The third section explores the different methods of analysing qualitative data, including tabulations, cut and paste, spider diagrams or mind maps, annotation and computerised analysis.

Topic list

What is qualitative research?	1
Qualitative data collection techniques	2
Analysing qualitative data	3

4.3	Identify and evaluate the various techniques for collecting qualitative data:
	■ Types of research most suited to qualitative research
	■ Individual depth interviews
	■ Group discussions (including basic guidelines on group moderation, stimulus material and projective techniques
	■ Using the Internet for qualitative research (online group discussions, chat rooms, blogs)
	■ Overview of approach to the analysis of qualitative research
5.1	Design a **basic** questionnaire and discussion guide to meet a project's research objectives:
	■ Discussion guide format
	■ The questionnaire design process
	■ Question and response formats
	■ Scaling techniques (Likert and semantic differential)
	■ Sequence and wording
	■ Design layout and appearance
	■ Questionnaire-generating software

1 What is qualitative research?

▶ **Key term**

Qualitative research generates contextually rich data. It is generally unstructured and only a small number of carefully selected individuals are used to produce non-quantifiable insights.

Qualitative research is a process which aims to collect primary data. Its main methods are the **open-ended interview**, whether this be a depth interview (one-to-one) or a group discussion (focus group), and **projective techniques**. The form of the data collected is narrative, rather than isolated statements reducible to numbers.

The main purpose is to understand consumer behaviour and perceptions rather than to measure them.

Qualitative research is 'research which is undertaken using an unstructured research approach with a small number of carefully selected individuals to produce non-quantifiable insights into behaviour, motivation and attitudes.' (Wilson, 2012).

The essential characteristics of qualitative research are:

- It is unquantifiable and is not representative of larger populations
- Data collection techniques are unstructured
- It involves small samples of individuals or groups of people
- It seeks to reveal opinions, motivations and attitudes
- It is about insight and depth of understanding
- It is subject to a high degree of interpretation by skilled researchers
- It often precedes quantitative work but can be independent of it
- It can inform the nature of quantitative research.

Typically qualitative work is carried out to explore what people need, care about or feel about a certain subject. In this sense it can be used for a variety of research objectives including:

- Exploratory research to help define problem areas and develop research objectives
- To uncover the context of decision making
- To reveal brand perceptions for our brands and competitors' brands
- To explore the reason why people behave in the way they do; to look at the underlying motivations and attitudes behind behaviour
- Exploring attitudes to elements of the marketing mix, for example advertising creatives or new product testing, product development and line extensions or pack designs
- Website design and usability

- Creative concept testing
- Motivational research to define areas for quantitative research
- Segmentation studies
- Positioning studies
- Brand and name development.

We'll begin this chapter by considering when it might be **appropriate** to conduct qualitative research. Then we go on to consider each of the main methods before considering how qualitative research can be analysed.

Qualitative research is particularly useful for new product research, marketing communications development and preliminary (exploratory) research prior to a more detailed, probably quantitative, study.

1.1 New products or services

New products and services (and also proposed improvements to existing products and services) have the disadvantage that there is **no existing data** to measure and perhaps **nothing more tangible than an idea** to present to people.

Qualitative research can help at the initial stages of development to help the company decide whether or not to continue with development at all, and later on, once there is a prototype of some kind, to find out what **further development** is necessary – what **other benefits** customers would like to see that could be included.

It may also help the company to decide **what part of the market** to target: the idea may be very warmly received by some groups but generate no interest whatever amongst others.

1.2 Advertising and promotion

Qualitative research is fairly widely used in the **development** of marketing communications messages to assess how consumers feel about a product or service and what sort of message they are most likely to respond to.

Qualitative methods can also be used to **pre-test** marketing communications messages to make sure the message is understood and that no unintended messages are conveyed.

1.3 Other exploratory research

For existing products and services, qualitative research may be used to find the answers to a variety of questions about customer attitudes and perceptions, segmentation and buying behaviour, often as a **preliminary** to help define the direction of **more detailed research**. For instance, if ultimately you want statistical data about the decision-making process amongst different buyer segments, you need to know what the different decision-making processes are in the first place, so you know what to measure.

Figure 6.1   Qualitative research methods

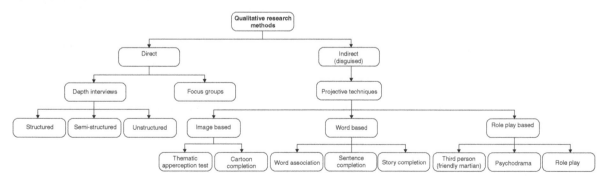

2 Qualitative data collection techniques

2.1 Unstructured interviews

> ▶ **Key term**
>
> **Unstructured interview:** An interview where neither interviewer nor respondent is bound by a structure of the questionnaire.

Interviewers may have a checklist of topics to cover in questioning, but they are free to word such questions as they wish. The order in which questions are covered may also be varied. This will allow the respondent to control the data flow and for the interviewer to explore, more thoroughly, particular views of the respondent and why they are held. Unstructured interviews are a very useful way of capturing data which is qualitative in nature. Such interviews may also provide the researcher with relevant questions which could be put to a wider audience of respondents using structured or semi-structured interview techniques, especially if quantitative data is required. (Chisnall, 2004)

2.2 Depth interviews

Motivational research often uses the psychoanalytic method of **depth interviews**. The pattern of questioning should assist the respondent to explore deeper levels of thought. Motives and explanations of behaviour often lie well **below the surface**. It is a **time-consuming** and **expensive** process. Taped interviews and analysis of transcripts are often used. A single individual or a small team may conduct depth interviewing. Depth interviews may have fewer than ten respondents although 20 seems to be a universally accepted rule of thumb. (Dillon *et al*, 1994)

The **strengths of depth interviews** include the following.

- **Longitudinal information** (such as information on decision-making processes) can be gathered from one respondent at a time, thereby aiding clarity of interpretation and analysis

- Intimate and **personal material** can be more easily accessed and discussed

- Respondents are **less likely to confine themselves** simply to reiterating socially acceptable attitudes.

There are, however, **disadvantages** of depth interviews.

- They are **time consuming** to conduct and to analyse. If each interview lasts between one and two hours, a maximum of three or four per day is often all that is possible. There is also a knock-on effect with regards to the time taken to analyse findings. Every hour of an in-depth interview can lead to around 30 pages of typed A4 paper!

- They are more **costly** than group discussions (due to time and travel expenses)

- There is a temptation to begin treating depth interviews as if they were simply another form of questionnaire survey, thinking in terms of quantitative questions like 'how many' rather than qualitative issues like 'how', 'why' or 'what'.

In a depth interview the key line of communication is between the interviewer and the respondent. They have an **open-ended conversation**, not constrained by a formal questionnaire, and the qualitative data is captured as narrative by means of an audio or video tape.

The factors to consider when planning a depth interview are as follows:

- Who should the respondent be?

    – The kind of person depends on the subject being discussed. It may be a consumer interview for discussion of consumer goods or an executive interview for discussing industrial buying

    – The number of people undergoing depth interviews in the course of the research should be considered in the light of the time they take. 10-15 is usually more than enough

    – Respondents for consumer interviews are pre recruited and asked to agree to the interview

- **What type of interview?** Although depth interviews are usually one-to-one, there may be more than one respondent and there may also be an informant, there to give *information* about tangible things (eg how big the organisation's purchase budget is) but not about his own *attitudes*.

- **How long should it be?** Genuine depth interviews interpret the meanings and implications of what is said and can therefore take some time. By contrast, a mini-depth interview may take only 15 minutes, because it can focus on one, predefined topic such as a pack design.

- **How structured should it be?** It can be totally open-ended, ranging over whatever topics come up, or it can be semi-structured with an interview guide and perhaps the use of show material.

- **What material should be used?** The type of material that is commonly used includes mock-ups or prototypes, storyboards or concept boards, narrative tapes and animatics, a form of cartoon.

- **Where should the interview take place?** Usually at home or in the workplace.

THE REAL WORLD

Using live research to obtain customer insights

Retail companies are incorporating live testing into their brand experience and using real-time insight to reduce the time it takes to launch first-class products. Marketers at retail brands in different sectors are gathering real-time consumer insight by incorporating live research techniques into their brand experience in order to create quality products faster than competitors.

Hotel Chocolat, a premium confectioner, used this technique and even charged customers for the privilege by running a members-only tasting club. This gave the company access to an informed and engaged, self-selecting research sample that fed back honest and useful insights on their needs.

ACTIVITY 6.1

Which do you think is preferable: audio or video recording of depth interviews?

2.3 Projective techniques

▶ **Key term**

Projective techniques: Research methods that attempt to draw out attitudes, opinions and motives by a variety of methods.

Many interview techniques rely on the assumption that you need only to ask people and they will tell you what you want to know. This is not always the case. People may respond differently to how they would act. People may tell you what they think you want to hear or give a different answer because their true answer may reflect badly on them or because they consider it too personal.

Alternatively, people may find difficulty in articulating their motives which lie buried deep within the sub-conscious mind. So as to overcome problems associated with articulating complex or sub-conscious motives,

researchers have borrowed techniques developed by psychologists in their studies of mentally disturbed people who have difficulty explaining why they do things.

These techniques are referred to as **projective techniques**. Attitudes, opinions and motives are drawn out from the individual in response to given stimuli.

A number of techniques might be employed.

- **Third person**, or 'friendly Martian' as it is sometimes called, is designed to get the respondent talking about issues which do not interest them. The researcher asks the respondent to describe what someone else might do (a friendly Martian). For example, if someone wanted to buy a house, what do they need to do? Can you describe the steps they would need to take?

- **Word association** is based on an assumption that if a question is answered quickly, it is spontaneous and sub-conscious thoughts are therefore revealed. The person's conscious mind does not have time to think up an alternative response.

- **Sentence completion** is a useful way to get people to respond quickly so that underlying attitudes and opinions are revealed.

  - Men who watch football are ....?
  - Women wear red are ....?
  - People who Morris dance are ....?

- In **thematic apperception tests** (TAT), people are shown a picture and asked to describe what is happening in the picture. They may be asked what happened just before or just after the picture. It is hoped that the descriptions reveal information about deeply held attitudes, beliefs, motives and opinions stored in the sub-conscious mind.

- **Story completion** allows the respondent to say what they think happens next and why.

- **Cartoon completion** is often used in competitions. There are usually speech balloons which need to be completed. A comment may be present in one and another left blank for the respondent to fill in.

- **Psychodrama** consists of fantasy situations. Respondents are often asked to imagine themselves as a product and describe their feelings about being used. Sometimes respondents are asked to imagine themselves as a brand and to describe particular attributes.

- **Mood boards** are collages of images that are cut from magazines and assembled together, either glued or pinned on a board. This technique can reveal the associations with other products' images and colours that may not come out in conventional research. The same objective lies behind asking respondents to model images relating to a brand in plasticine or clay or to draw them on paper.

- **Brand personality** asks respondents to describe a brand as a person. Another term is the 'brand CV' in which respondents write a mock curriculum vitae for the brand under consideration. This can be very useful in determining the accuracy of positioning in the market. Associations can also be made with objects or known people or celebrities; the reason for the association is the most important thing here. So when a car brand was described as 'Roger Moore' the researcher needed to probe to uncover the meaning of the association. Unfortunately, for the brand and Roger Moore, the association in this piece of work was due to the fact that 'he was once glamorous but now past it'.

- It is an extension of the brand personality test that involves multiple brands. Respondents are asked to identify key attributes or dimensions of a product sector and then position brands against those relative to the competition. This can be useful in identifying positioning and segmentation criteria and is very useful in identifying gaps in the market place. The alcopops sector was developed from this type of work. Consumers identify the fact that as children they drink fizzy, sweet, non-alcoholic drinks and as adults they drink flat, bitter or dry, alcoholic drinks. Alcopops filled the gap for sweet fizzy alcoholic drinks.

2.3.1 Problems and the value of projective research techniques

There are a few problems associated with projective techniques.

- Hard evidence of their validity is lacking. Highly exotic motives can be imputed to quite ordinary buying decisions. (One study concluded that women preferred spray to pellets when it came to killing cockroaches because being able to spray the cockroaches directly and watch them die was an expression of hostility towards, and control over, men!)

- As with other forms of intensive qualitative research, the samples of the population can only be very small, and it may not be possible to generalise findings to the market as a whole.

- Analysis of projective test findings – as with depth interviews – is highly **subjective** and prone to bias. Different analysts can produce different explanations for a single set of test results.

- Many of the tests were not developed for the study of marketing or consumer behaviour, and **may not therefore be considered scientifically valid** as methods of enquiry in those areas.

- There are **ethical problems** with 'invasion' of an individual's subconscious mind in conditions where he or she is often not made aware that he or she is exposing himself or herself to such probing. (On the other hand, one of the flaws in projective testing is that subjects may be all too well aware of the nature of the test. The identification of sexual images in inkblots has become a standard joke.)

The major drawback with projective techniques is that answers given by respondents require considerable and **skilled analysis and interpretation**. The techniques are most valuable in providing **insights** rather than **answers** to specific research questions.

However, motivational research is still in use. Emotion and subconscious motivation is still believed to be vitally important in consumer choice, and qualitative techniques can give marketers a deeper insight into those areas than conventional, quantitative marketing research.

Since motivational research often **reveals hidden motives** for product/brand purchase and usage, its main value lies in the following:

- Developing **new promotional messages** which will appeal to deep, often unrecognised, needs and associations

- Allowing the **testing of brand names**, symbols and advertising copy, to check for positive, negative and/or irrelevant associations and interpretations

- Providing **hypotheses which can be tested** on larger, more representative samples of the population, using more structured quantitative techniques (questionnaires, surveys).

2.4 Focus groups

The researcher must be careful not to generalise too much from such small-scale qualitative research. Group discussion is very dependent on the skill of the group moderator. It is inexpensive to conduct, it can be done quickly and it can provide useful, timely, qualitative data.

Focus groups are often used at the early stage of research to get a feel for the subject matter under discussion and to create possibilities for more structured research. Four to eight groups may be assembled and each group interviewed for one, two or three hours.

When planning qualitative research using focus groups, a number of factors need to be considered.

- **Type of group.** A standard group is of 7–9 respondents, but other types may also be used.

- **Membership.** Who takes part in the discussion depends on who the researcher wants to talk to (users or non-users, for instance) and whether they all need to be similar (homogenous).

- **Number of groups.** Having more than twelve groups in a research project would be very unusual, mainly because nothing new would come out of a thirteenth one!

- **Recruitment.** Usually on the basis of a quota sample: respondents are screened by a short questionnaire to see whether they are suitable. In order to persuade them to join in, the members are usually given an incentive plus expenses.

- **Discussion topics.** These will be decided by the researcher with regard to the purpose of the group discussion. There should be a number of topics, since the interviewer needs to be able to restart discussion once a topic has been fully explored.

2.4.1 Discussion guide

Topic guides can take many different forms, according to clients' preferences and the needs of the research, from loose lists of subject areas to be covered to more strictly structured lists of specific question areas.

According to Wilson (2012), a discussion guide tends to break the group discussion into three phases:

1. The introduction phase includes:

   - The objectives of the session
   - Explanation of the nature of a group discussion
   - The general agenda of topics to be followed
   - Prompts for the participants to introduce themselves

2. The discussive phase includes:

   - General topic areas to be discussed
   - Potential prompts and stimulus material

3. The summarising phase includes:

   - Prompts for summarising what has been discussed
   - Thanks to participants

Sample discussion guide: high fibre microwave pizza

Introduction

Introduce yourself and explain the ground rules you'll be operating under; remind the group that you will be (video)taping the discussion.

Ask participants to (briefly) introduce themselves, and describe, again briefly, the types of pizza they purchase or make, how often, the types of toppings, and the types of occasions when they have them.

Discussion

Ask the group to talk about the different styles of pizza that are on offer, and how (or if) this has changed over the years. They should discuss how (if) their own pizza-eating habits have changed – and why, if possible – cost, work style, time, etc.

The product

How many make pizzas at home? How many create from scratch, how many from finished stored or purchased product – and for these, how many of the various styles from frozen or chilled; oven or microwave? What else do they have by way of accompaniments – pepper, cheese, (type?); panini/ pitta/ bread sticks; extra toppings? Which?

Delve more deeply into some of the basic areas of cost and convenience.

Do all the family like the same, or compatible pizzas; or is everyone different?

Health etc

What about nutrition? What concerns do they have generally? About existing pizzas or other similar meals?

The current proposition has better nutritional content from whole wheat and bran crust, it is high in dietary fibre. It has a strong convenience position due to the ability to microwave effectively, rather than bake in oven – saving cost and time. Competitive price. Several flavours available.

What are their reactions?

Ensure you delve into central issues such as whether or not fibre is a concern – is this an opportunity to promote the product to specific users?

Is use of microwave a concern – do they raise issues of how brown and crusty the end product may be – or if it might be 'soggy' due to the steam?

Present the group with samples and discuss good and any negative points – especially identify any sensory issues – smell, appearance (colour, size, variety and density of ingredients, etc), weight.

Sum up, clarifying any uncertainties – and identify any suggestions for alternative flavours, variations, etc.

End discussion and go to retrieve incentives, etc – but allow group to continue to talk briefly 'in private' (taping is still continuing) ; note any comments for client feedback.

Summary

If necessary, continue discussion if new points have arisen from 'private' discussion. Otherwise close; thank participants for their time and distribute incentives.

▶ **Assessment tip**

The development of a discussion guide featured in the December 2009 assignment.

2.4.2 Moderator

Key to the success of a focus group will be the skill of the person running it, usually called the **moderator**.

- The moderator needs to be able to **build a rapport** between a group of people who have never met before

- He or she needs to make sure that **everyone gets an opportunity** to speak

- The moderator needs to ensure that the discussion **stays focused** on the topics at hand

- The moderator must be **sensitive to the mood** of the group throughout the discussion. It is likely to change a number of times, even during a relatively short meeting.

Dillon *et al* (1994) believes that the moderator plays the same role as a therapist does in group therapy. As such they should discuss topics within a time period but not in any set order. The role of a moderator is not to lead or direct the discussion but to keep it focussed on the topic of interest.

Moderator discussion guides should be flexible enough to be altered as the discussion progresses.

Wilson (2012) draws attention to the typical thinking process of a focus group.

- Initially there will be **anxieties and doubts**: participants won't know exactly why they are there or what is expected of them. The moderator needs to be aware of this and set their minds at rest: perhaps even ask them to share their doubts.

- Participants will **wish to feel included** so it is important to get contributions from each member early on.

- Especially because they are strangers, the group members are likely to want to **establish their own status**: what their experience of the matter under discussion is, why they should be listened to. This tends to die down after a while and participants are more interested in sharing and **relating to each other**. Depending on the individuals, however, intervention from the moderator may be required to prevent one or two people dominating the discussion.

- People are keen to feel that their **opinions are valued**: the moderator needs good listening skills (good eye contact, asking for points made to be developed).

- Sooner or later people will start to **wish to leave**, so the moderator needs to give indications of how much ground has been covered and what is left to be covered, at regular intervals.

2.4.3 Advantages and disadvantages of focus groups

The **key advantages** of focus groups include the following.

- The group environment with 'everybody in the same boat' can be **less intimidating** than other techniques of research which rely on one-to-one contact (such as depth interviews).

- What respondents say in a group often **sparks off experiences** or ideas on the part of others.

- **Differences between consumers** are highlighted, making it possible to understand a range of attitudes in a short space of time.

- It is **easier to observe groups** and there is more to observe simply because of the intricate behaviour patterns within a collection of people.

- **Social and cultural influences** are highlighted.

- Groups provide a **social context** that is a 'hot-house' reflection of the real world.

- Groups are **cheaper and faster** than depth interviews.

- **Technology** may help to facilitate and add value to the process.

  - Group discussions can be **video tape recorded** for later analysis and interpretation, or they may even be **shown 'live'** to the client via CCTV or webcam.

  - In business-to-business situations it may be possible to use **video-conferencing**, enabling opinions to be sought from a wider variety of locations.

- **Forums** and **chat rooms** on the web can be used.

The principal **disadvantages** of groups are as follows.

- Group processes may **inhibit some people from making a full contribution** and may encourage others to become exhibitionistic.

- Group processes **may stall** to the point where they cannot be retrieved by the moderator.

- Some groups may **take a life of their own**, so that what is said has validity only in the short-lived context of the group.

- It is not usually possible to identify **which group members said what**, unless the proceedings have been video recorded.

THE REAL WORLD

Customer insight at Sainsbury's

As one of the major players in the UK food retail industry, Sainsbury's needs a proper understanding of customer needs and how they are changing, to remain competitive in the industry.

At Sainsbury's all store managers run monthly listening groups with customers. They run accompanied shops and also spend a lot of time on the shop floor, watching customers, in order to understand their behaviour. The listening groups are both formal and informal. Formal listening groups normally involve some very selective recruitment, while informal sessions just involve recruiting customers on the day to talk about their shopping experience. The good thing about talking to customers is that they rarely hold back. They usually tell you exactly what they think about the store, the range of products available, the staff and other aspects of their shopping experience.

In addition to traditional qualitative and quantitative research, the company also listens to customers by watching their behaviour through the Nectar loyalty scheme. Nectar data allows the company to really see what customers are doing.

(Baker, 2011)

ACTIVITY 6.2

What are the advantages and disadvantages of group discussions and depth interviews?

2.5 Online qualitative research

In less than a decade, a third of US research agencies revenues has shifted to online research. Rather than the research industry being threatened by the new digital environment, Cooke and Buckley (2008) believed that it offers an opportunity to develop new research approaches. The researchers from agency GFK NOP identified Web 2.0 as one example of where innovative methods can be used to explore changing social environments. They clearly define Web 2.0 as:

'Web 2.0 refers to the new generation of tools and services that allow private individuals to publish and collaborate in ways previously available only to corporations with serious budgets, or to dedicated enthusiasts and semi-professional web builders.'

It is built around the concept of social software that enables people to collaborate and form online communities. Online communities combine one-to-one (email, instant messages), one-to-many (web pages, blogs) and many-to-many (social networking sites eg Wikis, Facebook, Second Life) communication modes.

The growth in social networking is significant for market researchers because within society a population is growing who are more willing to record and share their experiences with friends and other community members

for evaluation. This evaluation forms the basis of individuals' reputations and possibly self concept. Social networks also highlight human tribal behaviour. Earls (2003) suggested that market researchers have, in the past, overlooked the most important part of what it means to be human; we are herd animals. He argued that market researchers should study the interaction between individuals to make informed decisions about consumer behaviour.

Social software which supports group interaction can include: blogs, wikis, podcasts, peer-to-peer (P2P) file sharing, virtual worlds and social networks. Additional content is often generated following a 'mash up' where information is mixed from a number of disparate sources to create creative data. The key issue for researchers to grasp, according to Cooke and Buckley (2008), is that social networks are formed voluntarily and sub-groups develop as experiences are shared and reputations are built. Within these online environments, members set the agendas and conversations and therefore selectively only enter groups where there is a common interest.

The next generation of the web – Web 3.0 – is expected to significantly transform online market research. Rather than just creating links between people, Web 3.0 is expected to be much more about linking data. The technology is expected to make data more open, linkable and shareable.

ACTIVITY 6.3

Imagine you are investigating whether a new form of refrigerator, which is highly environmentally friendly with a negligible carbon footprint, could be an effective addition to your product range. You know through secondary research that this would appeal to a growing group of ecologically aware consumers but because the production costs are high, you need to conduct some detailed research into the price that target consumers would be willing to spend.

How might social networks help with this research?

For the market researcher, social networks can be created, or existing networks used where community members are already interested in the subjects being investigated. Both qualitative and quantitative research is possible and this provides a wealth of opportunity for not only increasing response rates as a result of precision sample selection and respondent interest, but the ability to hold more sophisticated extended focus groups and interactive panels (although to describe social network research in these two traditional terms could be considered to undermine their true value and future opportunity).

THE REAL WORLD

The virtual world Second Life has a growing number of established 'real-world' brands using its communities to pilot test product launches, idea generation, concept testing and customer experience research. Second Life enables users to create alternative realities from scratch and so they could technically be living a double life, one within the real world and one with a virtual existence alongside. As lifestyles are built within these virtual lives, brands are entering the virtual marketplace for members to purchase and conspicuously use, in order to develop their virtual self concept and reputation. Dell, for example, enables Second Life users to build their own bespoke computer to use in their virtual life and then to buy the finished product in the real world if they wish.

Lego, similarly, through their own website, enables member users to build their own models from over 500 pieces; this equates to a massive design team to assist with NPD.

(*Research*, 2008)

The Chartered Institute of Marketing

3 Analysing qualitative data

The qualitative data you have collected from focus groups and depth interviews and the like will most probably be in the form of **transcripts** of tapes and interviewers' notes. A large volume of such data may seem unmanageable at first, but there are a variety of techniques that you can use to make sense of it all. This is called '**content analysis**' (Miles and Huberman, 1994). It is 'the objective, systematic and quantitative description of the manifest content of a communication' (Malhotra, 2010). It Involves observing and analysing the content of advertising messages, newspaper and magazine articles, television and radio programmes and recorded conversations. According to Wilson (2012), it involves two main components:

1. Organisation of the data: Manual or computerised structuring and ordering of the data
2. Interpretation of the data: Determining what the data is saying in the light of the research objectives

There are various techniques:

- **Tabulation**. A table is created with columns for the different kinds of respondents and rows for the research objectives. Here is a very basic example.

Table 6.1   Sample tabulation example

	Men	Women
Attitude towards watching sports		
Attitude towards playing sports		

The comments and quotes from the transcripts are then entered into the appropriate box. This makes it much easier to make comparisons and can give rise to some quantitative data ('six out of ten women said ...').

Provided researchers are not allowed to add their own categories, the task can be shared between several people with consistent results. On the other hand, the method could be considered to be too inflexible: collected data that does not 'fit' anywhere might be discarded even though it is valuable.

- **Cut and paste**. This is identical to the tabular method except that data is not entered afresh but simply 'lifted' from the original transcript, so preserving accuracy. A word processing package or a spreadsheet would be used.

- **Spider diagrams** or **mind maps**. The research issue is placed at the centre of a sheet of paper and the key themes that emerge, and relevant quotes and comments from the transcripts, of are placed around it.

Figure 6.2   Factors influencing how customers assess price

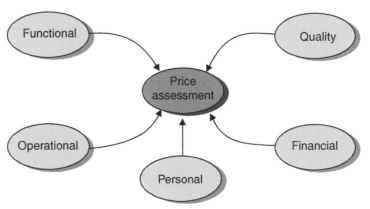

This makes it easier to include comments that don't 'fit' when using the tabulation method. The complexity of the interrelationships between items can be shown more clearly, via the placement of the comments and the use of interconnecting lines. Because the method is less rigid, there is no guarantee that two researchers would analyse the data in the same way, however.

- **Annotation.** As you might guess, this entails the researcher categorising the items in a transcript by adding marginal comments, or perhaps using different coloured highlighter pens (or the equivalent in a word processor or spreadsheet). This leaves the actual data intact, so it is still possible to see how the full conversation flowed.

- **Computerised analysis** is possible with varying degrees of sophistication. Some programs might simply count the number of times a particular word or phrase appears; others can recognise patterns and related concepts.

- Qualitative research is particularly useful for new product research, marketing communications development and preliminary (exploratory) research prior to a more detailed, probably quantitative study.

- The main method of qualitative research is the interview.

- Projective techniques attempt to draw out attitudes, opinions and motives by a variety of methods.

- Focus groups concentrate on discussion of chosen topics in an attempt to find out attitudes. They do have limitations, despite advantages such as the ability to observe a whole range of responses at the same time.

- Techniques for analysing qualitative data include tabulation, cut and paste, spider diagrams or mind maps, annotation and computerised analysis.

FURTHER READING

Chapters 7 and 9 of:

Bradley, N. (2010) *Marketing research: Tools & techniques.* 2nd edition. Oxford, Oxford University Press.

Chapter 5 of:

Wilson, A. (2012) *Marketing research: An integrated approach.* 3rd edition. Harlow, Financial Times Prentice Hall.

REFERENCES

Baker, R. (2011) Sainsbury's: 'Nectar data makes our c-stores stronger than rivals'. *Marketing Week,* http://www.marketingweek.co.uk [Accessed 12 June 2012].

Chisnall, P. (2004) *Marketing research.* 7th edition. Maidenhead, McGraw-Hill.

Cooke, N. and Buckley, N. (2008) Web 2.0, social networks and the future of market research. *International Journal of Market Research,* 50(2), pp267–292.

Dillon, W., Madden, T. and Firtle, N. (1994) *Marketing Research in a Marketing Environment.* 3rd edition. Illinois, Irwin.

Earls, M. (2003) 'Advertising to the herd: how understanding our true nature challenges the ways we thing about advertising and market research'. *International Journal of Market Research*, Vol 45, Issue 3, pp311–366.

Malhotra, N. (2010) *Marketing Research: An applied orientation.* 6th edition. New Jersey, Pearson.

Miles, M. and Huberman, A. (1994) *Qualitative data analysis: An expanded sourcebook.* London, Sage.

Wilson, A. (2012) *Marketing research: An integrated approach.* 3rd edition. Harlow, Financial Times Prentice Hall.

1   Qualitative research is particularly appropriate for which types of research project?

2   If you are stopped in the street and asked a series of questions by someone with a clipboard you have taken part in qualitative research. True or false? Explain your answer.

3   Which of the following is most likely to be a question asked in a depth interview?
     A   How often do you buy this product?
     B   Which product do you prefer?
     C   Why do you like this product?

4   What projective technique is being described in each case?
     –   Get someone talking about issues which do not interest them
     –   Subconscious thoughts may be revealed
     –   Underlying attitudes and opinions may be revealed
     –   What happens next
     –   What is happening in the picture
     –   What people think as opposed to what they say

5   List five factors that need to be considered when planning qualitative research using focus groups.

The Chartered Institute of Marketing

Activity 6.1

There is no definite answer, but people are more likely to be self-conscious about being captured on video than they are on tape and may even refuse to allow you to video them. If they are not comfortable it is less likely that you will get the information you require.

Activity 6.2

Table 6.2   Advantages and disadvantages of discussions and interview

Group discussions	Depth interview
Advantages	
Less intimidating	Decision-making *processes* can be analysed
Easily observed	Majority *and* minority opinion can be captured
Range of attitudes can be measured	Sensitive topics more easily discussed
Social aspect reflects real world	'Unusual' behaviour can be discussed
Dynamic and creative	
Cheaper	
Disadvantages	
Participants may not express what they really think – they may be inhibited or they may be showing off	Time consuming
	Less creative
Views may be unrealistic – meaningful in a group context but not for the individual	More expensive

Activity 6.3

There are a number of existing social networks which developed as individuals started to discuss their growing ecological concerns. The members of these online communities would be expected to be interested in debating and entering dialogue about such a refrigerator. These groups may also provide a strong referral market if the product was launched in the market

1   New product or service research, social research, marketing communications research and exploratory research.

2   Probably not: the person with the clipboard will most likely be asking a series of pre-defined questions and asking you to choose between pre-defined options. Qualitative research is supposed to allow the respondents to say whatever they feel and think in response to flexible, 'prompting' questioning.

3   Question C. 'Why do you like this product?'

     The other questions would be better asked as part of a questionnaire with pre-defined options, since there are only a limited number of possible answers.

4

Table 6.3   Projective techniques

Projective technique	Used to reveal
Third person or 'Friendly Martian	Get someone talking about issues which do not interest them
Word association	Subconscious thoughts may be revealed
Sentence completion	Underlying attitudes and opinions may be revealed
Story completion	What happens next
Thematic apperception tests	What is happening in the picture
Cartoon completion	What people think as opposed to what they say

5   We only asked for a list, but see if you can add a comment to each item.

(a)   Type of group   (d)   Recruitment
(b)   Membership   (e)   Discussion topics
(c)   Number of groups

The Chartered
Institute of Marketing

CHAPTER 7

Quantitative research

Introduction

Quantitative research is highly structured research conducted using large sample of respondents to provide quantifiable insights. It is the collection of information that can be easily counted or numbered. This chapter identifies and evaluates the various techniques for collecting quantitative data.

The first section defines quantitative research and identifies the different methods of collecting quantitative data. The second section discusses the different interview and survey methods used to collect quantitative data. These include street surveys, shop surveys, hall tests, placement tests, home interviews, business surveys, postal surveys, web surveys and omnibus surveys.

Topic list

4.4	Identify and evaluate the various techniques for collecting quantitative data:
	▪ Face-to-face survey methods
	▪ Telephone interviews
	▪ Postal surveys
	▪ Online surveys
	▪ Omnibus surveys
	▪ Forum voting (pressing voting buttons)

1 What is quantitative research?

▶ **Key terms**

Quantitative research is highly structured research conducted using a large sample of respondents to provide quantifiable insights.
Quantitative data: This is data that is measured or identified on a numerical scale.

Quantitative data are the best-known currency of marketing research. It is quantitative data that gives us the state of the opinion polls or allows companies to claim that nine out of ten customers prefer their product. According to ESOMAR (2010), it accounts for 80% of research turnover worldwide.

It is quantifiable because data is collected in a way that allows generalisations to be made about a general population from taking a sample of that population.

Questionnaires and surveys are key to collecting quantitative data. Surveys, however, can be administered in a number of different ways and the surveys that may be used therefore need to be produced in an appropriate style for that survey type. The following diagram highlights the alternative survey styles.

Figure 7.1   Alternative survey styles

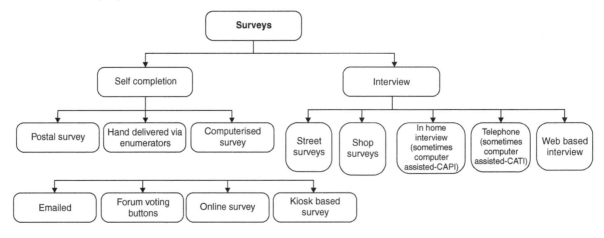

Quantitative research in fragrance testing

The international fragrance research agency ScentAnalysis has launched a new quantitative scent research tool, the Scent Choice Test. SCT is designed to evaluate not just whether people like a fragrance, but how effectively the fragrance conveys the image of the brand it is supposed to be associated with.

SCT enables respondents to rate fragrances according to particular attributes relevant to the brand or concept, so that the companies can see how close the fragrance matches customers' expectations of their brand and what changes they need to make to create a better fit.

(*Research*, 2011)

> **Assessment tip**
>
> A good understanding of quantitative research methods is essential as most assignments require you to decide on appropriate research methods in the process of writing a research proposal.

2 Interviews and surveys

Interviews are **classified according to where they occur** (in the street, in a shop, in the home). Despite possible interviewer bias, interviews can improve the quality and rate of responses.

Postal surveys are less costly and time consuming. **Telephone surveys** have some advantages, especially the ability to cover a wider geographical area, but have the disadvantage of lack of rapport and confusion with telesales.

2.1 Face-to-face interviews

Many surveys in UK market research take place as **face-to-face** interviews. The interviewers are often freelancers but can be employees of a market research organisation. An interview is a social encounter, where the personal interface between interviewee(s) and interviewer is crucial.

There are six main styles of interview, classified according to where they occur.

- **Street surveys** take place typically in busy town centres, with the interviewer approaching individuals as they pass by. They need to be brief (five minutes is too long for most people in their lunch break or going to or from work) and should not require too much concentration from the interviewees, so getting them to consider show material should be avoided. A survey taking place in a shopping centre requires the centre manager's permission, and a fee may be payable.

  Interviewing in the open air significantly affects the quality of the data obtained and respondents interviewed in bad weather may not be attentive to the questions being asked. In some cases, respondents have been known to provide quick, unreliable answers in order to complete the survey and get away from the interviewer as soon as possible. It is also becoming more difficult to recruit respondents as shoppers intentionally avoid interviewers and mistake them for charity fundraisers.

- **Shop surveys** take place inside or just outside a particular shop, obviously with the shop's permission.

- **Hall tests** take place in a pre-booked location such as a hotel, where people are invited to attend to answer a few questions, usually being recruited from the street and being enticed by a giveaway or refreshments. More complex tasks can be performed by the interviewee, for instance a display can be permanently set up and considered. Sometimes they may be carried out in a natural place for a particular product's consumption or usage: for example, a new brand of alcohol may be tested in pubs or restaurants.

- **Placement tests.** Respondents for these tests are recruited from omnibus surveys or street interviews, and are provided with the product to test in their own home, or whatever location is appropriate.

- **Home interviews** are held in the interviewee's home (or doorstep), with the interviewer recruiting simply by knocking on doors. They can be pre-arranged by phone or by dropping a note through the door. Larger, in-depth interviews often result but they are time-consuming, expensive and prone to interruption. Many people are reluctant even to answer their doors let alone let an interviewer in, so recruiting for home interviews is often frustrating for the interviewer. In recent years the amount of time it takes to get the interviews and the increased number of houses that must be visited has resulted in a significant reduction in the use of this method.

- **Business surveys** take place on the interviewee's business premises and are always pre-arranged. Again they are prone to interruption and/or last-minute cancellation.

ACTIVITY 7.1

The next time you see someone conducting interviews in the street don't cross the road or avert your eyes: volunteer to take part and (without being too obvious about it) try to take note of the way questions are phrased, how much depends on the skill of the interviewer, and how easy the interviewer (who may or not be well-trained) finds it to record your responses. Don't forget to make notes when you get the opportunity.

It must always be remembered that people taking part in interview surveys are **doing the researcher a favour**, so the least one can do is ensure that the interviewer is well-prepared and does not make the interviewee feel that his or her time is being wasted. Good preparation will also save time in the long run and reduce the costs of hiring freelance interviewers. Finally, it will result in getting the data that is actually needed. It is vital, therefore, that the questionnaire or interview schedule is clear, unambiguous, and accurate.

The interviewer's other tasks are:

- To **locate respondents** (stopping in street, or calling house-to-house as instructed by the researcher)

- To **obtain respondents' agreement** to the interview (no mean feat)

- To **ask questions** (usually sticking strictly to the interview schedule/questionnaire's wording) and take down answers

- To **complete records**.

Since the desired outcome of the survey is useful data, it is important to consider whether **interviewer bias** may affect the outcome. This comes about in selection of respondents (stopping people who look 'nice' rather than a reasonable cross-section) and handling the interview (not annoying the respondent so his or her answers are affected).

The **advantages** of face-to-face contact methods are:

- There is **greater acceptance** of the validity of the research if an interviewer can introduce the reasons for the research and show professional membership cards

- The interview process is **more efficient** as non-eligible respondents can be screened out more effectively

The Chartered
Institute of Marketing

- They **improve response rates**, as the interviewer can answer questions or help with any difficulty in completing the questionnaire

- Personal contact creates a **sense of obligation** and this can be useful with long surveys. This can reduce the incidence of incomplete or unfinished interviews

- **Complexity** can be introduced into the survey – for example, the use of show cards or other stimuli material is more easily managed

- Empathy and encouragement can enable **deeper consideration** of the questions and ensure accuracy of some claims – for example, gender and age.

There are some **disadvantages**:

- Costs, particularly in B2B research, may be high, but this must be offset against a higher response rate

- It can take a considerable amount of time to complete a survey

- Interviewers may be demotivated and may take short cuts to ensure that their quota of completed surveys is made

- Interview bias is a problem. Bias may affect:

  - Who is interviewed – interviewers may select those people who want to be interviewed.

  - The way questions are asked – with a negative inflection or a preceding ad-libbed comment, eg 'I know this sounds stupid, but …'

  - The way an interviewer responds verbally and visually to an answer – a raised eyebrow or an expression of shock is not required!

  - The way an answer is recorded; the interpretation of a response may be biased

- Safety of interviewing staff may be an issue in some areas

- The training and control of field staff is important and adds to costs

- A dispersed sample geographically, for example regional store managers, is clearly difficult to administer in this way and other data collection methods might need to be considered.

2.1.1 What makes a good interviewer?

From the above, it is clear that the weak point in the collection of survey data is often the interviewer. The Interviewer Quality Control Scheme (IQCS) is an independent organisation working to maintain standards.

There are many factors which must be carefully considered when selecting or recruiting interviewers.

Gender

The majority are women. At the risk of sounding sexist, there are several reasons for this. Part-time work-interview work is flexible and fits around other responsibilities. Women tend to have better listening skills and find it easier to elicit information from respondents.

Age

The ideal age requirements for entry to consumer interviewing is between 25 and 45 years. In B2B markets, older, more experienced interviewers may be required.

Social background

It is useful if the interviewer is not obviously from any social class. It helps if the interviewer has the ability to be 'chameleon-like' so as to be able to fit in with the respondent. Politically, interviewers should be aware but not activists. It is usual, when interviewers are recruited, for them to be screened for political activity if they are likely to be employed in asking political questions.

Education

Interviewers should be numerate and literate. Interviewers should have at least GCSE level English and Maths. In certain B2B projects it may be useful to have some business education.

Experience

Some experience of dealing with people and B2B interviewing experience in the sector under review may be desirable. Training in research interviewing is not vital but IQCS-accredited interviewers are required to be trained. MRS training is available via the Accredited Interviewer Training Scheme. Interviewers are awarded the MRS Certificate in Interviewing Skills for Market & Social Research if they complete the MRS training. Information can be found at http://www.mrs.org.uk/training and follow the link to AITS.

Personality

The ideal researcher is gregarious and outgoing but not overbearing. They should be a good listener capable of empathy. They should be capable of multitasking, that is listening and recording data simultaneously.

THE REAL WORLD

Understanding non-native British consumers

Over the past three decades, the UK population has become much more diverse. Non-native British consumers now represent a significant proportion of the target market for many consumer goods companies.

A new study known as Culture Watch has been commissioned to examine the basic dynamics of a sample of non-native British consumers, their attitudes to branding and advertising, their awareness and purchasing across key market sectors and their media consumption. It includes a syndicated quantitative study of groups of non-native British consumers, including people from Poland, China, the Indian sub-continent and Latin America. Face-to-face interviews will also be conducted to gather more detailed information.

For more information, check out http://www.ipa.co.uk/news/Culture-watch-joins-forces-with-Future-Foundation

---

2.2 Postal surveys

Approximately 25% of market research questionnaires are completed by postal survey. We are using the term 'postal' survey to cover all methods in which the questionnaire is given to the respondent and returned to the investigator without personal contact. Such questionnaires could be sent by post but might also be left near a store exit or delivered via door drops.

Postal questionnaires have the following **advantages** over personal interviews.

- The **cost per person** is likely **to be less**, so more people can be sampled, and central control is facilitated

- It is usually possible to **ask more questions** because the people completing the forms (the respondents) can do so in their own time

- **All respondents are presented with questions in the same way**. There is no opportunity for an interviewer to influence responses (interviewer bias) or to misrecord them

- It may be **easier to ask personal or embarrassing questions** in a postal questionnaire than in a personal interview

- Respondents **may need to look up information for the questionnaire**. This will be easier if the questionnaire is sent to their homes or places of work.

The Chartered
Institute of Marketing

There are **disadvantages**:

- Response rates may be low, sometimes as low as 1–2%. They can be increased through time-limited incentives and appeals to a sense of duty; in these circumstances rates can be as high as 50–60% and sometimes even higher

- Research design is limited

- They may take time to complete and this can lead to low response

- The availability of lists to form a sample frame may be limited in certain markets

- There is limited control over the respondent and a higher incidence of incomplete questionnaires or inconsistent answers may be expected. This can be alleviated through good questionnaire design and careful piloting

- There is potential for bias in responders as those who respond may be those who feel strongly about an issue.

While postal survey response rates may be low, these can be increased in the following ways:

- **Pre-screening** – Calls can be made to respondents prior to sending the questionnaire. This could confirm details and create a sense of expectation and commitment to the process.

- **Reminder calls** or letters to encourage the respondent to reply – These may take place at a specified time after the questionnaire has been sent. Some agencies will send duplicate copies of the research questionnaires.

- **Provide incentives** – In consumer markets, coupons or vouchers can be used; in B2B markets access to an executive summary of the final report may be offered as an incentive.

- **Personalise the survey** – Postal research response rates tend to be higher when the research is part of an existing relationship. Data collection methods need to reflect the nature of the population under consideration.

The covering letter is crucial to introduce the research and the organisation carrying out the research. It may contain a letter of reference or professional membership symbols.

ACTIVITY 7.2

What are the advantages of personal interviews over postal questionnaires?

2.2.1 Enumerators

An **enumerator** will **deliver the questionnaire** and **encourage the respondent to complete it**. He or she will later visit the respondent again to collect the completed questionnaire and perhaps to help with the interpretation of difficult questions. This method results in a better response rate than for postal questionnaires.

2.3 Telephone surveys

Telephone research involves interviewing respondents over the telephone. This may be done at home but more usually is managed via a call or contact centre. The use of the telephone in market research is significant: 18% of research turnover was accounted for by the telephone in 2008 (ESOMAR, 2010). This is due to a number of factors:

- **Changing environment** – We are contactable all the time via our mobile phones. Automation has meant that the costs of calling have come down and automated dialling and digital research accounted for 17% of research spend in 2008 (ESOMAR, 2010).

- **The way we work** – Telephone research mirrors many business processes and distribution networks. Business is changing. People are used to transacting over the telephone.

- We are comfortable discussing personal matter over the telephone.

- An estimated 3% of the entire UK workforce is employed in the 'contact centre' industry. This is more than mining, fishing and agriculture combined.

- The United Kingdom is the largest user of call centres in Europe employing 39% of the total agents in Europe.

- The United Kingdom has 5,000–16,000 call centres depending on the definition used.

- Legislation and de-regulation have opened up, the market for telephone services and the cost of calls has fallen.

- Mobile phones and mobile internet mean that research can use a range of methods to reach and stimulate respondents.

- Technology enables very efficient calling procedures. These include computer telephony integration (CTI) linking the call centre to the marketing database, computer-assisted telephone interviewing (CATI) systems, bespoke systems for the management of telephone research and interactive voice recognition (IVR) that enables calls to be made automatically.

Surveys conducted over the phone, rather than face-to-face, have the following **advantages**:

- The response is **rapid**

- There is a **standard sampling frame** – the **telephone directory**, which can be systematically or randomly sampled

- A **wide geographical area** can be covered fairly cheaply

- It may be **easier to ask sensitive or embarrassing questions**.

But there are considerable **disadvantages** as well.

- A **biased sample** may result from the fact that a significant proportion (about 10%) of people do not have telephones (representing certain portions of the population such as old people or students) and many of those who do are ex-directory.

- It is not possible to use 'showcards' or pictures.

- Due to the reputation of telesales, the refusal rate is much higher than with face-to-face interviews, and the interview is often cut short.

- It is not possible to see the interviewee's expressions or to develop the rapport that is possible with personal interviews.

- The interview **must be short**.

2.4 Online surveys

Online surveys are becoming more and more common. The internet is ideal for surveys in some respects, but far less so in others.

- Questionnaires can be **generated dynamically** in response to the respondent's answers. For example, if the respondent indicates no interest whatever in a particular topic then any questions relating to that topic can be skipped by the computer without the respondent even knowing the questions existed. Alternatively, if they indicate strong interest they may get additional questions that others would not see. This saves time for everybody.

- On the other hand **web users may not be typical** of the target market (not all of whom may have access to the internet). **Design issues** are even more crucial than with paper-based questionnaires. All the same issues and pitfalls apply, but with several **additional factors** such as speed of processing, intuitive navigation through the questionnaire and security concerns.

Respondents can be recruited to participate in web-based surveys through:

- Self-selection, when they notice a link or a pop-up on a website they have visited
- An email request with a link to the site
- A non-electronic invitation to participate, eg by letter

Online methods have a number of **advantages**:

- They are cheap to administer, design, deliver and analyse

- They are flexible in content and can include image and sound files

- They are fast to administer and to report on

- They have immediate and low-cost global reach

- They can replicate customer behaviour in both consumer and business markets

- They can be used automatically as pop-up, as a browser scrolls over a certain part of the site. Dell have used this system on their website – a service designed by Opinionlabs (http://www.opinionlabs.com)

- They are easy to control

- They can be completed at the respondents' convenience.

There are several **disadvantages**:

- Technology is varied and the use of attachments or HTML e-mails may not be supported by all devices

- The amount of unsolicited e-mails or spam may affect perception of the questionnaire

- Samples might be difficult to construct as e-mail lists are not very reliable and there is limited access to the internet and e-mail – especially in the lower socio-economic groups and in certain international markets

- It may be hard to validate who has responded as anybody could be using the computer

- People remain suspicious of the internet and confidentiality needs to be ensured

- There may be a cost to the respondent, especially if the questionnaire takes time to download

- The ease of use in some organisations has led to very poor 'research' being carried out on an ad hoc basis.

2.4.1 Forum voting (voting buttons)

Voting buttons are also popular in order to gather quick answers to just one or two key questions. Voting buttons can be sent by email or placed within a website. Clearly the use of voting buttons cannot be used where there are a number of complex research objectives, but they are useful in quickly measuring a key issue.

2.4.2 Kiosk surveys

Kiosk surveys are essentially similar in terms of the look and design of the overall survey. The difference is that touch-sensitive computer station are located in areas where sample respondents are likely to be passing. The kiosks are used frequently in research into exhibitions for example. Whereas previously footfall may have been measured and survey interviewers may have approached visitors as they left an exhibition, kiosks offer the opportunity for respondents to participate in research independently. Retailers and public services locations are also key users of kiosk-based surveys.

2.5   Continuous research

The object of continuous research is to **take measurements regularly** so as to monitor **changes in the market**, either consumer, business or internally. Often syndicated because of the set-up costs, continuous research is usually undertaken by a large market research organisation. It can focus on the same consumers over time (panel research) or on a changing body of consumers.

Some research is continuous in the sense that measurement takes place every day, while in other cases measurements are taken at regular intervals.

2.5.1 Omnibus surveys

> ▶ **Key term**
>
> An **omnibus survey** is a master questionnaire run by market research companies who 'sell' space on the questionnaire to marketing organisations who need data.

Because the market research companies undertake the sampling, administration, processing and analysis, and spread the cost over the organisations needing data, Omnibus surveys are a cost-effective method of research for all concerned. Like panel-based surveys, omnibus surveys are increasingly popular because of the development of Web 2.0.

The master questionnaire usually contains some of the same questions (age, gender, occupation) every time, while the remainder of the questions are either continuous (the same questions in the same place on the questionnaire as were asked of a different group, say, one week earlier) or *ad hoc* (inserted on a first-come-first-served basis but in a sensible order).

Omnibus surveys have a number of advantages:

- They are cheap: typically, a simple question can be placed for around £1,200; more complex questions will cost more
- Quantified analysis can be accessed extremely quickly
- Representative of a market and statistically valid
- Gives access to 'hard to research' markets – for example, directors or small business owners.

Disadvantages:

- The sample cannot be changed.
- Questions must be phrased simply.
- Not suitable for opinions or attitudes.
- Question order may affect responses.

2.5.2 Market tracking surveys

Where the market research company designs the whole questionnaire seeking data on a particular market from regular samples of respondents, rather than a panel, there is a **market tracking survey**. The results are sold by the company to as many marketing organisations as possible. Sometimes information on product usage is combined with data on media exposure.

2.5.3 In-store testing

Product testing in store may be a **relatively quick and inexpensive method** of gathering information about customer attitudes towards a particular product. In-store testing can be a useful, convenient way to gain insights into expected consumer behaviour before a full product launch is implemented. Selected stores can be chosen to test a product and gather information about likely buyer behaviour when the product is launched. In-store testing is also a way of promoting the product before, during and after a launch.

2.6   Incentives

It may be advisable to take active steps to **encourage better response rates** from questionnaires, surveys and telephone studies. Methods of achieving this include putting all respondents' names into a **prize draw** or offering a product or service **discount** to all respondents. A whole host of incentives exist and the key is to use an incentive which is valued by the respondents (Dillon *et al*, 1994). There is a lot of debate within marketing research about whether incentives work. A key issue to consider however is that it is probably fair to assume that respondents have come to expect some form of incentive in return for their time and opinions. It is probably not worth the risk of reducing response rates further by not including one.

ACTIVITY 7.3

Explain the difference between quantitative and qualitative methods of marketing research.

CHAPTER ROUNDUP

- Quantitative data is the best-known currency of marketing research.

- Interviews are classified according to where they occur (in the street, in a shop, in the home). Despite possible interviewer bias interviews can improve the quality and rate of responses. Postal surveys are less costly and time consuming. Telephone surveys have some advantages, especially the ability to cover a wider geographical area, but have the disadvantage of lack of rapport and confusion with telesales.

- Online surveys are becoming more and more common.

- Omnibus surveys may be a cost-effective way of obtaining certain types of information.

- Incentives can be used to encourage better response rates.

FURTHER READING

Chapters 4 and 8 of:

Bradley, N. (2010) *Marketing research: Tools & techniques*. 2nd edition. Oxford, Oxford University Press.

Chapter 6 of:

Wilson, A. (2012) *Marketing research: An integrated approach.* 3rd edition. Harlow, Financial Times Prentice Hall.

REFERENCES

Anon (2011) ScentAnalysis launches qualitative fragrance test. *Research*, http://www.research-live.com/news/technology/scentanalysis-launches-quantitative-fragrance-test/4005369.article [Accessed May 2012].

Bain, R. (2012) IPA backs UK cultural diversity study. *Research*, http://www.research-live.com/news/news-headlines/ipa-backs-uk-cultural-diversity-study/4006664.article [Accessed May 2012].

Dillon, W., Madden, T. and Firtle, N. (1994) *Marketing research in a marketing environment.* 3rd edition. Illinois, Irwin.

Verinder, J (2011) Paradigm sample unveils iPhone app. *Research*, http://www.research-live.com/news/technology/paradigm-sample-unveils-iphone-app/4005357.article [Accessed 12 June 2012].

The Chartered
Institute of Marketing

1   What is quantitative research?
2   What are the five main styles of interviews?
3   What are the disadvantages of face-to-face contact methods?
4   What strategies can be used to increase the response rate for postal surveys?
5   Outline five advantages of online surveys.
6   What is an omnibus survey?
7   What are the advantages of using omnibus surveys to collect data?

ACTIVITY DEBRIEFS

Activity 7.1

This is a practical, ongoing exercise.

Activity 7.2

Large numbers of postal questionnaires may not be returned, may be returned only partly completed or may be returned very late. This may lead to biased results if those replying are not representative of all people in the survey. Response rates are likely to be higher with personal interviews, and the interviewer can encourage people to answer all questions. Low response rates are a major problem with postal questionnaires, but low response rates can be avoided by:

- Providing a stamped and addressed envelope or a box for the return of the questionnaire
- Giving a date by which you require the completed questionnaire
- Providing an incentive such as a lottery ticket for those who return questionnaires on time
- Using a good covering letter.

Misunderstanding is less likely with personal interviews because the interviewer can explain questions which the interviewee does not understand.

Personal interviews are more suitable when deep or detailed questions are to be asked, since the interviewer can take the time required with each interviewee to explain the implications of the question. Also, the interviewer can probe for further information and encourage the respondent to think more deeply.

Activity 7.3

Qualitative methods tend to be used when suitable concrete statistical data is not available or when it is considered unable to provide an adequate basis for forecasting on its own. Qualitative research is useful for 'depth interviews', 'focus groups', 'repertory grid' and 'observation'. These are the techniques that involve the use of human judgement, flair and experience.

Quantitative methods use statistical techniques based on the analysis of past numeric data. Quantitative research is useful for experimentation, sampling and surveys. The techniques used could include sampling theory, probability and the normal distribution.

1   It is highly structured research conducted using a large sample of respondents to provide quantifiable insights.

2   Street surveys, shop surveys, hall tests, placement tests and home interviews.

3   High costs, can take considerable amount of time to complete the survey, interviewers may be demotivated and interviewer bias.

4   Pre-screening, reminder calls or letters, provide incentives and personalise the survey

5   Cheap to administer, design, deliver and analyse, flexible in content, fast to administer and report on, immediate and low-cost global reach and easy to control.

6   A master questionnaire run by market research companies who sell space on the questionnaire to marketing organisations who need data.

7   They are cheap, they are representative of a market and statistically valid, they give access to hard-to-reach markets and quantified analysis can be accessed extremely quickly.

CHAPTER 8

Sampling

Introduction

Having designed a good questionnaire and selected the appropriate research method, the researcher must address the all-important question of how to select the individuals or groups that will participate in the study. This chapter explains and evaluates different basic sampling approaches designed to maximise the benefit of market research. The first section explains the concept of sampling and its importance in marketing research.

The second section discusses the different stages of the sampling process. The stages of the process are: define the population of interest, determine the sampling frame, select the sampling method, determine the sample size and, finally, implement sampling as part of the research plan.

The final section explores the problems with sample data and how to deal with them in order to ensure that the result of the survey is valid and reliable.

Topic list

What is sampling? ① 1

The sampling process ② 2

Problems with sample data and research design ③ 3

5.2	Explain and evaluate different **basic** sampling approaches designed to maximise the benefit of market research activities:
	■ The sample process
	■ Difference between probability and non-probability samples
	■ Knowledge of convenience, judgemental and quota samples
	■ Determining sample size
	■ Sampling and non-sampling error
	■ Panels

1 What is sampling?

▶ **Key term**

A **sample** is 'a part or subset of a population taken to be representative of the population as a whole for the investigative purposes of research'. (MRS, 2010)

A **population** in statistics simply means the set of individuals, items or data from which a statistical sample is taken. For example you might send a questionnaire to a sample of 100 people who are aged 30 to 40: the population is ALL people aged 30 to 40.

Sampling is one of the most important tools of marketing research because in most practical situations a population will be far too large to carry out a complete survey.

The key to sampling is to remember the practical issues, and its purpose. Once you have decided who you need to invite to participate in research they should be referred to as the **'population of interest'**.

A familiar example of sampling is a poll taken to try to predict the results of an election. It is not practical to ask everyone of voting age how they are going to vote week after week: it would take too long and cost too much. So a sample of voters is taken, and the results from the sample are used to estimate the voting intentions of everyone eligible to vote.

Occasionally a population (set of items) is small enough that **all of it can be examined**: for example, the examination results of one class of students. When the complete population is examined, the survey is called a **census**. This type of survey is quite rare, however, and usually the researcher has to choose some sort of sample.

A sample is also preferable to researchers who do not have the resources, or the need, to conduct a census. There is often a lot of wastage in conducting a census. Let's think about a practical everyday scenario to demonstrate the benefits of a sample. Imagine you are cooking a pot of pasta. To test whether it was cooked you wouldn't eat the whole pot and then decide if it was ready, because it is likely that you could tell just by testing a small amount. The chances are that if you test a fair proportion of the pasta then you will know if it is cooked or not. This, however, presupposes that each of the pieces of pasta were sufficiently alike in their characteristics – don't, for example, try cooking fusili and expecting it to cook at the same rate as a whole sheet of lasagne in the same pan. The same is true of people; if there are characteristics which are sufficiently alike within a specific group (population of interest), then it is possible to assume they may have similar beliefs and attitudes. Therefore, you will only need to include a proportion of these within your research.

You may think that using a sample is very much a **compromise**, but you should consider the following points.

■ It can be shown mathematically that once a certain sample size has been reached, **very little extra accuracy** is gained by examining more items

■ It is possible to **ask more questions** with a sample

■ The **higher cost** of a census may **exceed the value** of results

■ **Things are always changing**. Even if you took a census it could be out of date by the time you completed it.

2 The sampling process

When designing your sample, you will need to address just five key questions :

- **Who** do we need to research? (Population of interest)
- **Where** do we find them?
- How should we **select** individual respondents? In other words what sampling technique should be used?
- **How many** respondents do we need? This will determine on sample size.
- Will research respondent views be **representative** of the views of everybody else in that situation?

The diagram outlines the sampling process.

Figure 8.1   The sampling process

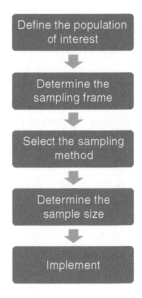

(Adapted from Malhotra 2004)

2.1   Define the population of interest

It is essential to correctly define the population of interest; eg if the researcher wishes to elicit responses from dedicated gym goers then they should clearly define what constitutes 'dedicated' and plan to only include those individuals in the research.

We may be interested in all car dealers, we may be interested in Renault dealers, or we may be interested in Renault dealers in London and the south-east.

The definition of the population of interest is of vital importance. It is possible that the definition will produce a very low number of people in the sample. This has implications that we will explore below.

The key thing is that the definition of the population informs the whole research process. It will determine the methodology, the nature of questions asked and the interview process. The interviewer will be given screening criteria on which to select and deselect potential respondents.

2.2 Determine the sampling frame

Sampling frames are lists or set of directions for identifying the population of interest.

The term sampling frame originates from science. You may remember your science classes at school when you were given a rectangular frame (similar to an empty picture frame) and were then asked to throw it randomly on the ground. Typical experiments then included counting the number of bugs or plants that you found within that sampling frame.

THE REAL WORLD

You may have been approached by a survey interviewer whilst walking in a shopping centre. The researcher will have been given specific instructions in terms of the time and location from which they should approach shoppers. The directions they would have been given is the sampling frame.

In market research terms, the picture frame equivalent is usually something tangible from which you can select respondents, such as a database, a directory or instructions about a specific location to visit or stand.

ACTIVITY 8.1

Why is a telephone directory an unsuitable sampling frame?

2.3 Select the sampling method

The technique you use to select your sample is broadly grouped into one of two types, either a probability sample, which is taken at random, or a non-probability sample, where respondents are selected on characteristics rather than by pure chance.

Table 8.1   Sampling methods

Factors affecting sampling approach	Non-probability sampling	Probability sampling
Nature of research	Exploratory	Conclusive
Research flaws likely to be due to sampling or non-sampling errors	Non-sampling errors are larger	Sampling errors are larger
Similarity in population characteristics	Homogenous (similar)	Heterogeneous (different)
Statistical analyses	Not as statistically sound	Statistically sound
Operational issues	Convenient, cost effective, fast	Expensive, time consuming

(Adapted from Malhotra 2004)

The Chartered
Institute of Marketing

The diagram below shows the most common types of sample selection methods.

Figure 8.2   Sampling methods

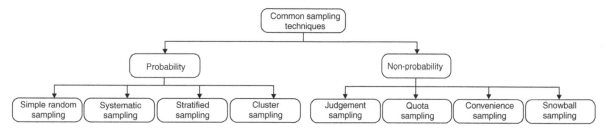

2.3.1 Probability random sampling

To ensure that the sample selected is **free from bias**, random sampling must be used. Inferences about the population being sampled can then be made validly.

■   A **simple random sample** is a sample selected in such a way that every item in the population has an equal chance of being included.

For example, if you wanted to take a random sample of library books, it would **not be good enough to pick them off the shelves, even if you picked them at random**. This is because the **books which were out on loan** would stand no chance of being chosen. You would either have to make sure that all the books were on the shelves before taking your sample, or find some other way of sampling (for example, using the library index cards).

A random sample is **not necessarily a perfect sample**. For example, you might pick what you believe to be a completely random selection of library books, and find that every one of them is a detective thriller. It is a remote possibility, but it could happen. The only way to eliminate the possibility altogether is to take a 100% survey (a census) of the books, which, unless it is a tiny library, is impractical.

In many situations it might be **too expensive** to obtain a random sample, in which case quasi-random sampling is necessary, or else it may not be possible to draw up a sampling frame.

■   **Systematic sampling**: sampling units are chosen from the sampling frame at a uniform rate (eg every tenth item from a chosen start point in a directory of names

■   **Stratified sampling**: the population is divided into mutually exclusive groups (eg income) and a random sample is taken from each group

■   **Cluster sampling**: clusters are chosen using a range of measures – such as geography, income, age – and individuals within the clusters are chosen at random.

2.3.2 Non-probability sampling

Non-random sampling is used when a sampling frame cannot be established.

Non-probability sampling involves a subjective selection of respondents. Therefore, the probability of selecting respondents is unknown. This means that because the sample is not chosen objectively it is not possible to state results with any degree of statistical certainty.

Non-probability sampling has advantages and disadvantages.

Advantages:

■   Lower cost
■   Faster
■   Smaller sample sizes
■   Important respondents can be targeted.

Disadvantages:

- Results are purely indicative
- Sampling error cannot be computed
- The degree of representativeness of the sample to the population is not known
- Assumptions need to be made about the groupings with the population of interest.

There are four forms this can take:

Judgemental sampling

Judgemental sampling involves selecting respondents because they possess particular characteristics which the researcher believes are representative of the population of interest as a whole. 'Typical' residents for example may be selected from a selection of streets that a researcher believes are representative of an entire neighbourhood.

Snowball sampling

Sometimes considered to be a form of judgemental sampling (Dillon *et al*, 1996) because this method involves the respondent suggesting other individuals for selection because they are similar to themselves. Snowball sampling is used when respondents are hard to find and tends to be only relevant for small samples in qualitative studies.

Convenience sampling

Convenience sampling refers to samples that are selected because the population of interest are easy to access by the researcher. Convenience samples are sometimes considered to be biased and unprofessional (Wilson, 2012) however if the easiest to access respondents who are reasonably similar to the population of interest, then it can be a justifiable method on a cost and resource basis.

Many online surveys use convenience sampling because it is difficult to establish common patterns between users of websites (Wilson, 2012).

Quota sampling

In quota sampling randomness is forfeited in the interests of **cheapness and administrative simplicity**. Investigators are told to interview all the people they meet up to a certain quota. A large degree of bias could be introduced accidentally. For example, an interviewer in a shopping centre may fill his or her quota by only meeting people who can go shopping during the week. In practice, this problem can be **partly overcome by subdividing the quota** into different types of people, for example on the basis of age, gender and income, to ensure that the sample mirrors the structure or stratification of the population. The interviewer is then told to interview, for example, 30 males between the ages of 30 and 40 from social class B. The actual choice of the individuals to be interviewed, within the limits of the **quota controls**, is left to the fieldworker.

ACTIVITY 8.2

The number of marketers and their sex in each type of work in a particular country are as follows.

	Female	Male	Total
Lecturers	100	100	200
Commercial companies	400	300	700
Public sector	100	200	300
Marketing research and agencies	500	300	800
			2,000

What would an investigator's quota be, assuming that a sample of 200 is required?

Advantages include the following:

- Speed and cost.

- Allows sampling to take place where a sample frame may not be available but key characteristics of the population are known – for example, in overseas B2B research.

- Interviewers do not have to interview named individuals; they are screened in or out via a small number of classification questions.

- The data, when compared to random methods which are perhaps double the cost, has been proved to be acceptable provided that the research is managed effectively.

- Cost savings may be used to improve the quality of research through increasing sample sizes or using a different method in support of the survey.

- Its popularity shows that it works!

Disadvantages include the following:

- Whilst known characteristics may be distributed in correct proportions, unknown characteristics that may be relevant to the survey may not be. Hidden bias may exist that is not discovered.

- Researchers may be biased as to the type of respondents they choose to interview or the location where they choose to carry out the interviews. A quota for young people may be filled at just one youth club but will not be truly representative of the population as a whole.

THE REAL WORLD

Improving sampling in dual-frame telephone surveys

The German research association ADM has commissioned a study to develop empirically supported standards for conducting dual-frame telephone surveys. Dual-frame telephone surveys involve the application of sampling methods to populations comprising landline and mobile phone users. The study will help researchers to know what proportion of samples should be made up of landline and mobile users, and also provide detailed guidance on how to weight samples.

The ADM believes that the study is important because the number of mobile-only users has increased significantly in different sections of the population and needs to be appropriately reflected so that sampling is representative of the population.

▶ **Assessment tip**

Within your syllabus the senior examiner has specified that you will only be expected to know the difference between probability and non-probability samples. You will also be able to explain and outline when you could use convenience, judgement and quota sampling methods. The June 2009/September 2009 assignment included a task on sampling.

2.4 Determine the sample size

Determining the sample size involves answering the question 'How many people should we interview?' It is a challenging question for many interviewers because it involves finding the right balance between a number of financial, managerial and statistical issues. While a larger sample may reduce the sampling error associated with a study, it is likely to increase the cost and time involved in the data collection process. Therefore, researchers and clients must determine the relative importance of precision against time and cost considerations.

In determining the sample size, researchers can use statistical techniques or a number of ad hoc methods (Aaker *et al*, 2011):

- Rules of thumb or industry standard: Certain industries assume particular benchmark sizes, eg. 200–300 for a product test (Dillon *et al*, 1994). Some researchers suggest that the sample should be large

enough so that when it is divided into groups, each group will have a minimum sample size of 100 or more (Sudman, 1980).

- Budget constraints: In most situations, the sample size is determined by the amount of money that is available for the project.

- Comparable studies: Another method is to find similar studies and use their sample size as a guide. Ideally, such studies should be comparable in terms of the number of groups into which the sample is divided for the purpose of comparison.

According to Aaker *et al* (2011), there are four main factors that really determine the sample size:

- The number of groups and sub-groups in the sample that is being analysed.

- The value of the information in the study and the degree of precision or accuracy required.

- The cost of the sample. This means that researchers and managers must apply a cost-benefit analysis in deciding the appropriate size of the sample.

- The variability of the population.

2.4.1 Statistical techniques for determining sample size

For probability samples, statistical methods are used to establish sample sizes.

We need three pieces of information to work this out.

- Variance and the degree of variability of the population, known as **standard deviation**
- The required limit of accuracy or **sampling error**
- The required **level of confidence** that the results will fall within a certain range.

Variance is a measure of how spread out a data set is. We work it out by looking at the average squared deviation of each number from its mean.

There are different formulae for working out variance, but the one most commonly used in market research takes into account the potential bias in a sample.

The formula is

$$s^2 = \sum_{i=1}^{n} \frac{(X_i - \overline{X})^2}{n-1}$$

where X is the individual value in an array of data

$$\overline{X}$$

is the mean of the array and n is the number of values in an array.

For example, for the numbers 1, 3, 6, 4 and 1, the number of values is 5, and the variance is 4.5.

Value	Mean	Deviation	Deviation squared
1	3	(2)	4
3	3	0	0
6	3	3	9
4	3	1	1
1	3	(2)	4
Total			18

Sum of squared differences divided by number of observations less 1 is 18/(5 – 1) = 4.5.
This is the variance.

Standard deviation is used to compare the spread of data sets. The more spread a set of values, the higher the standard deviation.

Standard deviation is the square root of the variance which we calculated above. You can see that the formula within the square root symbol is the formula we used to calculate variance.

$$SD = \sqrt{\frac{\sum (X_i - \overline{X})^2}{n-1}}$$

X_i = the value of each data point</P>

$\overline{X}$ = the average of all the data points

σ = the Greek letter sigma, meaning 'sum of' and

n = the total number of data points.

Value	Mean	Deviation	Deviation squared
1	3	(2)	4
3	3	0	0
6	3	3	9
4	3	1	1
1	3	(2)	4
Total			18

Sum of squared differences divided by number of observations less 1 is 18/(5 − 1) = 4.5.
This is the variance.
The standard deviation is the square root of the variance or 2.12.

2.4.2 Normal distribution

Standard deviation is a measure of how widely values are dispersed from the average value (the mean). The higher the standard deviation, the more widely the values are spread. This allows us to use standard deviation to compare data sets.

In order to apply this to the determination of sample size, we need to understand another concept. That is normal distribution. Normal distribution is an important concept. What it implies is that the distribution of values within any data set will be similar, for example shoe size, height or income, and will follow the pattern known as a bell-shaped curve.

So what does this mean? The area under the curve represents all occurrences. The line through the centre of the curve is the mean value.

Normal distribution has another key characteristic. Sixty-eight per cent of all occurrences fall within one standard deviation of the mean.

Normal distribution also tells us that 95% of occurrences would fall between 1.96 standard deviations. This is very important as, for the most part, market researchers work at this level of certainty. What it means effectively is that there is a 1 in 20 chance of an occurrence falling outside this predicted range. Normal distribution also tells us that 99% of occurrences fall within 2.58 standard deviations.

The key point is that for any normal distribution, for any data set, the distribution of values is the same.

To repeat:

- 68% of values fall within 1 standard deviation.
- 95% fall within 1.96 standard deviations.
- 99% fall within 2.58 standard deviations.

These percentages (68, 95 and 99%) are known as confidence levels and are the same for all data sets that conform to a normal distribution. There are other types of distribution but you need not go further into this for the course.

For our purpose, marketers generally use 95 or 99% confidence limits. These relate to 1.96 and 2.58 standard deviations and these are the confidence levels also known as Z values that are used. The upper and lower limit of the range that they indicate (e.g. = ±1.96) is called the confidence limit. The range itself is the confidence interval. Together these represent the most valuable tools for working out occurrences in the total market from a smaller sample.

There are two different ways of working out sample sizes for random samples, and these depend on whether we are measuring **averages** or **proportions**.

2.4.3 For studies involving averages or means

The formula to work out sample size is

$$N = \frac{Z^2 \delta^2}{E^2}$$

- – where Z is the confidence level
- – δ is the population standard deviation
- – E is the acceptable level of precision.

- **Specify the level of precision**

  The level of precision is worked out by clients and researchers and reflects the budget available and the acceptable margin of error or degree of risk attached to the outcome of the research. If there is a need for accurate data, the sample size may be larger and the level of precision would be tighter.

- **Determine the acceptable confidence interval**

  As we have seen above, the standard level of confidence is 95%. Remember, this means that at the 95% confidence interval there is a 1 in 20 chance of the sample being wrong. If the level of risk was high, then we could work at the 99% confidence level; here there is a 1 in a 100 chance of the sample being wrong.

- **Estimate the standard deviation**

  It is impossible to know this before carrying out the survey, so an estimate is required. This can be based upon:

  - – Previous studies
  - – Secondary research
  - – The result of pilot surveys
  - – Judgement.

Once the study is completed, the sample mean and standard deviation can be calculated, and the exact confidence level and limits of error can be worked out.

Remember the formula, and work through the example

$$N = \frac{Z^2 \delta^2}{E^2}$$

The sample required is 443.

2.4.4 Studies involving proportions

Studies measuring the proportion of a population having a certain characteristic are often required in marketing and in surveys; for example, the proportion responding to a promotion or the number of voters against university top-up fees. To determine sample size here a different formula is needed.

Remember Z is our confidence level; let us use the standard marketing confidence level – so Z is 1.96 or the 95% confidence level.

E is the limit of error. In this case we need the results to be correct to within let us say $\pm 3\%$, written as a decimal ± 0.03.

P is the estimated percentage of the population who have the characteristic. In this case we will look at the number of people who may respond to a test mailing and we estimate that 15% may respond. This again is written as a decimal 0.15.

So, let us work this through:

$$N = \frac{1.96 \times 1.96[0.15(1 - 0.15)]}{0.03^2}$$

We would therefore need a sample of 544 to be 95% confident of our 15% response rate on roll out of the campaign.

If we reduced the limits of error to $\pm 1\%$ the sample size would increase to 4,896.

If the estimated response was 2% we can see the sample size would decrease to 750. The figure reduces because the variance in the population is lower.

If the estimated response rate went to 20%, then the sample required would be 6,144.

2.4.5 Adjustment for larger samples

We have said that there is no direct relationship between population and sample size to estimate a characteristic with a level of error and confidence.

The assumption is that sample elements are drawn independent of one another. This cannot be assumed when the sample is higher than 10% of the population. If this is the case, an adjustment is made, called the finite population correction factor.

The calculation reduces the required sample:

$$N_1 = \frac{nN}{N+n-1}$$

- N_1 is the revised sample size
- n is the original sample size
- N is the population size.

For example, if the population has 2,000 elements and the original sample size is 400, then,

$$N = \frac{400 \times 2000}{2000 + 400 - 1}$$
$$N = 333$$

Other rules-of-thumb factors to consider in setting sample sizes:

- Trade off cost against reliability and accuracy.

- Minimum subgroup sizes should be more than 100 respondents. It is difficult to be confident in figures lower than this.

- The average sample size in national surveys in the United Kingdom is around 1,000–2,000 respondents. Minimum sample sizes in the FMCG markets are 300–500 respondents.

2.5 Implement the sampling procedure

Once the sample size is worked out, the researcher can start to gather data. We have already discussed the fact that a sample will always vary in some way from the population.

ACTIVITY 8.3

Although there are statistical methods for determining the size of a sample in marketing research, frequently other means are used. What means are these?

---

3 Problems with sample data and research design

There are many **potential problems** with sample data including **bias**, **unrepresentative data**, and **insufficient data**, perhaps because of non-response.

There are several faults or weaknesses which might occur in the design or collection of sample data. These are as follows.

- **Bias**. In choosing a sample, unless the method used to select the sample is the random sampling method, or a quasi-random sampling method, there will be a likelihood that some 'units' (individuals or households, etc) will have a poor, or even zero chance of being selected for the sample. Where this occurs, samples are said to be biased. A biased sample may occur in the following situations.

    - The sampling frame is out of date, and excludes a number of individuals or 'units' new to the population.

    - Some individuals selected for the sample decline to respond. If a questionnaire is sent to 1,000 households, but only 600 reply, the failure of the other 400 to reply will make the sample of 600 replies inevitably biased.

    - A questionnaire contains leading questions, or a personal interviewer tries to get respondents to answer questions in a particular way.

- **Insufficient data**. The sample may be too small to be reliable as a source of information about an entire population.

- **Unrepresentative data**. Data collected might be unrepresentative of normal conditions. For example, if an employee is asked to teach a trainee how to do a particular job, data concerning the employee's output and productivity during the time he is acting as trainer will not be representative of his normal output and productivity.

- **Omission of an important factor**. Data might be incomplete because an important item has been omitted in the design of the 'questions'.

- **Carelessness**. Data might be provided without any due care and attention. An investigator might also be careless in the way he or she gathers data.

- **Confusion of cause and effect (or association)**. It may be tempting to assume that if two variables appear to be related, one variable is the cause of the other. Variables may be associated but it is not necessarily true that one causes the other.

- Where questions call for something **more than simple 'one-word' replies**, there may be difficulty in interpreting the results correctly. This is especially true of 'depth interviews' which try to determine the reasons for human behaviour.

One method of checking the accuracy of replies is to insert control questions in the questionnaire, so that the reply to one question should be compatible with the reply to another. If they are not, the value of the interviewee's responses are dubious, and may be ignored. On the other hand, the information that the interviewee is genuinely confused about something, and so offers contradictory answers, may be valuable information itself, or it may reflect the way the questions are structured.

3.1 Non-sampling error

A non-sampling error is an error that results solely from the manner in which the observations are made, and leads to inaccurate conclusions being drawn from the group being studied. In other words, there is a problem with the way the data is collected. It can occur whether a total population or a sample is being used. The simplest example of a non-sampling error is inaccurate measurements due to poor procedures or data input errors. Unintended errors may result from any of the following.

- The manner in which the response is elicited – no two interviewers are alike, and questions may be worded poorly

- The suitability of the persons surveyed – some may give deliberately inaccurate answers

- The purpose of the study – if the respondent knows what it is, it may affect the responses given

- The personal biases of the interviewer or survey writer – questionnaires must be designed to draw out useful responses

- Non-response – either through refusal or non-availability.

3.2 Non-response

Non-response (of a sample member) cannot be avoided. It can, however, (apart from in mail surveys) be kept at a reasonable level. Experience has shown that the non-response part of a survey often differs considerably from the rest. The types of non-response are as follows.

- **Units outside the population.** Where the field investigation shows that units no longer exist (eg demolished houses), these units should be considered as outside the population and should be subtracted from the sample size before calculating the non-response rate.

- **Unsuitable for interview.** This is where people who should be interviewed are too infirm or too unfamiliar with the language to be interviewed.

- **Movers.** People who have changed address since the list was drawn up cannot be interviewed.

- **Refusals.** Some people refuse to co-operate.

- **Away from home.** People might be away from home for longer than the field work period and call-back might not be possible.

- **Out at time of call.**

These sort of problems occur chiefly in **random** sample surveys. Some of the above do not apply when interviewing is done in factories, colleges or offices. In quota sampling 'movers', 'away', and 'out' do not appear. Although the interviewer may miss some people for these reasons, he or she simply continues until he or she fills the quota.

Social change can influence the level of non-response. Rising crime means that householders may be afraid to answer the door to strangers and there are other employment opportunities for 'doorstep interviewers'. Response rates are therefore slipping as more people either refuse to be, or cannot be, interviewed.

Another problem is that of **'data fatigue'**, as the public becomes tired of filling in questionnaires and more cynical about the real motives of 'market researchers' because of 'sugging' (selling under the guise of research) and 'frugging' (fundraising under the guise of research).

3.3 Dealing with non-response

Taking **substitutes** (such as the next house along) is no answer because the substitutes may differ from the non-respondents. Instead the interviewer can try to increase the response rate.

- Little can be done about **people not suitable** for interview.

- **People who have moved** are a special category. It is usually not practical to track them down. It is acceptable to select an individual from the new household against some rigorously defined procedure.

- To minimise **'refusals'**, keep questionnaires as brief as possible, use financial incentives, and highly skilled interviewers. Refusal rates tend to be low (3–5 per cent).

- People **'away from home'** may be contacted later, if this is possible.

- People **'out at time of call'** is a common problem. The researcher should plan the calling time sensibly (for example, as most breadwinnners are out at work in the day-time, call in the evening). Try to establish a good time to call back – or arrange an appointment.

THE REAL WORLD

A smarter response to survey challenges

Survey data collection costs are rising as researchers go to great lengths to entice non-responders to take part. But Gerry Nicolaas says efforts to increase response rates need to be better informed and better targeted. Responsive design can help.

For random sample surveys, it's long been considered not only good practice but absolutely essential to strive for a high response rate if we are to draw valid conclusions about the population we are studying. The long-term decline in response rates worries researchers who fear that those who aren't taking part in surveys are somehow different from those who are, and that these differences will introduce bias in the data.

As a result, data collection agencies have adopted expensive strategies for increasing response rates, such as increasing the number of calls to non-contacts, refusal conversion attempts and respondent incentives. To some extent these efforts have paid off. At NatCen Social Research we've seen the speed of decline slowing and some indication of it having halted on a number of surveys.

But it has taken a lot of money to get where we are – and rising fieldwork costs are particularly problematic at a time when research buyers of all types, be they private or public sector, are looking to reduce costs.

(*Research*, 2012)

The Chartered
Institute of Marketing

3.4 Panels

The use of panels is an important part of the marketing research industry and there are a range of panels covering everything from media consumption to B2B purchasing.

Information may be gathered by questionnaire, telephone interviews, diaries (documents where the respondent records their behaviour and purchases over a period such as a week or a month), barcode readers or through the internet.

The key tasks involved in undertaking panel research are as follows:

- The recruitment of a representative sample of the population that is willing and capable of doing the task
- The maintenance of the members of the panel once recruited
- Replacement of panel members who leave with similar respondents so as to maintain consistency.

Panels may be used rather than one-off surveys in order to obtain dynamic information on the following:

- Broad trends in a market (eg are people moving from buying white bread to brown bread; which television programmes are more or less popular than previously).
- Case histories of specific respondents (eg level of repeat purchases, brand switching, reaction to special offers and advertising).
- Attitudes and reactions over time to particular products or services (a placement test is a type of panel where people's reactions to a new type of vacuum cleaner or car can be measured over time).

CHAPTER ROUNDUP

- Sampling is a key topic in marketing research.

- A sample can be selected using random sampling, quasi-random sampling (systematic, stratified and multistage sampling) or non-random sampling (quota and cluster sampling).

- The stages of the sampling process are: define the population of interest, determine the sampling frame, select the sampling method, determine the sample size and implement.

- There are many potential problems with sample data including bias, unrepresentative data, and insufficient data, perhaps because of non-response.

- Non-sampling errors occur as a result of the way the data is collected or inaccurate responses being given or recorded.

FURTHER READING

Chapter 5 of:

Bradley, N. (2010) *Marketing research: Tools & techniques*. 2nd edition. Oxford, Oxford University Press.

Chapter 8 of:

Wilson, A. (2012) *Marketing research: An integrated approach.* 3rd edition. Harlow, Financial Times Prentice Hall.

REFERENCES

Aaker, D., Kuman V., Day, G. and Leone, R. (2011) *Marketing Research.* 10th edition. New Jersey, Wiley.

Dillon, W., Madden, T. and Firtle, N. (1994) *Marketing research in a marketing environment.* 3rd edition. Illinois, Irwin.

Malhotra, N. (2004) *Marketing research: An applied orientation.* 4th edition. Upper Saddle River, NJ, Prentice Hall.

Nicolaas, G. (2012) A smarter response to survey challenges. *Research*, http://www.research-live.com/comment/a-smarter-response-to-survey-challenges/4006999.article [Accessed May 2012].

Sudman, S. (1980) Improving the quality of shopping centre sampling. *Journal of Marketing Research*. 17 November, pp423–431.

Wilson, A. (2012) *Marketing research: An integrated approach.* 3rd edition. Harlow, Financial Times Prentice Hall.

The Chartered Institute of Marketing

1   What is a simple random sample?
2   What is a sampling frame?
3   What is stratified sampling?
4   What is cluster sampling?
5   What is the standard error of the mean at the 95% confidence level?
6   How can knowing the standard error of the mean be useful in sampling?
7   Is this information about the standard error of the mean useful for all sampling methods?
8   List five problems that may occur in the collection of sample data.
9   List three ways of improving response rates.

ACTIVITY DEBRIEFS

Activity 8.1

Not everyone has a telephone and not all of those who do have a telephone are listed.

Activity 8.2

The investigator needs to interview 200/2,000 × 100% = 10% of the population.

Using quota sampling, the investigator would interview the first 10 (100 × 10%) male marketing lecturers that he met, and the first 40 (400 × 10%) female marketers in commercial companies.

	Female	Male	Total
Lecturers	10	10	20
Commercial companies	40	30	70
Other commercial	10	20	30
Marketing research and agencies	50	30	80
			200

Activity 8.3

Ideally, statistical calculations will be carried out to help determine the size of sample required in a survey, as samples that are too small can produce misleading data and ones that are too large can waste resources.

Although it is true to say that the larger the sample the less the sampling error, the level of error decreases at a rate equal to the square root of the increase in sample size. In other words, to halve the sampling error, the sample will need to be four times the size. This is clearly expensive as the costs of interviewing and analysis will increase proportionately. It should be noted that statistical means of calculating the sample size can really only be applied to random samples (ie where everybody in the 'population' has an equal and non-zero chance of being picked).

There are, however, other ways of deciding upon the size of the sample.

- Budget available. Frequently this is the most important factor. In an ideal world, the appropriate size of sample would be calculated and the research costed accordingly. However, in most cases, the budget is already allocated and therefore the sample is the size that can be afforded. To achieve a larger sample, it might be possible to look at alternative cheaper means of data collection: interviewing in the high street rather than door-to-door, or by telephone rather than in the street. However, the method of data collection should not be altered if this is going to lead to incorrect or inadequate data. It would be better to recommend that the research is not done at all in that case.

- Rule of thumb or gut feeling. Frequently managers commissioning research will demand a sample of 300 or 500. It may be based on past experience or other similar research or it may not be based on any sound reasoning at all, except that it sounds about right.

- Number of sub-groups. To mean anything, each major sub-group should contain at least 50 members and each minor sub-group at least 20.

If, for example, the sample is to be based on smokers and non-smokers, and then age within those two categories, there would have to be at least 20 non-smokers and 20 smokers under 25, at least 20 of each between the age of 25 and 34 and so on. If there were five age bands, the minimum sample size would be $2 \times 5 \times 20$, ie 200 respondents.

1   A sample selected in such a way that every member (or item) of the population has an equal chance of being included.

2   A numbered list of all the members or items in the population.

3   A random sampling technique in which the population is divided into subsets or strata which are based on like characteristics, such as same gender or same location. Each strata is then sampled using a random sampling technique.

4   A random sampling technique in which one definable sub-section of the population is taken to be representative of the population of interest, such as the location. Can be used where there is no suitable sampling frame.

5   The standard error of the mean at the 95% confidence level is plus or minus 1.96.

6   You can establish the confidence levels, the confidence limits and the confidence interval or margin of error of the results of the sample. You can also use this to find the size of the sample you need given a certain confidence level and margin of error.

7   No – you can only use this for probability based or random samples.

8   Bias; insufficient data; unrepresentative data; omission of an important factor; carelessness; confusion of cause and effect; ambiguity.

9   Choose three from this list: Improving response rates by better survey design, better interviewer skills and training, offering a reward or incentive to respondents, reducing the time cost to the respondents, improving the trust of the respondents.

CHAPTER 9

Questionnaire design

Introduction

The main tool for collecting quantitative data in most research projects is the questionnaire. A properly designed questionnaire is essential for the researcher to collect the data that is required to properly address the research questions. This chapter explores the process involved in designing a basic questionnaire to meet a project's research objectives. The first section discusses the steps involved in designing questionnaires, including: develop question topics, select question and response formats and wording, determine sequence, design layout and the pilot test.

The second section explains the importance of survey-generating software in constructing and designing surveys.

Topic list

5.1	Design a **basic** questionnaire and discussion guide to meet a project's research objective:
	▪ Discussion guide format
	▪ The questionnaire design process
	▪ Question and response formats
	▪ Scaling techniques (Likert and semantic differential)
	▪ Sequence and wording
	▪ Design layout and appearance
	▪ Questionnaire-generating software

1 The questionnaire design process

> ▶ **Key term**
>
> A **questionnaire** is a structured data-collection mechanism involving a range of question formats and completed orally, online or in print. Questionnaires may be administered by interviewers or self-completed by the respondent.

The questionnaire is driven by the objectives of the research. It is important to design the questionnaire with this in mind. Often it is tempting to ask more questions than is strictly needed but respondents will not spend time completing a poorly constructed and unfocussed questionnaire.

As we have seen, questionnaires may be administered by interviewers or self-completed by the respondent. The design of the questionnaire is a key task in the research and proves that good design can make the difference between a successful project and a failure.

The questionnaire has four main purposes. It is designed to:

▪ Collect relevant data
▪ Remove bias
▪ Make data comparable
▪ Motivate the respondent.

Questionnaire design should be done methodically: develop question topics; select question and response formats and take care with wording; determine the sequence; design the layout; and pilot test.

In the majority of research projects, the most critical technical issue is likely to be the **quality of the research techniques that have been used**. Where research findings are suspect, this is most commonly because there are fundamental **flaws in the design of the questionnaire**. In this section, therefore, we will spend some time looking at some of the key issues involved in designing an effective questionnaire.

Wilson (2012) recommends a methodical approach to designing questionnaires, with the following steps.

▪ Develop **question topics**: these will derive from the research **objectives** and may be refined by initial **qualitative research**. We have covered these topics in earlier chapters

▪ Select question and response **formats and wording**

▪ Determine **sequence**

▪ Design **layout**

▪ **Pilot test**.

Google enters the market research sector

The world's number one search engine has entered into the market research sector with a new product called Google Consumer Surveys. Google Consumer Surveys uses a 'surveywall' to quiz respondents as they browse the internet.

The new product allows users to design a survey which is then sent out and appears to respondents as a 'surveywall' when they try to access premium content, like news or videos, around the web. The publisher of the site hosting the premium content and survey is paid every time somebody completes the questionnaire.

On completion of the questionnaire, Google collates and analyses the responses in order to provide feedback to users in real time.

The Texas Tribune, a US publisher, has generated a significant amount of revenue from the service. The newspaper places surveys in its data section which brings in 60% of its 600,000 unique visitors per month. It is this 60% of the newspaper's readers that come in mostly through search engines that get to see the Google-powered survey. To gain access to the content they are looking for, readers can either answer one question or provide their email address to receive a minimum of one alert per month. If they choose to do nothing they will be unable to get access to the content they require. In addition to providing revenue for publishers, the service represents a cost-effective way for researchers to get the data they need.

(*The Next Web*, 2012)

▶ **Assessment tip**

Within your assignment it is highly likely that you will have to design a questionnaire.

1.1 Developing question topics

This process will draw on the results of any exploratory, desk or qualitative research carried out already. The research objectives laid down in the research brief and proposal will also be drawn on to inform the process. The idea is to make the questionnaire as efficient as possible. The questionnaire should produce the maximum amount of required information at minimum time.

The characteristics of the respondents should also be considered:

- Do they have the information we are asking for?

- Will they be able to remember the information?

- Are they likely to tell us the information we are asking for? Is it particularly sensitive data, for example income, sexual practices and so on?

- How literate and numerate are they? Will they be able to articulate the information?

- Will they understand the questions?

- Will they be interested in the survey?

- Question and response formats.

- What does the questionnaire contain?

There are **three parts** to any questionnaire:

- **Identification data**. This is usually completed by the interviewer. It contains identification of the respondent: maybe, name, address and a contact number.

  It will also include the time, date and place of the interview and the name of the interviewer. It may also include a unique number to identify the questionnaire itself.

This data is required to allow check backs to be made. It is important to note that the MRS code of conduct aims to ensure the anonymity of the respondent.

- **Classification data**. This is the data that is required to classify respondents. It may include the following:

  - Age
  - Gender
  - Income
  - Job title
  - Marital status.

  This allows the information to be analysed effectively and also to help the interviewer ensure that the respondent has the characteristics of the sample that is required to be interviewed.

  Both identification and classification questions may be kept to the end of the questionnaire to allow sufficient rapport to be built up between the interviewer and the respondent. The exception to this is classification data which may be needed to establish quotas or exclusions from the questionnaire.

- **Subject data** – It refers to the nature of the information that is being gathered to meet the survey objectives. This may be laid down in a flow diagram which allows us to begin to plan the question sequence.

This flow chart is a route map through the questionnaire to be created in outline and allows the designer to introduce what are known as 'skip' or 'filter' questions to take the respondent through the questionnaire.

For example:

Do you drink wine?

If YES go to Q.2
If NO go to Q.9

Care needs to be taken in the use of skip questions; too many can be confusing to a respondent who is self-completing or to an inexperienced interviewer. The use of CATI and CAPI systems (computer-assisted telephone or personal interviewing) can help here as the computer will go to the appropriate question automatically, given the response to the skip question.

'Cushion statements' help with the flow and management of the questionnaire, for example:

> *That complete the first part of the questionnaire. I am now going to ask you some questions about the store.*

Cushion statements and skip and routing questions are often printed in a different colour to distinguish them from the questionnaire itself.

1.2   Question and response formats and wording

Questions need to be **worded with precision**, avoiding ambiguity and lack of clarity, not conflating multiple issues, not making unjustified assumptions, making it easy and clear for respondents to answer.

1.2.1 Precision

Even though most marketing research questionnaires explore comparatively straightforward issues, **precision** should always be a primary concern.

The principles set out in the following paragraphs may sound so obvious as to be hardly worth stating and yet, in many questionnaires, these apparently self-evident points are **routinely disregarded**. All too often, there is little clarity about the information that is required, there is woolliness and imprecision in the framing of questions and there are confusions both about the meaning of the question and about the interpretation of the response.

The potential causes of this imprecision are numerous, but there are a number of common pitfalls that are worth highlighting.

- **Ambiguity and uncertainty about language or terminology**. In framing a question, managers will often assume a common understanding of words or phrases, where no such commonality actually exists.

- **Lack of clarity about the information required**. Questionnaires are frequently weakened by a lack of clarity about the nature and detail of the information they are intended to collect. You should always stop and ask yourself some fundamental questions, such as:

  - Why am I asking this question?
  - What is it intended to find out?
  - What exactly do I want to know?
  - Will this question give me the information I need?

  These questions are often not explicitly addressed, with the result that the wrong question (or only part of the right question) is asked. In one employee survey, for example, the questionnaire asked:

Figure 9.1   Imprecision question

> Which of the following do you feel are barriers to your undertaking further training or development in your own time?
>
> - Lack of spare time
> - Lack of motivation
> - Personal/domestic commitments
> - Cost

Not surprisingly, many respondents ticked most if not all of these options. The questionnaire designer really wanted to ask not **whether** these factors were seen as barriers, but **which** were the most significant barriers and **how** significant they were.

- **Conflation of multiple questions into one**. In one survey, for example, respondents were asked, 'How often does your workgroup meet to discuss performance, quality and safety issues?' The assumption behind this question – which was part of the evaluation of a team development programme – was that managers called workgroups together to discuss all three of these issues, as they were required to do. In fact, practice varied considerably across the organisation. Some workgroups did not meet at all, some met infrequently and many met relatively often but only discussed performance issues. However, this fact, which was crucial to evaluating the effectiveness of the programme, only emerged during a subsequent focus group.

- **Making unjustified assumptions**. Similar problems can arise when the phrasing of the question implies an assumption of a preconception that is not justified by the evidence available to you. It is not uncommon, for instance, to encounter questions such as, 'In reviewing your performance, which of the following methods does your manager use?' The assumption here, of course, is that the manager reviews the respondent's performance at all.

1.2.2 Open and closed questions

In conversation and information gathering they help to establish the basic facts.

Figure 9.2   Closed question

Title	Mr ☐	Mrs ☐	Miss ☐	Ms ☐	Dr ☐	Other ☐
Would you like a sales representative to call you?				Yes ☐	No ☐	

- The advantage is that you will get short, relevant answers that are easy to analyse
- The disadvantage is that the choices may be too restrictive to cover every possibility.

▶ **Key term**

Open questions let people respond in their own words.

Typically an open question begins with 'Why ...?' or 'How ...?' or a phrase like 'Could you describe...' or 'Tell me more about ..'.

- The advantage of this type of question is that it is less likely to lead people into giving the answer they think you want.
- The disadvantage is that you may end up collecting a large amount of subjective data. This may or may not be relevant, and you will need to spend time reading and interpreting it to find out.

For instance, suppose you design a questionnaire with the following (open) question and put a large blank box underneath for the answer.

Figure 9.3   Open question

> **What method(s) of communication did you use the last time you arranged to meet someone or a group of other people?**
>
>

Some people would simply respond 'PHONE & E-MAIL', but (depending on the size of the blank box) others may be tempted to scribble you a little story about what the event was, who was there, how the initial idea for the event was a spontaneous conversation in the kitchen at work, how the news spread like wildfire by phone and e-mail – all of which you would have to decipher, read and interpret, but almost all of which you do not need to know!

A much better way to get the information you want is to offer a limited range of possible responses to the question, something along these lines.

Figure 9.4   Modified open question

Please indicate what methods of communication you used the last time you arranged to meet someone or a group of other people (✓ *Tick all boxes that apply*)			
E-mail	☐	I do not meet other people	☐
Telephone conversation	☐	Message pinned on notice board	☐
Post	☐	Website/chat-room	☐
Text message	☐	Face-to-face	☐
Other (please give brief details)			
....			

The Chartered Institute of Marketing

The answers to this (almost closed) question will be much easier to analyse, and it will be much quicker for people to answer the question if they do not have to think up their own words.

- So far as possible, you should avoid putting the choices in the order that you think reflects their popularity: note the two-column layout, which tries to avoid this

- Note that the text and the associated boxes to tick are closely aligned and shaded so that it is clear which box belongs to which option

- It is also clear in this example that you want a tick, not a cross. Actually it probably doesn't matter what mark people use, but remember that lots of people are scared of forms: save them from worrying and make it clear for them

- If the answer is 'Other' it is clear from the wording and the limited space for the answer that you do not want much detail.

THE REAL WORLD

Online surveys with SurveyMonkey

SurveyMonkey is the world's leading provider of web-based survey solutions. The company is trusted by millions of companies, organisations and individuals to obtain the insights that they need to make vital decisions. Their customers include all Fortune 100 companies, as well as other small, medium and large businesses, academic institutions and organisations.

SurveyMonkey provides an easy-to-use platform for any type of research. Try out SurveyMonkey for yourself at http://www.surveymonkey.com

1.2.3 Leading questions

▶ **Key term**

Leading questions: Questions that appear to encourage the respondent to answer in a particular way.

Even when the question has been very carefully and precisely planned, it may still provide misleading or inaccurate data if it appears to be **leading the respondent towards a particular answer**. People may still feel **uncertain** about its outcomes and they may still feel **suspicious of your motives** for conducting it. In such cases, some may feel very keen to give the 'right' answer – the answer that they believe the organisation wants to hear. Regardless of your care in drafting the questionnaire, you may not be able to avoid this problem entirely.

This problem occurs most commonly when respondents are asked to **indicate their level of agreement or disagreement** with a particular statement. The preferences or prejudices of the questionnaire designer can appear too obvious to the respondent. It is prudent, therefore, to include a **mixture of positive and negative statements**, which do not suggest any intrinsic preference.

In some cases, the choice of statement can **significantly undermine the value of the information obtained**. In one questionnaire, for instance, respondents were asked to indicate their agreement or disagreement with the statement, 'The quality of work in my department is generally excellent'. If the respondent agreed with this statement the meaning was clear – that he or she thought the quality of work in the department was generally excellent. However, if the respondent **disagreed** with the statement, the meaning was less clear. Did they think the quality was moderate or even poor? From the information provided by the question, there was no way of telling.

1.2.4 Formats

Question types include **Yes/No, multiple choice, ratings** and **scales**: the primary purpose is to facilitate statistical analysis. Two of the best known scales are the Likert scale and the Semantic Differential scale.

Apart from a simple **'Yes/No' closed question** format, there are various **other ways** of structuring questions. In general, the questions in a written questionnaire often contain **multiple choice** type, so providing the basis for quantitative analysis. The primary purpose of a written questionnaire is to facilitate **precise statistical analysis**. If the questionnaire includes too many narrative or open questions, analysis becomes very difficult. There is a fine balance when designing questionnaires in terms of the need to keep questions varied to avoid respondent boredom and also ensuring that the analysis is not overly complex. Open-ended qualitative-style questions can be used within surveys, although they should be kept to a minimum.

Questions can be divided into two broad categories; those **exploring attitudes** or opinions and those **seeking some form of factual information**. In the former category would generally fall, for example, the 'agree/disagree' format, such as 'Safety is always a paramount concern for the organisation. Do you agree strongly/agree slightly/disagree slightly/disagree strongly'. In the latter category might fall questions about, say, the frequency of workgroup meetings or about recent experience of training.

Within these two broad categories, a number of formats can be applied. Questions on attitude or opinion generally ask the respondent to indicate both the direction and the strength of feeling – say, 'strongly agree' to 'strongly disagree'. Alternatively, you might ask for the range of opinion relating to a given topic with a question like 'Do you think the quality of work in your department is generally excellent/good/fair/poor?' In such cases, where you are effectively asking respondents to commit themselves to a specific opinion, you need to be aware of what is sometimes called, in an experimental content, the 'error of the central tendency'.

In other words, **respondents are commonly reluctant to give extreme responses** and prefer to hover around the middle ground. If you have an odd number of items in your scale, you may find that respondents disproportionately opt for the neutral option. There are benefits in forcing respondents off the fence by **offering only an even number of options**, so that the respondent has to choose between, say, 'agree slightly' and 'disagree slightly'. In this way, you gain a clearer perspective on the **true direction of opinion**.

Where you are asking to identify preferences from among a number of options, you may ask respondents to **rank the options against a given criterion**, such as 'Which of the following do you think are the most important contributors to high workgroup performance? (Please rank in order of importance.)'

- If you use this format, you should remember to **indicate how the ranking should be applied**. Is number 1 the **most** or the **least** important factor? Ranking questions can seem **confusing** to respondents and are best used sparingly. In any cases, it is rarely worth asking respondents to rank more than the first three or four items. Beyond that, rankings usually become fairly arbitrary.

- A more straightforward approach is to ask respondents simply to **select one item** – 'Which of the following do you think is the single most important contributor to high workgroup performance? (Please tick one only.)' Although slightly less detailed, this question is easier both to complete and to analyse.

In collecting **factual** information, you may again wish to **use scales** where the required information lies on a continuum. For example, 'How many days have you spent training in the past twelve months? Fewer than 4 days/4–6 days/7–10 days/more than 10 days.'

Be especially careful of 'overlapping' values. If the previous question had been phrased as 'How many days have you spent training in the past twelve months? Fewer that 3 days/4–6 days/6–10 days/more than 10 days?' Which option would you choose if you had spent 3 days in training? Or 6?

Where you are exploring more discrete items of information, you may simply ask respondents to **select the most relevant items**. For example, you might ask, 'Which of the following types of training have you undertaken in the last year? (Please tick any that apply.)' In this case, you are not asking respondents to evaluate the options against one another, but simply to make a choice between those that are and those that are not significant. This format can also be applied in cases of **opinions and attitudes**.

1.2.5 The Likert scale

This approach can be summarised in three steps.

- A list of statements is prepared about the topic being researched, and a test group of respondents is asked to rate each statement on a scale from strong agreement to strong disagreement.

- A numerical value is given to each response:

  5   Strongly agree
  4   Agree
  3   Don't know
  2   Disagree
  1   Strongly disagree

- Each respondent's scores for all the statements are added up to give a total score for the topic, which may reflect overall positive or negative attitudes: responses to individual statements can also be analysed to get more meaningful information about the pattern of responses.

Likert scales are simple to prepare and administer. You may have been asked to complete such an inventory test over the telephone, or seen one in a magazine. However, again you should be aware that scale values have no absolute meaning, and are limited in their statistical uses, on an 'interval' scale.

ACTIVITY 9.1

Create a list of 10 statements for a Likert scale about a product of your choice.

Test this list on a friend or colleague. How effective was your list? What have you learned from the test?

1.2.6 The Semantic Differential scale

- Scales are constructed on a number of **'dimensions'** – pairs of opposite attributes or qualities, expressed as adjectives – valued on a continuum from +3 to –3.

Figure 9.5   Semantic differential example

Profile of Car Model X

	+3	+2	+1	0	–1	–2	–3	
Modern								Old-fashioned
Fast								Slow
Attractive								Unattractive
Powerful								Weak
Responsive								Unresponsive
Glamorous								Ordinary

- Respondents are asked to **select the position of the object** being researched (in this case the car) on each continuum, according to the degree to which they think the adjective describes the object. (If the car is very powerful but not terribly responsive, say, it might rate +3 on the powerful-weak dimension, and +1 on the responsive-unresponsive scale.)

- A **'profile'** is thus built up by each respondent.

The main problem with Semantic Differential scales is the **subjectivity attached to language**. Words mean different things to different people. (The word 'old-fashioned' in our car profile may mean 'old-hat' to some and 'classic' to others.)

The other problem of measuring responses to, and perceptions of, different attributes of the same thing is that **one attribute can influence our perception of other attributes** and some attributes bring clusters of other assumed attributes with them (stereotypes). Think, for example, about our model X car: if it looks sleek and attractive, we may perceive it as a fast car – whether it is or not – and if we think of old-fashioned cars as glamorous (because of stereotypes of 'classic' cars and the people who drive them) we might distort our glamour rating.

1.2.7 Other rules on questionnaire wording

- Use clear and simple language. Use words of one or two syllables. Use simple English:
    - Instead of 'observe', use 'look'
    - Instead of 'construct', use 'build'
    - Instead of 'regarding', use 'about'
    - Instead of 'at this moment in time', use 'now'.

- Use what is known as demotic language or the language of your audience. It is very easy to produce stiff and inaccessible written words.

- Remember, very often the questionnaire will be read out loud. It is good practice to speak the question.

- Avoid ambiguity:
    - 'Do you buy a newspaper regularly?'
    - What does regularly mean? Every day? Once a month? Once a year?

- Avoid two questions in one:
    - 'What do you think of our prices and product quality?'
    - This is impossible to be answered accurately.

- Avoid leading or loaded questions:
    - 'Should the council spend money regenerating the poor environment in Brookmill ward?' It is hard for anyone to disagree with this question.
    - 'Most people think that our membership of the European Union is a good thing, Do you?' is a leading question. The aim has to be to reduce the potential to lead respondents.

- Avoid assumptions:
    - 'When driving, do you listen to your CD player?'
    - This makes a number of assumptions about the respondent: That he drives, that his car has a CD player, even that he is not hearing impaired!!

- Avoid generalisation:
    - 'How much do you usually spend on beer in a week?'
    - There are much better observational or panel methodologies to ensure accuracy here.

- Avoid negative questions:
    - 'You don't think that drink-driving should be more strictly regulated, do you?' is confusing and leads to problems.

- Avoid hypothetical questions:
    - 'If West Ham were relegated, would you still buy a season ticket?'
    - Speculation and guesswork is an outcome of this type of question.

Figure 9.6   Question format and wording

Name	Description	Example

CLOSED-END QUESTIONS

Dichotomous	A question with two possible answers.	'In arranging this trip, did you personally phone British Airways?' Yes ☐ No ☐
Multiple choice	A question with three or more answers.	'With whom are you travelling on this flight?' No one ☐ Children only ☐ Spouse ☐ Business associates/ Spouse and friends/relatives ☐ children ☐ An organised tour group ☐

| *Likert scale* | A statement with which the respondent shows the amount of agreement/ | 'Small airlines generally give better service |

Strongly disagree 1	Disagree 2	Neither agree nor disagree 3	Agree 4	Strongly agree 5
☐	☐	☐	☐	☐

British Airways

| *Semantic differential* | A scale connecting two bipolar words, where the respondent selects the point | Large _ _ _ _ _ _ _ _ _ _ _ _ _ _ _ _ _ _ Small
Experienced _ _ _ _ _ _ _ _ _ _ _ _ _ Inexperienced
Modern   Old-fashioned |

| *Importance scale* | A scale that rates the importance of some attribute. | |

Extremely important 1	Very important 2	Somewhat important 3	Not very important 4	Not at all important 5
☐	☐	☐	☐	☐

| *Rating scale* | A scale that rates some attribute from 'poor' to 'excellent'. | |

Excellent	Very good	Good	Fair	Poor

| *Intention-to-buy scale* | A scale that describes the respondent's intention to buy. | 'If an inflight telephone was available on a long flight, I would' |

Definitely buy 1	Probably buy 2	Not sure 3	Probably not buy 4	Definitely not buy 5
☐	☐	☐	☐	☐

OPEN-END QUESTIONS

| *Completely unstructured* | A question that respondents can answer in an almost unlimited number of ways. | 'What is your opinion of British Airways?' |

Using the rules above try to work out what is wrong with the following questions:

Are you single?

What is your average weekly disposable income?

How regularly do you come here?

Do you buy green vegetables?

Do you by frozen and canned foods?

What about our chilled and ambient ready meals?

How much did you spend on food last year?

Does your husband come with you?

When do you leave the car?

Are you against drug abuse?

You don't think council tax is too high, do you?

If we moved to the high street would you come more often?

1.3 Sequence

The overall structure of the questionnaire can take a number of forms, depending on the purpose and nature of the research. As a general rule, when you are exploring a given topic, you should aim to be as systematic as possible in **progressing from the general to the specific**. Typically, your initial aim should be to gain an understanding of the **broad context** within which opinions are held. You can then progress to gaining an understanding of the **nature and strength of opinion** in a given area. Finally, you can move, step by step, towards identifying the **detail that underpins these**.

To illustrate this, let us take a specific example – and one where you can easily put yourself in the position of the customer, assuming you enjoy being paid by your organisation! This is a staff questionnaire (staff are **internal customers**, of course) designed to explore attitudes to reward and recognition. The questionnaire might begin, for example, by asking a question about perceptions of reward and recognition in the organisation generally.

Figure 9.7   General perception

> How satisfied are you with the level of recognition and reward you receive for your achievements at work?
>
> Very satisfied
> Fairly satisfied
> Fairly unsatisfied
> Very dissatisfied?

The **responses** to this question will help provide you with a **context** within which you can interpret the more detailed information you will obtain from subsequent questions.

Having defined the broad organisational context, you can begin to focus more precisely on the detail of the specific topic. The next question might be:

Figure 9.8   Current perception

> If you feel that your work achievements are recognised, what form does this recognition generally take? (Please tick any that apply.)
>
> Increased basic pay
> Bonus payment

```
Other financial reward
Promotion
Verbal congratulations
Non-financial reward
Other (please specify)
```

This will provide you with an understanding of the **current perceptions of the topic** – what respondents' perceptions of the rewards they typically receive for work achievements are. It is important not to make assumptions (in this case it would be all too easy to assume that **your** perceptions and perspective reflect those of the wider workforce, but that may not be the case). The broad rule, as in most aspects of research, is **do not make assumptions**. If you have any doubts at all about people's views or perceptions, test them out.

Having identified people's perceptions of the current state of play in the specific area, you can then move to the next level of detail and begin to explore, for example, internal customers' **preferences** for reward and recognition. You might ask:

Figure 9.9   Preferences

```
Which of the following forms of recognition for work achievements do you find most motivating? (Please tick
one only.)

Increased basic pay
Bonus payment
Other financial reward
Promotion
Verbal congratulations
Non-financial reward
Other (please specify)
```

As a general rule a questionnaire should **progress from the general to the particular** (funnelling). It may be helpful to avoid a pattern of negative responses by distributing questions about respective topics throughout the questionnaire rather than bunching them together.

Mapping these expressed preferences against the current perceived position should indicate very clearly **if or where there is gap between the current and the desired positions**. This, in turn, will enable the organisation to focus its future activities very precisely on these areas, where they are likely to bring maximum pay-back. Having identified the most important issues in this way, you can then, of course, move on to look in detail at specific aspects of the topic (Dillon *et al*, 1994).

This process of moving from the general to the specific is sometimes known as **'funnelling'**. Clearly, it is an important device for **ensuring precision in interpretation**. In addition, it may also help you to provide a meaningful interpretation of responses that may be influenced by extraneous factors, such as **self-interest**. The use of broad, contextual questions, however, will help you to interpret such responses against a range of other issues and concerns. You might, for instance, ask respondents, initially, to rank areas of potential dissatisfaction in order of significance. This will then provide you with a basis on which to evaluate any specific expression of dissatisfaction with the really important issue.

Other questionnaire structures can also be used, to **minimise the influence of external factors**. If you are exploring a range of issues, for example, it can be helpful to distribute questions about each respective issue throughout the questionnaire, rather than bunching them in discrete sections. This can help reduce what is sometimes known as the **'halo effect'**, which is when overall positive or negative feelings about a given issue influence responses to individual questions. For example, if customers generally feel unhappy about delivery times, they may feel inclined to give negative responses to **all** questions relating to delivery, even though they may actually be highly satisfied with, say, quality of packaging. Distributing questions about delivery throughout the questionnaire may help to prevent such respondents establishing a **pattern of negative responses**.

It is important to think carefully about the order in which questions will appear in the questionnaire. Here are some general principles:

- In order to get the most important data from non-finishers, try to put the most important items in the first half of the questionnaire

- Don't start the questionnaire with awkward or embarrassing questions

- Questions should ideally progress from the general to the particular; from the factual to the abstract, and from closed to open questions

- Leave demographic and personal questions until the end.

1.4 Questionnaire length and layout

Questionnaire **length** will depend on the circumstances, but **short is better than long**. Clear instructions and layout are vital.

One of the most common questions asked by those conducting or commissioning research is, 'What length of questionnaire is acceptable?' As with sampling, there is **no straightforward answer**. It depends on the nature and complexity of the **questions** being asked. It depends on the **population** being researched, and their familiarity and confidence with questionnaires. It depends on the **methods being used** to administer the questionnaire. It is also true that the appliance and format of the questionnaire may be just as important as its length. Everything else being equal, a well-designed and clearly laid out questionnaire can afford to be longer than a poorly constructed equivalent.

Above all, of course, there is generally a trade-off between questionnaire length and the level of response. The **longer and more detailed** the questionnaire, the **more likely** you are to encounter **resistance** from potential respondents. Ultimately, you will need to balance these two factors. In some cases, for instance, you may feel that a smaller response is justified by the need to obtain a higher level of detail from the questionnaire.

Despite these caveats, the following crude guidelines for different forms of questionnaire administration may be helpful.

- **Cold surveys**. Where the questionnaire is being sent out with no preparation and where respondents have no particular incentive to respond, you should aim for an absolute maximum of four sides of paper and no more than 15 to 20 questions (including sub-questions), but in many cases, it will be preferable to aim for just one or two sides of paper and even fewer questions. The key issue here is likely to be one of presentation. You will want to suggest that the questionnaire is easy to complete and will involve comparatively little of the respondent's time. Therefore, simple, 'user-friendly' layout is likely to be an even more significant issue than the overall length.

- **Postal questionnaires**. Where respondents have been briefed and prepared, but are nevertheless expected to complete the questionnaire entirely in their own time, you should generally aim for a questionnaire of some six to eight sides of paper, ideally with no more than 30 to 40 questions. You will still need to ensure that the form is not unduly intimidating or off-putting and, ideally, respondents should feel encouraged to complete it immediately rather than delaying. If potential respondents put the questionnaire to one side, the chances are that a substantial proportion will not get around to completing it at all.

Some other general points about questionnaire design are also worth stressing. First, make sure that you provide **clear instructions** throughout, indicating precisely how the questionnaire should be completed. These should be simply phrased and as concise as possible. It is also a good idea to **provide some examples** of

specific question types and how they should be completed. As always, one good example is worth several dozen words of explanation.

Try to **avoid over-complicated instructions**. In some cases, a degree of complexity may be inevitable – particularly where, for example, some respondents are required to skip a number of the questions. Nevertheless, the most effective questionnaires, in terms of ease of response, are those where all respondents are able to proceed straightforwardly through the questionnaire from the first question to the last.

1.4.1 Laying out the questionnaire

- If respondents have to complete the questionnaire themselves, it must be approachable and as short as possible. Consider the use of **lines, boxes, different typefaces and print sizes and small pictures**. Use plenty of space.

- Consider the use of **tick boxes**. Is it clear where ticks go or how to respond in each case? For analysis, will it be easy to transfer responses from the forms to a summary sheet or a computer? Consider pre-coding the answers.

- Explain the **purpose of the research** at the beginning of the questionnaire and where possible guarantee confidentiality. Emphasise the date by which it must be returned and where it should be returned.

- At the end of the questionnaire, **thank the respondent** and make it clear what they should do with the completed questionnaire.

1.4.2 Showcards

Showcards are used to help respondents remember options read to them in face-to-face surveys. They are used as prompts and can include a list of scale points, phrases to select from, logos to recognise, lists of items, pictorial images or anything else that the researcher needs (Brace, 2004).

The increased use of computer-assisted personal interviewing has meant that the researcher will not necessarily need to use physical cards (similar to children's flashcards) as previously but they can make use of more interactive computerised prompts.

ACTIVITY 9.3

Using a range of techniques, design a questionnaire with the objective of obtaining feedback on the customers' satisfaction on the services provided by a club/bar/discotheque.

1.5 Pilot tests

> **Key term**
>
> **Pilot test**: This is the process of testing the questionnaire for mistakes and ambiguities by administering it on a small group of respondents in conditions that are as close as possible to the real thing.

Finally, it is **vital** to pilot test questionnaires since mistakes, ambiguities and embarrassments in a questionnaire can be extremely expensive once the main data collection phase has been entered. The **conditions** for the test should be the **same as**, or as close as possible to, the intended conditions for **the real thing**: respondents of the type you really want to test, using interviewers or self-administered questionnaires.

Piloting or testing the questionnaire is crucial for the following reasons:

- Allows problems to be corrected
- Helps with the coding process
- Improves question sequencing
- Improves wording of questions.

Piloting can be done with a small sample but it must be done. If many changes are made, the revised questionnaire should also be piloted. Piloting should be carried out by the staff who will administer the questionnaire, in a comparable environment and with respondents who share the characteristics of the sample.

- The **debriefing** method means the respondents should be asked after completing the questionnaire what their thought processes were as they completed the questionnaires

- The protocol method allows the respondent to talk through the process of completing the questionnaire as they are completing it.

2 Survey generating software

There are many IT packages available which help researchers to construct, design, select appropriate question formats and also analyse questionnaires for use as a paper version, in computer-assisted surveying form or online.

THE REAL WORLD

Snap Solo is just one example of a growing number of survey creating software packages.

The main package enables:

Questionnaire design

- » Survey Constructor wizard
- » WYSIWYG questionnaire design
- » Questionnaire templates
- » Set response types
- » Access to SurveyPak question libraries
- » Question routing
- » Add images and logos

Data entry

- » Four data entry modes
- » Browsing of selected cases
- » Verification of entered data
- » Editing and cleaning

Results analysis

- » Easy-to-read summary report
- » Cross-tabulations
- » Frequency, grid and holecount tables
- » 2D and 3D charts
- » Statistical analysis
- » Filtering / subsets
- » Weighting
- » Derived / recode variables
- » Analysis of literals
- » Templates for tables and charts
- » Printed and electronic reports
- » Volume batch reporting
- » Exporting results

(Snap Surveys, 2012)

- Questionnaire design should be done methodically: develop question topics; select question and response formats and take care with wording; determine the sequence; design the layout and pilot test.

- Questions need to be worded with precision, avoiding ambiguity and lack of clarity, not conflating multiple issues, not making unjustified assumptions, making it easy and clear for respondents to answer.

- Question types include Yes/No, multiple choice, ratings and scales: the primary purpose is to facilitate statistical analysis. Two of the best-known scales are the Likert scale and the Semantic Differential scale.

- As a general rule a questionnaire should progress from the general to the particular (funnelling). It may be helpful to avoid a pattern of negative responses by distributing questions about related topics throughout the questionnaire rather than bunching them together.

- Questionnaire length will depend on the circumstances, but short is better than long. Clear instructions and layout are vital.

- There are many IT packages that researchers can use to construct and design good questionnaires.

FURTHER READING

Chapter 6 of:

Bradley, N. (2010) *Marketing research: Tools & techniques*. 2nd edition. Oxford, Oxford University Press.

Chapter 7 of:

Wilson, A. (2012) *Marketing research: An integrated approach.* 3rd edition. Harlow, Financial Times Prentice Hall.

REFERENCES

Brace, I. (2004) *Questionnaire design: how to plan, structure and write survey material for effective market research (Market Research in Practice series).* London, Kogan Page.

Dillon, W., Madden, T. and Firtle, N. (1994) *Marketing Research in a Marketing Environment*. 3rd edition. Illinois, Irwin.

Messieh, N. (2012) Google's consumer surveys are bringing in one publisher $5,000 a month. *The Next Web*, http://thenextweb.com/google/2012/04/12/googles-consumer-surveys-are-bringing-in-one-publisher-5000-a-month/ [Accessed 12 June 2012].

Snap Surveys (2012) http://www.snapsurveys.com/ [Accessed 02 July 2012].

Wilson, A. (2012) *Marketing research: An integrated approach*. 3rd edition. Harlow, Financial Times Prentice Hall.

1.   At what point in the questionnaire design process should you 'determine sequence'?
2.   What are the three choices of question and response formats?
3.   Write an example of a closed question.
4.   What is wrong with this question?
     A   CIM Study Texts are excellent.
     B   CIM Study Texts are very useful.
     C   CIM Study Texts cover the syllabus very closely.
     D   CIM Study Texts are user friendly.
5.   Rewrite option A in the previous question using a Likert scale.
6.   What are the steps involved in designing a questionnaire?
7.   What are the three main parts of a questionnaire?
8.   Outline five rules for questionnaire wording.

ACTIVITY DEBRIEFS

Activity 9.1

The following statements are for a local supermarket chain:

Extra Supermarket offers a wide range of quality products (eg food, clothing, electrical, etc)

Extra Supermarket offers a large choice of items within each product range (eg food – fruit & veg, chilled, frozen, etc)

Extra Supermarket is competitive on price

Extra Supermarket has a high level of presence in the market (store locations, advertising, etc)

The staff at Extra Supermarket are polite and customer friendly

Extra Supermarket provides adequate information to customers about its products and services

Extra Supermarkets have convenient and adequate parking facilities

Extra Supermarket's own label products are as good or better than the major brands

Extra Supermarket provides a good level of nutritional information about its products

The staff at Extra Supermarket deal with complaints promptly and effectively.

Activity 9.2

Are you single?

(A sensitive question; ask the respondent to state what their marital status is. Also ambiguous – what is 'single'? Unmarried, divorced, separated, or a break?)

What is your average weekly disposable income?

(A sensitive question and hard for respondents to work out.)

How regularly do you come here?

(Ambiguous. Once a year or once a week.)

Do you buy green vegetables?

(Cabbage, fair trade or organics?)

Do you by frozen and canned foods?

(Spelling is poor, and two questions in one.)

What about our chilled and ambient ready meals?

(Two questions in one, and what are ambient ready meals? Will the respondent understand the question?)

How much did you spend on food last year?

(Can you remember this?)

Does your husband come with you?

(Assumption about gender and marital status.)

When do you leave the car?

(Assumption and 'when' does the researcher mean? – Overnight? When we go on holiday?)

Are you against drug abuse?

(A leading question, this would not produce a varied response.)

You don't think council tax is too high, do you?

(Use of negative and a leading question.)

If we moved to the high street would you come more often?

(A hypothetical question.)

XYZ club questionnaire

As someone who has visited XYZ club, we wish to find out your opinion on the range of services we offer, to help us improve our services. We shall be grateful if you will take a little time to complete this questionnaire.

Have you visited XYZ nightclub in the last 28 days?   ☐ Yes ☐ No

What is your gender?   ☐ Male ☐ Female

What is your age? (tick one box)

18–20 years ☐

21–23 years ☐

24–26 years ☐

27–30 years ☐

> 30 years ☐

How did you find out about XYZ nightclub?

Local newspaper advertisements ☐

Handbill / Flyer received in street ☐

Word of mouth ☐

Other ☐

For how long have you been visiting XYZ nightclub? (tick one box)

< 1 month ☐

1–3 months ☐

4–6 months ☐

7–12 months ☐

>12 months ☐

Your welcome to the club

Thinking about your entry to the club and the welcome you received, how do you rate your welcome?

Very unwelcoming	Unwelcoming	Neither welcoming nor unwelcoming	Welcoming	Very welcoming
☐	☐	☐	☐	☐

The bar

How do you rate the selection of drinks on offer at the bar? (please circle one alternative)

Poor selection   1   2   3   4   5   Excellent selection

Music

How do you rate the selection of the music played at the club? Please circle the alternative that best describes your opinion.

Poor   1   2   3   4   5   Excellent

The Chartered Institute of Marketing

Optional

Please add your name and address if you would like to enter the monthly draw of completed surveys for a free admission voucher.

Club facilities

Consider your attitude to the following club facilities and for each of the following statements state whether you strongly agree, agree, neither agree nor disagree, disagree or strongly disagree by placing a tick in the appropriate box for each statement.

Table 9.1

	Strongly agree	Agree	Neither agree nor disagree	Disagree	Strongly disagree
The rest room facilities are good					
The general club atmosphere is good					
The club experience is good value for money					
The dance floor is about the right size					

Your opinion

Finally, what improvements would you like to see XYZ club make to the services it provides?

End

Thank you for taking the time to complete this questionnaire.

1   The fourth step after you have determined the question topics, decided on question and answer formats and decided the wording, but before designing the layout of the questions.

2   Open, Closed, Scaling

3   A closed question can be answered Yes or No or with a very short factual answer. For example, 'What is your date of birth?'

4   This is intended to be an example of a very bad question. There is no indication of what to do (tick one or more options? Ring round one or more letters?). Option B in particular is far too vague: what does 'useful' mean? It is also a highly leading question, since there is no opportunity to do anything other than praise BPP Study Texts.

5   The CIM Study Texts are excellent.

    5   Strongly agree
    4   Agree
    3   Don't know
    2   Disagree
    1   Strongly disagree

6   Develop question topics, select question and response formats and wording, determine sequence, design layout and pilot test.

7   Identification data, classification data and subject data.

8   Use clear simple wording, avoid ambiguity, avoid two questions in one, avoid leading or loaded questions and avoid assumptions.

CHAPTER 10

The presentation of results

Introduction

This chapter explores the key elements and formats involved in reporting or presenting marketing information to decision-makers. It provides valuable guidance on how to bring together the information derived from the activities discussed in the previous chapters, and present it to managers in a format that is easy to understand. The first section identifies the factors that the researcher should take into account in order to understand the thinking sequence of the audience and communicate effectively with them.

The second section identifies the elements of a report and outlines the techniques that can be used to make the content easy to read and digest. The third section explains different ways of presenting research data in order to make it easy for readers to understand.

Finally, the fourth section explores the different issues involved in delivering effective oral presentations of research reports.

Topic list

The audience thinking sequence   (1)

Research reports   (2)

Presenting findings   (3)

Oral presentations   (4)

1.4	Review the key elements and formats when reporting or presenting marketing information to decision-makers:
	▪ Understanding the audience/audience thinking sequence
	▪ Physical and online research report format
	▪ Oral presentation format
	▪ Using tables and graphs

1 The audience thinking sequence

Wilson (2012) suggests that the researcher should take account of the typical 'thinking sequence' that people go through when you are communicating with them.

- **Respect the client's importance**: in other words don't waste their time with irrelevant, badly structured or presented, over-long information.

- **Consider the client's needs**: the client needs to make a marketing decision.

- **Demonstrate how your information helps the client**: relate the research findings to the original objectives.

- **Explain the detail that underpins your information**: why should your findings be believed? Because you have evidence that 'Nine out of ten dogs prefer ...' or whatever. This is the place for tables and charts and apt quotes from respondents.

- **Remind the client of the key points**

- **Suggest what the client should do now**: there will usually be a variety of options. It is the client's decision, but it is usual to give recommendations.

The researcher knows more about the subject matter of the report or presentation than the report user. It is important that this information should be communicated impartially, so that the report user can make his or her own judgements.

- Any assumptions, evaluations and recommendations should be clearly signalled as such

- Points should not be over-weighted (or omitted as irrelevant) without honestly evaluating how objective the selection is

- Facts and findings should be balanced against each other

- A firm conclusion should, if possible, be reached. It should be clear how and why it was reached.

The researcher must also recognise the needs and abilities of the audience.

- Beware of 'jargon', overly technical terms and specialist knowledge the user may not share

- Keep your vocabulary, sentence and paragraph structures as simple as possible, for clarity (without patronising an intelligent user)

- Bear in mind the type and level of detail that will interest the user and be relevant to his/her purpose

- The audience may range from senior manager to junior operational staff to complete layman (a non-executive director, say). Your vocabulary, syntax and presentation, the amount of detail you can go into, the technical matter you can include and the formality of your report structure should all be influenced by such concerns.

2 Research reports

A research report typically has the following elements: Title page; list of contents; executive summary; introduction/problem definition; research method (and limitations); research findings; conclusions; appendices.

Birn (2004) believes that the key to effectively presented research is to make managers want to use it. He argues that too much research is conducted only to be left to get dusty on the marketers shelf, the key to it being used he argues it to make it meaningful.

Various techniques can be used to make the content of a research report easy to identify and digest.

- The material in the report should be in a logical order
- The relative importance of points should be signalled by headings
- Each point may be numbered in some way to help with cross-reference
- The document should be easy on the eye, helped by different font sizes, bold, italics, capitals, spacing.

A typical report structure covers:

- **Headings**. There is a 'hierarchy' of headings: there is an overall title and the report as a whole is divided into sections. Within each section main points have a heading in bold capitals, sub-points have a heading in bold lower-case and sub-sub-points have a heading in italics. (Three levels of headings within a main section is usually considered the maximum number that readers can cope with.) It is not necessary to underline headings.

- **References**. Sections are lettered, A, B etc. Main points are numbered 1, 2 and so on, and within each division paragraphs are numbered 1.1, 1.2, 2.1, 2.2. Sub-paragraphs inherit their references from the paragraph above. For instance the first sub-paragraph under paragraph 1.2 is numbered 1.2.1.

- **Fonts**. Word processors offer you a wealth of fonts these days, but it is best to avoid the temptation. It is often a good idea to put headings in a different font to the main text, but stop there: two fonts is quite enough!

You might also choose to reference sub-paragraphs, eg 1.2(a), 1.2(b). You might use Roman numerals, although we advise against this. If your report turns out to be longer than you expected and you get up to paragraph XLVIII you are likely to confuse many of your readers.

A detailed report on an extensive research study may run to many pages, and may therefore require these elements.

- **Title page** (also giving contact information)

- A **list of contents**: the major headings and sub-headings. Most word processing software can produce these automatically.

- A **summary** of findings (to give the reader an initial idea of what the report is about). This is usually called the **executive summary**, the implication being that senior managers don't have time to read it all.

- **Introduction/problem definition**: this is likely to be very similar to the rationale and objectives set out in the research brief and proposal.

- **Research method (and limitations)**: again this is likely to be similar to the equivalent section in the proposal, although it must be updated if anything had to be changed during the implementation of the research or if the research did not go to plan (eg lower than expected response rates).

- **Research findings**: this is the main body of the report

- **Conclusions**: this section should point out the implications of the findings for the client with reference to the initial problem.

- Supporting **appendices**: these might include the questionnaire used or the original discussion document, more detailed tables of figures, lists of secondary sources used. Appendices contain subsidiary detailed material that may well be of interest to some readers, but which might lessen the impact of the findings if presented in full detail in the body of the report.

- Possibly, an **index**.

3 Presenting findings

Tables, **graphs**, **charts** and **illustrations** of various kinds can **greatly enhance** the **value** of a report because they make it easier to take in information at a glance.

3.1 Tables

Tables present data in rows and columns. This form of presentation makes it easier to understand large amounts of data. A railway timetable is a familiar example.

Table 10.1   Typical table of data

Charing Cross	15:38	16:08	16:18	16:28	16:37	16:45	16:58
Waterloo	15:41	16:11	16:21	16:31	16:40	16:48	17:01
London Bridge	15:49	16:19	16:29	16:39	16:48	16:56	17:09
New Cross	16:01	16:31	16:41	-	17:00	17:08	17:21
Lewisham	16:06	16:36	16:46	16:50	17:05	17:13	17:26

Suppose you arrive at London Bridge at 16:42 and you want to go to Lewisham. Using a table like the one above there are at least three things that this timetable tells you.

- You can **look up a specific value** by seeing where rows and columns meet. Since you know it is 16:42 you can quickly see from the timetable that your next train is due in six minutes (at 16:48) and will arrive in Lewisham at 17:05.

- You can work your way around the table from your original starting point and **test out other scenarios**. For instance, you can see that if you had arrived at London Bridge a few minutes earlier you could have got a fast train. If you are not sure that six minutes is long enough to buy a cup of coffee and a bar of chocolate you can get a slightly later train to Lewisham which will give you 14 minutes.

- You can read across rows (or down columns) and **compare values**. For future reference you can note (by reading right across the London Bridge row) that from 16:19 onwards there is a train to Lewisham roughly every ten minutes.

Tables are a simple way of presenting numerical information. Figures are displayed, and can be compared with each other: relevant totals, subtotals, percentages can also be presented as a summary for analysis.

A table is two-dimensional (rows and columns): so it can only show two variables: a sales analysis for a year, for example, might have rows for months, and columns for products.

Table 10.2 Rows and columns

SALES FIGURES FOR 201X					
	Product A	Product B	Product C	Product D	Total
Jan	370	651	782	899	2,702
Feb	718	312	748	594	2,372
Mar	548	204	585	200	1,537
Apr	382	616	276	359	1,633
May	132	241	184	223	780
Jun	381	216	321	123	1,041
Jul	679	612	733	592	2,616
Aug	116	631	343	271	1,361
Sep	421	661	868	428	2,378
Oct	211	158	653	479	1,501
Nov	306	243	676	404	1,659
Dec	898	759	796	394	2,847
Total	5,162	5,334	6,965	4,966	22,427

You are likely to present data in tabular form very often. Here are the key points to remember.

- The table should have a clear **title**

- All columns and rows should be clearly **labelled**

- Where appropriate, there should be **sub-totals** and a **right-hand total column** for comparison

- A total figure is often advisable at the **bottom of each column** of figures also, for comparison. It is usual to double-underline totals at the foot of columns

- **Numbers** should be **right-aligned** and they are easier to read if you use the **comma separator** for thousands

- **Decimal points should line up**, either by using a decimal tab or by adding extra noughts (the latter is preferable, in our opinion)

- A grid or border is optional: see what looks best and is easiest to read

- Tables should not be packed with too much data. If you try to get too much in, the information presented will be difficult to read.

3.1.1 Columns or rows?

Often it will be obvious what information should go in the columns and what should go in rows. Sometimes, it won't matter too much which way round you have the rows and columns. Here are some points to remember.

(a) It is usually easier to read across a short line than a long one. That means that it is usually **better to have a long thin table** than a short wide one: lots of rows rather than lots of columns. If you had a price list of five hundred products each of which came in 3 different sizes. You would probably tabulate the information like this, without even considering the other possibility (it wouldn't fit on the paper or screen, anyway, if you had products in columns).

Table 10.3 Rows and columns (1)

Product	Large	Medium	Small
A001	12.95	11.65	9.35
A002	14.50	12.50	10.50
A003	Etc.	Etc.	Etc.
A004			
A005			
Etc.			

- However, most people find it easier to compare figures by reading across than by reading down. For example, in the previous version of the sales figures (Table 10.2) it is easier to compare *product* totals, but in Table 10.4 it is easier to compare *monthly* totals.

Table 10.4 Rows and columns (2)

	Jan	Feb	Mar	Apr	May	Jun	Jul	Aug	Sep	Oct	Nov	Dec	Total
Product A	370	718	548	382	132	381	679	116	421	211	306	898	5,162
Product B	651	312	204	616	241	216	612	631	661	158	243	759	5,334
Product C	782	748	585	276	184	321	733	343	868	653	676	796	6,965
Product D	899	594	200	359	223	123	592	271	428	479	404	394	4,966
Total	2,702	2,372	1,537	1,633	780	1,041	2,616	1,361	2,378	1,501	1,659	2,847	22,427

- If you are not sure what your audience will most want to compare, it might be helpful to give them both versions, if practicable.

> ▶ **Assessment tip**
>
> Tables, graphs, charts and illustrations of various kinds can greatly enhance the value of a report because they make it easier to take in information at a glance

3.2 Line graphs

In business, line graphs are usually used to illustrate **trends over time** of figures such as sales or customer complaints.

Figure 10.1 Single line graph

The figures are plotted on a grid and then joined by a line that reflects the 'ups and downs' of the figure, over a period of time. Note that it is conventional to show **time** on the **horizontal** axis.

Now the trend in sales is shown instantly, in a way that is probably not immediately apparent from a column or row of figures. This **encourages us to ask questions**: for instance why did sales drop in the early months of the year and suddenly shoot up in June and July?

By using different symbols for the plotted points, or preferably by using different colours, several lines can be drawn on a line graph before it gets too overcrowded, and that means that **several trends** (for example the sales performance of different products) can be compared, as shown in Figure 10.2.

Figure 10.2   Multiple line graph

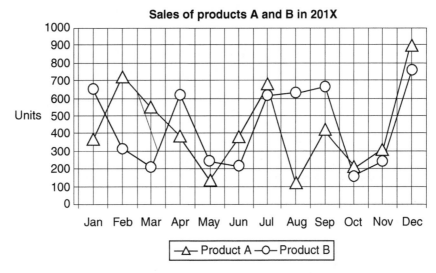

The scale of the vertical axis should be just large enough for you to tell with reasonable accuracy the sales figure at any given point during the period. In the example above we have used a scale of 100 and you can tell, for instance, that sales of product A in April were a little less than 400 (check in the table given above).

3.3 Charts

3.3.1 Bar charts

The bar chart is one of the most common methods of visual presentation. Data is shown in the form of bars which are the same in width but variable in height. Each bar represents a different item, for example the annual production cost of different products, or the number of hours required to produce a product by different workteams.

Figure 10.3   Bar chart (vertical)

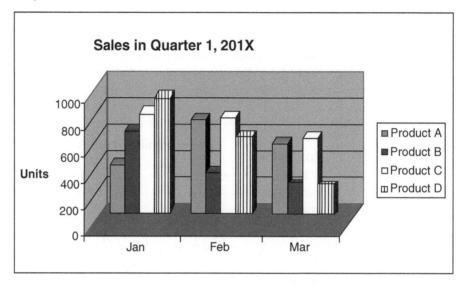

As you can see, here we are more interested in comparing a few individual items in a few individual months (although you can still get a visual impression of trends over time).

Horizontal presentation is also possible.

Figure 10.4   Bar chart (horizontal)

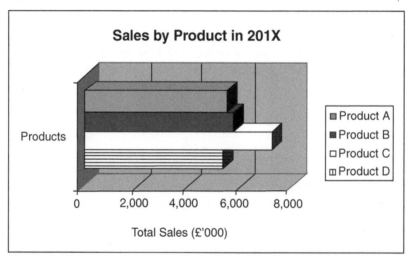

There are no hard-and-fast rules about whether you should use vertical or horizontal presentation. However, these guidelines may help.

- If you are showing **trends over time** (for instance January to March) **vertical bars** look best

- If you are showing **differences at a single point in time** (the end of 201X, for instance) you might prefer **horizontal** bars.

3.3.2 Pie charts

A pie chart shows the **relative** sizes of the things that make up a total.

Pie charts are most effective where the number of slices is small enough to keep the chart simple, and where the difference in the size of the slices is large enough for the eye to judge without too much extra information.

Figure 10.5 Pie chart

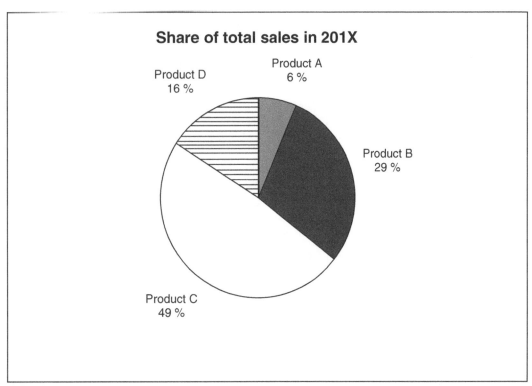

THE REAL WORLD

Create Impressive Excel & PowerPoint Charts

Deciding on the right way to present data on your slides can be sometimes be a challenge. Chart Chooser from Juice Analytics is an innovative tool that enables you to create Excel and PowerPoint charts and choose the characteristics that you wish to highlight in your data. Chart Chooser filters the selections highlighting the possible charts for your needs. When you have decided on your selection, Chart Chooser will display options to download templates for Excel and PowerPoint. The downloaded files will also have random data filled for you to get an idea of how the data is presented and where you will be able to enter your own figures. Find out more at http://www.juiceanalytics.com/chart-chooser

3.4 Flow charts, organisation charts and other labelled diagrams

Flow charts and organisation charts are useful ways of presenting and summarising information that involves a series of **steps** and **choices** and/or **relationships** between the different items.

On the following pages there are some examples of this type of presentation.

If you choose any of these forms of presentation here are some points to bear in mind.

- Be consistent in your use of layout and symbols (and colours, if used). For instance, in Figure 10.6 a decision symbol is consistently a diamond with italic text; a YES decision consistently flows downwards; a NO decision consistently flows to the right.

- Keep the number of connecting lines to a minimum and avoid lines that 'jump over' each other at all costs.

- Keep the labels or other text brief and simple.

- Hand-drawn diagrams should be as neat and legible as possible. If they are likely to be seen by a lot of people (not just your team) it is better to use a business graphics programme like Microsoft Visio.

- Everyone can draw ... but only so well. If you are not expert you can waste an enormous amount of time playing with computer graphics. If it needs to be really beautifully presented and you are not an expert sketch it quickly by hand and then give it to a professional!

Figure 10.6   A flowchart

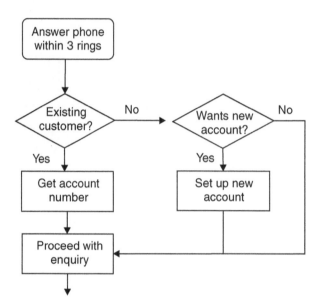

Figure 10.7   An organisation chart

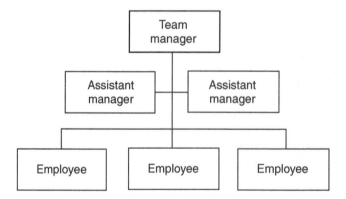

The Chartered
Institute of Marketing

3.5 Pictograms

A pictogram is a simple graphic image in which the **data is represented by a picture or symbol**, with a clear key to the items and quantities intended. Different pictures can be used on the same pictogram to represent different elements of the data. For example a pictogram showing the number of people employed by an organisation might use pictures of … people!

Figure 10.8   Pictogram (1)

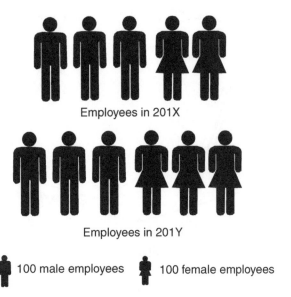

Employees in 201X

Employees in 201Y

100 male employees   100 female employees

You can see quite easily that the workforce has grown and that the organisation employs far more female workers than before.

Pictograms present data in a simple and appealing way. They are **often used on television**. Watch out for them next time you are watching a news item involving numbers (number of trains late, number of new jobs created, and so on).

- The symbols must be clear and simple
- There should be a key showing the number that each symbol represents
- Bigger quantities are usually shown by more symbols, not bigger symbols.

Bear in mind, however, that pictograms are **not appropriate** if you need to give **precise** figures. You can use portions of a symbol to represent smaller quantities, but there are limits to what you can do.

Figure 10.9   Pictogram (2)

     150 female employees   *Over 100 employees, mostly male. But how many others and what sex are they?*

3.6 Drawings and graphics

A labelled drawing may sometimes be the best way of presenting a lot of information in a small space. Imagine how difficult it would be to explain all the information you get from Figure 10.10 if you could only use words!

Figure 10.10   Graphic display

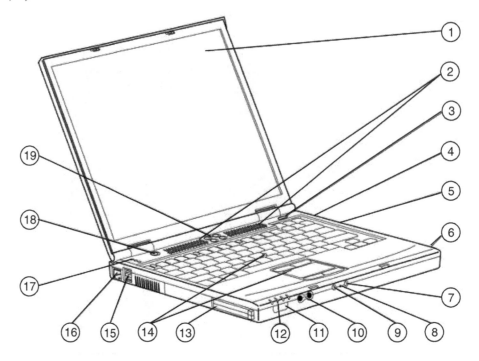

1. Color Display	10. Volume Controls
2. Stereo Speakers	11. Infrared Port
3. Power Switch	12. System LEDs
4. RJ-11 (Modem)	13. PC Card Slots (2)
5. MultiBay	14. Touchpad + Pointstick
6. Cable Lock Connector	15. USB (2)
7. Audio-In	16. RJ-45 (NIC)
8. Microphone	17. Keyboard LEDs
9. Headphone-Out	18. Suspend Button
	19. Easy Access Internet Button

3.7 Product positioning maps

Although they may be called **'maps'** these are really a form of **scatter diagram**. **Two key attributes** of a product are taken and competing products are graded to fit between the extremes of *possessing* an attribute or *not possessing* it.

For example a package delivery service may be **fast** or **slow**, and it may deal with **large** or **small** packages.

Figure 10.11   Product positioning map

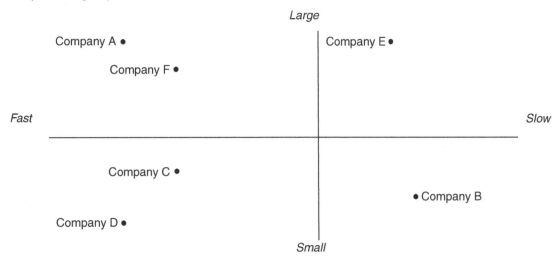

Interpret the diagram at Figure 10.12.

---

4 Oral presentations

An oral presentation would have the following structure: Introduction; Explanation of research methodology; Key findings; Conclusions/recommendations; Questions.

This is not unlike the structure of a report, and many of the same points apply. However, **live interaction** with the audience has its own issues.

Matters to consider when preparing and delivering presentations include **audience motivation**, **physical factors** in the presentation room, **content**, **clarity**, adding **emphasis and interest**, and **controlling nerves** and **body language**.

What presentations, conferences, or speech-making occasions have you attended recently? For each, note:

- The style of speech (formal/informal etc)
- The length of the speech
- Any visual aids used

How effective was the speaker in targeting each of these elements to

- The purpose of the speech
- The needs of the audience?

THE REAL WORLD

In an effort to help people who aren't young anymore understand those who are, MTV and Microsoft commissioned OTX to conduct an 18-month research project to study 24,000 youngsters in their natural habitats. The researchers presented their findings in an exhibition in London's Brick Lane.

As interesting as the study itself is the fact that the findings have been presented in a fun, funky exhibition open to the public, as well as targeting clients of MTV and OTX. This approach was a much better way to grab clients' attention than even the most brilliantly crafted PowerPoint presentation.

OTX researcher and ex-MTV employee Graham Saxton told *Research*: 'The point is to showcase a lot of insights about global youth culture that would be hard to present in more traditional ways. Researchers beat themselves up about adding value and getting findings in front of clients and yet most research is presented in the same old way, so we're trying to get away from that, and we'd love to do more of it.'

Saxton then planned to take the exhibition to the US, where he suggested that presentation of research tends to be 'more traditional' than in Europe.

'Clients are always looking for more engaging ways of research being communicated and this is one way of doing that – although it is an expensive way!'

The research findings identified that concerned parents might see kids retreating from the 'real world' into technology, but youngsters are actually just connecting with the world in a way that, to them, is just as 'real' as anything else.

The researchers also found that to think that young people 'like' technology is wrong. In fact, most don't even notice it. Mobiles, computers and social networks are just ways for them to stay in touch with their friends.

(*Research*, 2008)

▶ **Assessment tip**

General points here about presentation may be familiar from your earlier studies, but it does no harm to be reminded: that is one of the principles of good communication! Although your assignment does not include an oral presentation, you will, however, be expected to create professional slides and possibly even give advice about how to formally present for maximum effect.

4.1 Audience

The audience's **motivations** and **expectations** in attending a presentation will, as we have seen, influence their perceptions of you and your message. Why might they be at your presentation?

- **They need specific information from the presentation.** An audience which is deliberately seeking information, and intending to use it to further their own objectives, is highly motivated. If their objectives

match the speaker's (say, in a training seminar, where both trainer and trainees want improved job performance as the outcome), this motivation aids the speaker. It is therefore important to gauge, as far as possible, what this highly-motivated group **want** to hear from you, and **why**.

- **They are interested in the topic of the presentation**. The audience may have a general expectation that they will learn something new, interesting, or useful on a topic that they are pre-disposed to gather information about: it is up to the speaker to hold their attention by satisfying the desire for relevant information. They may also have some prior knowledge, on which the speaker can build: there will be a fine line to tread between boring the audience by telling them what they already know, and losing them by assuming more knowledge than they possess.

- **They are required to be there**.

  - Attendance may be **compulsory**, whether or not those attending are motivated or interested in the subject matter. In this case, you can at least find out the size and composition of your audience, but unless motivation and interest can be stimulated by the presentation, compulsory attendance may simply create resistance to the message.

  - Attendance may be **recommended by a superior**, in which case even if the participants are not interested in the subject matter, they may be motivated to pay attention because they perceive it to be in their own interest to do so.

    This is known as a **captive audience**. Note that it is a double-edged sword: the audience may be compelled to listen to you, but they are actually **less** likely to listen attentively, co-operatively and with positive results, unless you can motivate them to do so once you have them in front of you.

- **They expect to be entertained**. The topic of the presentation may be entertaining or the audience may expect the speaker to put information across in an entertaining manner – perhaps using humour or illustration. The organisation culture may encourage the idea that attending meetings and conferences is equivalent to rest and recreation: a bit of a 'day out' for the participants, more useful for the networking in the coffee breaks than the technical content of the presentations. As a speaker, you will have to ensure that you do not fulfil such expectations at the expense of your primary objectives – but be aware that the entertainment-seekers are also a potential audience for your message: it may be possible to arouse more motivated interest.

Taking into account any **specific** audience needs and expectations, your message needs to have the following qualities.

- **Interest**. It should be lively/entertaining/varied and relevant to the audience's needs and interests, or preferably both.

- **Congeniality**. This usually means positive, supportive or helpful in some way (eg in making a difficult decision easier, or satisfying a need).

- **Credibility**. It should be **consistent** in itself, and with known **facts**; apparently **objective**; and from a source perceived to be **trustworthy**.

- **Accessibility**. This means both:

  - **Audible/visible**. (Do you need to be closer to the audience? Do you need a microphone? Enlarged visual aids? Clearer articulation and projection?)

  - **Understandable**. (What is the audience's level of knowledge/education/ experience in general? Of the topic at hand? What technical terms will need to be avoided or explained? What concepts or ideas will need to be explained?)

4.2 Physical preparation

At the planning stage, you might also consider physical factors which will affect the audience's concentration: their ability and willingness to keep listening attentively and positively to your message. Some of these may not be in your control, if you are not planning the meeting or conference or arranging the venue but, as far as possible, give attention to the following.

- **Listening conditions**. Try and cut out background noise – conversations outside the room, traffic, loud air conditioning or rattling slide projector, say. (There may be a trade-off between peace and quiet, and good ventilation, also required for alertness: be sensible about the need to open a door or window or switch on a fan.)

- **Freedom from interruption and distraction**. Do not let the focus shift from the speaker and the message to outside views of people passing by. Arrange not to be disturbed by others entering the room. Announce, if appropriate, that questions and comments will be invited at the end of the session.

- **Ventilation, heating and lighting**. A room that is too stuffy, or draughty, too hot or cold, too bright or too dim to see properly, can create physical discomfort, which shifts attention from the speaker and the message to the listener.

- **Seating and desking**. Excessive comfort can impair alertness – but uncomfortable seating is a distraction. Combined with inadequate arrangements for writing (since many people may wish or need to take notes), it can cause severe strain over a lengthy talk.

- **Audibility and visibility**. Inadequate speaking volume or amplification is a distraction and a strain, even if it does not render the message completely inaccessible. Excessive volume and electronic noise is equally irritating. Visibility requires planning not just of effective visual aids (clear projection in suitable light, adequately enlarged) but also of seating plans, allowing unobstructed 'sight lines' for each participant.

- **Seating layout**. Depending on the purpose and style of your presentation, you may choose formal classroom-like rows of seating, with the speaker in front behind a podium, or informal group seating in a circle or cluster in which the speaker is included. The formal layout enhances the speaker's credibility, and may encourage attention to information, while the informal layout may be more congenial, encouraging involvement and input from the whole group.

- **Time**. Listeners get tired over time – however interesting the presentation: their concentration span is limited, and they will not be able to listen effectively for a long period without a break.

    - If you have the choice (and a limited volume of information to impart), a ten-minute presentation will be more effective than a one-hour presentation.

    - If the volume of information or time allotted dictate a lengthy talk, you will need to build in reinforcements, breaks and 'breathers' for your listeners, by using repetition, summary, jokes/anecdotes and question-and-answer breaks.

    - Bear in mind, too, that the time of day will affect your listeners' concentration, even if your presentation is a brief one: you will have to work harder if your talk is first thing in the morning, late in the day (or week), or approaching lunchtime.

- **The speaker's appearance**. It should already be obvious that the appearance of the speaker may sabotage his or her efforts if it is uncongenial or unappealing, lacks credibility or the authority expected by the audience or is distracting in some way.

In what other research circumstances besides the final presentation might the researcher find it useful to think about physical factors that will affect his or her audience's concentration?

4.3 Content

Armed with your clearly-stated objectives and audience profile, you can plan the **content** of your presentation.

One approach which may help to clarify your thinking is as follows.

Table 10.5   Presentation overview

Prioritise	Select the key points of the subject, and a storyline or theme that gives your argument a unified sense of 'direction'. The fewer points you make (with the most emphasis) and the clearer the direction in which your thoughts are heading, the easier it will be for the audience to grasp and retain your message.
Structure	Make notes for your presentation which illustrate simply the logical order or pattern of the key points of your speech.
Outline	Following your structured notes, flesh out your message. ■ Introduction ■ Supporting evidence, examples and illustrations ■ Notes where visual aids will be used ■ Conclusion.
Practise	Rehearsals should indicate difficult logical leaps, dull patches, unexplained terms and other problems: adjust your outline or style. They will also help you gauge and adjust the length of your presentation.
Cue	Your outline may be too detailed to act as a cue or aide-memoire for the talk itself. Small cards, which fit into the palm of the hand may be used to give you: ■ Key words for each topic, and the logical links between them ■ Reminders for when to use visual aids ■ The full text of any detailed information you need to quote.

An effective presentation requires two key structural elements.

- An **introduction** which:
    - Establishes your credibility
    - Establishes rapport with the audience
    - Gains the audience's attention and interest (sets up the problem to be solved, uses curiosity or surprise)
    - Gives the audience an overview of the **shape** of your presentation, to guide them through it: a bit like the scanning process in reading.

- A **conclusion** which:
    - **Clarifies and draws together** the points you have made into one main idea (using an example, anecdote, review, summary)
    - **States or implies what you want/expect your audience to do** following your presentation

– Reinforces the audience's **recall** (using repetition, a joke, quotation or surprising statistic to make your main message **memorable**).

4.4 Clarity

Your structured notes and outline should contain cues which clarify the **logical order**, shape or progression of your information or argument. This will help the audience to **follow you** at each stage of your argument, so that they arrive with you at the conclusion. You can signal these logical links to the audience as follows.

- **Linking words or phrases**

  Therefore ... [conclusion, result or effect, arising from previous point]

  As a result ...

  However ... [contradiction or alternative to previous point]

  On the other hand ...

  Similarly ... [confirmation or additional example of previous point]

  Again ...

  Moreover ... [building on the previous point]

- **Framework**: setting up the structure

  'Of course, this isn't a perfect solution: There are advantages and disadvantages to it. It has the advantages of ... . But there are also disadvantages, in that ... '

- You can use more **elaborate devices** which summarise or repeat the previous point and lead the audience to the next. These also have the advantage of giving you, and the listener, a 'breather' in which to gather your thoughts.

Other ways in which content can be used to clarify the message include the following.

- **Examples and illustrations** – showing how an idea works in practice

- **Anecdotes** – inviting the audience to relate an idea to a real-life situation

- **Questions** – rhetorical, or requiring the audience to answer, raising particular points that may need clarification

- **Explanation** – showing how or why something has happened or is so, to help the audience understand the principles behind your point

- **Description** – helping the audience to visualise the person, object or setting you are describing

- **Definition** – explaining the precise meaning of terms that may not be shared or understood by the audience

- The use of **facts, quotations or statistics** – to 'prove' your point.

Your **vocabulary and style** in general should contribute to the clarity of the message. Remember to use short, simple sentences and non-technical words (unless the audience is sure to know them): avoid jargon, clichés, unexplained acronyms, colloquialisms, double meanings and vague expressions (like 'rather', 'good'). Remember, too, that this is **oral** communication, not written: use words and grammatical forms that you would **normally use in speaking** to someone – bearing in mind the audience's ability to understand you, and the formality of the occasion.

Visual aids will also be an important aspect of content used to signal the structure and clarify the meaning of your message. We discuss them specifically below.

4.5 Adding emphasis

Emphasis is the 'weight', importance or impact given to particular words or ideas. This can largely be achieved through delivery – the tone and volume of your voice, strong eye contact, emphatic gestures – but can be reinforced in the content and wording of your speech. Emphasis can be achieved by a number of means.

- **Repetition:** 'If value for money is what the market wants, then value for money is what this brand must represent.' or 'One in five customers has had a quality complaint. That's right: one in five.'

- **Rhetorical questions:** 'Do you know how many of your customers have a quality complaint? One in five. Do you think that's acceptable?'

- **Quotation:** '"Product quality is the number one issue in customer care in the new millennium." That's the conclusion of our survey report.'

- **Statistical evidence:** 'One in five of your customers this year have had a quality complaint: that's 10% more complaints than last year. If the trend continues, you will have one complaint for every two satisfied customers – next year!'

- **Exaggeration:** 'We have to look at our quality control system. Because if the current trend continues, we are going to end up without any customers at all.'

4.6 Adding interest

Simple, clear information often lacks impact, and will only be interesting to those already motivated by the desire for the information. The speaker will need to balance the need for clarity with the need to get the key points across. All the devices discussed so far can be used for impact.

Here are some further suggestions.

- **Analogy, metaphor, simile** etc – comparing something to something else which is in itself more colourful or interesting

- **Anecdote or narrative** – as already mentioned, telling a story which illustrates or makes the point, using suspense, humour or a more human context

- **Curiosity or surprise** – from incongruity, anticlimax or controversy. Verbatim quotes from customers can be very useful in this respect

- **Humour.** This is often used for entertainment value, but also serves as a useful 'breather' for listeners, and may help to get them on the speaker's side. (Humour may not travel well, however: the audience may not be on the speaker's wavelength at all, especially in formal contexts. Use with caution.)

4.7 Controlling nerves

Stage-fright can be experienced before making a phone call, going into an interview or meeting, or even writing a letter, but it is considerably more acute, for most people, before standing up to talk in front of a group or crowd of people. Common fears are to do with **making a fool of oneself**, forgetting one's **lines**, being unable to answer **questions**, or being faced by blank incomprehension or **lack of response**. Fear can make vocal delivery hesitant or stilted and **body language** stiff and unconvincing.

A **controlled amount of fear**, or stress, is actually **good for you**: it stimulates the production of **adrenaline**, which can contribute to alertness and dynamic action. Only at excessive levels is stress harmful, degenerating into **strain**. If you can **manage your stress** or stage-fright, it will help you to be **alert** to feedback from your audience, to think 'on your feet' in response to questions, and to project vitality and enthusiasm.

- Reduce uncertainty and risk. This means:

    - **Preparing thoroughly** for your talk, including rehearsal, and anticipating questions

- **Checking** the venue and facilities meet your expectations

- **Preparing** whatever is necessary for your own confidence and comfort (glass of water, handkerchief, note cards)

- **Keeping your notes to hand**, and in order, during your presentation.

- **Have confidence in your message.** Concentrate on the desired outcome: that is why you are there. Believe in what you are saying. It will also make it easier to project enthusiasm and energy.

- **Control physical symptoms.** Breathe deeply and evenly. Control your gestures and body movements. Put down a piece of paper that is visibly shaking in your hand. Pause to collect your thoughts if necessary. Smile, and maintain eye contact with members of the audience. If you **act** as if you are calm, the calm will **follow**.

4.8 Non-verbal messages

Any number of body language factors may contribute to a speaker **looking confident and relaxed**, or nervous, shifty and uncertain. **Cues** which indicate confidence – without arrogance – may be as follows.

- An upright – but not stiff – **posture**: slouching gives an impression of shyness or carelessness.

- **Movement** that is purposeful and dynamic, used sparingly: not constant or aimless pacing, which looks nervous.

- **Gestures** that are relevant, purposeful and flowing: not indecisive, aggressive, incomplete or compulsive. Use gestures **deliberately** to reinforce your message, and if possible keep your hands up so that gestures do not distract the audience from watching your face. In a large venue, gestures will have to be exaggerated – but practise making them look **natural**. Watch out for habitual, irrelevant gestures you may tend to make.

- **Eye-contact** with the audience maintains credibility, maintains the involvement of the audience and allows you to gather audience feedback as to how well you are getting your message across. Eye-contact should be **established immediately**, and **re-established** after periods when you have had to look away, to consult notes or use visual aids.

The most effective technique is to let our gaze wander (purposefully) across the whole audience, **involving** them all, without intimidating anybody: establish eye-contact long enough for it to be registered, to accompany a point you are making, and then move on.

4.9 Visual aids

Visual aids include slides (acetates and PowerPoint), videos, flipcharts, handouts and props and demonstrations.

The term **visual aids** covers a wide variety of forms which share two characteristics.

- They use a visual image

- They act as an aid to communication. This may seem obvious, but it is important to remember that visual aids are not supposed to be impressive or clever for their own sake, but to support the message and speaker in achieving their purpose.

A number of media and devices are available for using visual aids. They may be summarised as follows.

Table 10.6   Different types of visual aid

Equipment/medium	Advantages	Disadvantages
Slides: photographs, text or diagrams projected onto a screen or other surface	■ Allow colour photos: good for mood, impact and realism ■ Pre-prepared: no speaker 'down time' during talk ■ Controllable sequence/ timing: pace content/audience needs	■ Require a darkened room: may hinder note-taking ■ Malfunction and/or incompetent use: frustration and distraction
Film/video shown on a screen or TV monitor	■ Moving images: realism, impact: can enhance credibility (eye witness effect)	■ Less flexible in allowing interruption, pause or speeding up to pace audience needs
Overheads: films or acetates (hand drawn or printed) projected by light box onto a screen behind/above the presenter	■ Versatility of content and presentation ■ Low cost (for example, if hand written) ■ Clear sheets: can be used to build up images as points added	■ Require physical handling: can be distracting ■ Risk of technical breakdown: not readily adaptable to other means of projection
Presentation software: for example, Microsoft PowerPoint. PC-generated slide show (with animation, sound) projected from PC to screen via data projector	■ Versatility of multi-media: impact, interest ■ Professional design and functioning (smooth transitions) ■ Use of animation to build, link and emphasise as points added	■ Requires PC, data projector: expensive, may not be available ■ Risk of technical breakdown: not readily adaptable to other means of projection ■ Temptation to over-complexity and over-use: distraction
Flip charts: large paper pad mounted on frame – sheets are 'flipped' to the back when finished with	■ Low cost, low-risk ■ Allows use during session (for example, to 'map' audience views, ideas) ■ Can be pre-prepared (for example, advertising 'story boards') ■ Easy to refer back	■ Smaller, still, paper-based image: less impact ■ Hand-prepared: may lack perceived quality (compared to more sophisticated methods)
Handouts: supporting notes handed out for reference during or after the session	■ Pre-prepared ■ Audience doesn't need to take as many notes: reminder provided	■ Audience doesn't need to take as many notes: may encourage passive listening.
Props and demonstrations: objects or processes referred to are themselves shown to the audience	■ Enhances credibility (eye witness effect) ■ Enhances impact (sensory solidity)	■ May not be available ■ Risk of self-defeating 'hitches'

The following illustrations show two of the media discussed in Table 10.6, demonstrating some of their key features – and showing how a picture can be a helpful 'break' from reading or hearing lots of verbal content!

Figure 10.12   Slide presentation

Figure 10.13   Flipchart

Whatever medium or device you are using, visual aids are **versatile** with regard to **content**: maps, diagrams, flowcharts, verbal notes, drawings and photographs.

When planning and using visual aids, consider the following points.

- Visual aids are **simplified and concrete**: they are easier to grasp than the spoken word, allowing the audience to absorb complex relationships and information.

- Visual aids are **stimulating** to the imagination and emotions, and therefore useful in gaining attention and recall.

- Visual aids can also be **distracting** for the audience – and for the presenter, who has to draw/write/organise/operate them. They can add complexity and ambiguity to the presentation if not carefully designed for relevance and clarity.

- Visual aids impose **practical requirements**.

  - The medium you choose must be **suitable** for the needs of your **audience**. Demonstrations, or handing round a small number of samples, is not going to work for a large audience. A flipchart

The Chartered
Institute of Marketing

will not be visible at the back of a large room; a slide projector can be overwhelming in a small room. A darkened room, to show video or slides, will not allow the audience to take notes.

- **Skill, time and resources** must be available for any pre-preparation of aids that may be required in advance of the presentation.

- **The equipment, materials and facilities** you require must be available in the venue, and you must **know** how to **use** them. (No good turning up with a slide projector if there is no power source, or film when there is no overhead projector, or without proper pens for a particular type of board.)

The following are some **guidelines** for effective use of visual aids.

- Ensure that the aid is:

    - **Appropriate** to your message, in content and style or mood
    - **Easy to see** and understand
    - Only used when there is **support** to be gained from it.

- Ensure that all **equipment** and materials are **available and working** and that you can (and do) operate them efficiently and confidently. This includes having all your slides/acetates/notes with you, in the right order and the right way up.

- Ensure that the aid does not become a **distraction**.

    - Show each image **long enough** to be absorbed and noted, but not so long as to merge with the following idea.

    - Maintain **voice and eye contact** with your audience, so they know that it is you who are the communicator, not the machine.

    - **Introduce** your aids and what they are for, placing the focus on the verbal presentation.

    - Hand out **supporting material** either well before the presentation (to allow reading beforehand) or at the relevant point: if you hand it out just before, it will distract or daunt the audience with information they do not yet understand.

    - **Write or draw**, if you need to do so during the presentation, as quickly and efficiently as possible (given the need for legibility and neatness).

The look of presentation slides (or other visual aids) is very important. Make sure that they are:

- **Simple**: not too many points

- **Visually appealing**: use graphics and type styles to create an effect

- **Neat**: especially if you are preparing them by hand.

Issues to consider when using visual aids

- Do use colour, at least for your slides. Monochrome looks boring, and it can be hard to differentiate the content – how do you make certain words or values stand out?

- Check the colour! Something that looks great on your laptop may not work on a large screen, especially if there is a lot of light. So avoid pale colours, such as yellow or light pastel shades. Always check your presentation for legibility before you 'go live'.

- Be aware, too, of the incidence of colour blindness. In Britain just under 3 million people are affected to some degree – mainly men. For some helpful examples of the use of inappropriate colour, visit: http://www.colourblindawareness.org

- Don't use too many words on a slide. The audience has come to listen to you, not read your slides! If necessary, additional and detailed information can be on a handout. Bullet points that can be rapidly assimilated and remembered are far more effective.

- Do be aware of typefaces – styles and size. In general don't use more than two or three style, and don't use sizes less than 22 point.

- Keep the elements on a slide consistent – same style, and position, for headings; same style of bullets; same relative position on the slide for bulleted lists, etc. Minor variations of positioning on a laptop screen are magnified enormously on a large screen.

- Be aware of graphics, colours and overlapping items; it may be easy to differentiate the text and picture on your laptop, but this may not work so effectively when you are presenting.

- Do, however, try to introduce a little, consistent, graphic content. Don't use cartoons or clip art on one slide, photographs on another, and sketches on another.

- Do check the content! Make sure there are no typographic errors. Check your slides, and then get someone else to check them. Even if audience members don't spot the error (and someone will!) it is likely to throw you when you notice it.

- Be aware of symbols, jargon or abbreviations. Ensure you know exactly what the item means – someone will ask you!

- Ideally, ensure you have a 'slide controller' – a small handheld device that allows you to remotely control the computer. This ensures you can change slides easily, wherever you are, without having to reach and fumble for the keyboard, or shout 'next' to the computer operator.

- Don't turn your back on the audience. Ever! Some of the worst presentations are when the speaker faces the screen, and reads what is on the slides. Either have the computer positioned so that you can see a duplicate of what is on the screen, or have printed 'presenter thumbnails' on the lectern, so you always know what each slide contains.

- Obtain a laser pointer or long stick if you must point to specific items on the slide – don't stand in front of the screen and try to use your hand.

- If you have handouts, or can allow users to receive a copy of the presentation, let the audience know at the beginning – it can save a lot of time in taking notes.

- Consider giving your handouts in batches, or at the end – this prevents the audience 'reading ahead' or concentrating on the handout instead of your talk.

4.10 Handling questions

Questions are important to help clarify misunderstandings and overcome doubts. It is important that the speaker maintains **credibility**.

Inviting or accepting questions is usually the final part of a presentation.

- In informative presentations, questions offer an **opportunity to clarify any misunderstandings**, or gaps that the audience may have perceived

- In persuasive presentations, questions offer an opportunity to address and overcome specific doubts or resistance that the audience may have, which the speaker may not have been able to anticipate.

The manner in which you 'field' questions may be crucial to your **credibility**. Everyone knows you have prepared your presentation carefully: ignorance, bluster or hesitation in the face of a question may cast doubt on your expertise, or sincerity, or both. Moreover, this is usually the last stage of the presentation, and so leaves a lasting impression.

The only way to tackle questions effectively is to **anticipate** them. Put yourself in your audience's shoes, or, more specifically, in the shoes of an ignorant member of the audience and a hostile member of the audience and a member of the audience with a particular axe to grind: what questions might they ask and why? When questions arise, listen to them carefully, assess the questioner's manner, and draw the questioner out if necessary, in order to ascertain exactly what is being asked, and why. People might ask questions:

- To **seek additional information** of particular interest to them, or to the group – if you have left it out of your talk

- To seek **clarification** of a point that is not clear

- To **add information** of their own, which may be relevant, helpful and accurate – or not

- To **lead the discussion into another area** (or away from an uncomfortable one)

- To display their **own knowledge or cleverness**

- To **undermine** the speaker's authority or argument, to 'catch him out'.

If you have anticipated questions of the first two kinds in the planning of your talk, they should not arise: incorporate the answers in your outline.

The important points about **answering questions** are as follows.

- You may **seek feedback** throughout your talk, as to whether your message is getting across clearly – and it is common to invite the audience to let you know if anything is unclear – but by and large, you should encourage questions only at the end of your presentation. That way, disruptive, rambling, hostile and attention-seeking questions will not be allowed to disrupt your message to the audience as a whole.

- You should **add or clarify** information if required to achieve your purpose. An honest query deserves a co-operative answer.

- You need to **maintain your credibility** and authority as the speaker. Strong tactics may be required for you to stay in control, without in any way ridiculing or 'putting down' the questioner.

  - If a question is based on a **false premise** or incorrect information, **correct it**. An answer may, or may not, then be required.

  - If a question is **rambling**: interrupt, clarify what the question, or main question (if it is a multiple query) is, and answer that. If it is completely irrelevant, say politely that it is outside the scope of the presentation: you may or may not offer to deal with it informally afterwards.

- If a question is **hostile or argumentative**, you may wish to show understanding of how the questioner has reached his or her conclusion, or why he or she feels as he or she does. However, you then need to reinforce, repeat or explain your own view.

- If a question tries to **pin you down** or 'corner' you on an area in which you do not wish to be specific or to make promises, be straightforward about it.

- If a question exposes an area in which you do not know the answer, **admit your limitations** with honesty and dignity, and invite help from members of the audience, if appropriate.

- Try and answer all questions with **points already made** in your speech, or related to them. This reinforces the impression that your speech was in fact complete and correct.

- **Repeat** any question that you think might not have been **audible** to everyone in the room.

- **Clarify** any question that you think is lengthy, complex, ambiguous or uses jargon not shared by the audience as a whole.

- **Answer briefly**, keeping strictly to the point of the question (while relating it, if possible, to what you have already said). If your answer needs to be lengthy, structure it as you would a small talk: introduce what you are going to say, say it, then confirm what you have said!

- Keep an eye on the **overall time-limit** for your talk or for the question-and-answer session. Move on if a questioner is taking up too much time, and call a halt, courteously, when required. 'I'll take one more question ... ' or 'I'm afraid that's all we have time for' is standard practice which offends few listeners.

 The Chartered Institute of Marketing

CHAPTER ROUNDUP

- Whenever you are communicating you should take into account the audience's thinking sequence: respect the client's importance; consider the client's needs; demonstrate how your information helps the client; explain the detail that underpins your information; remind the client of the key points; suggest what the client should do now.

- A research report typically has the following elements: Title page; list of contents; executive summary; introduction/problem definition; research method (and limitations); research findings; conclusions; appendices.

- Tables, graphs, charts and illustrations of various kinds can greatly enhance the value of a report because they make it easier to take in information at a glance.

- An oral presentation would have the following structure: introduction; explanation of research methodology; key findings; conclusions/recommendations; questions.

- Matters to consider when preparing and delivering presentations include audience motivation, physical factors in the presentation room, content, clarity, adding emphasis and interest, and controlling nerves and body language.

- Visual aids include slides (acetates and PowerPoint), videos, flipcharts, handouts and props and demonstrations.

- Questions are important to help clarify misunderstandings and overcome doubts. It is important that the speaker maintains credibility.

FURTHER READING

Chapter 10 of each of the following books:

Bradley, N. (2010) *Marketing research: Tools & techniques*. 2nd edition. Oxford, Oxford University Press.

Wilson, A. (2012) *Marketing research: An integrated approach*. 3rd edition. Harlow, Financial Times Prentice Hall.

REFERENCES

Bain, R. (2008) MTV dissects the youth of today: London exhibition reveals findings of global youth culture study. *Research,* http://www.research-live.com/news/mtv-dissects-the-youth-of-today/3003769.article [Accessed 12 June 2012] .

Birn, R. (2004) *The effective use of market research: How to drive and focus better business decisions*. London, Kogan Page.

Wilson, A. (2012) *Marketing research: An integrated approach*. 3rd edition. Harlow, Financial Times Prentice Hall.

1   The use of a graph or bar chart illustrates that the writer or presenter is aware of what part of the audience thinking sequence?

2   Which part of a report contains a summary of findings?

3   A graphic aid used to show processes and relationships is a _____ chart.

4   If 💰 represents $100m, draw a pictogram for $550m.

5   List five techniques that can be used to add emphasis.

6   List five reasons why people might ask questions when attending a presentation.

7   What are the typical elements of a research report?

8   Outline five physical factors that you should consider in preparing for a presentation.

ACTIVITY DEBRIEFS

Activity 10.1

Company A specialises in delivering quite large packages quickly
Company B delivers smaller packages fairly slowly
Company C delivers smaller packages quite quickly
Company D delivers fairly small packages slightly more quickly than average
Company E delivers very large packages very slowly
Company F delivers medium to large packages more quickly than average

Activity 10.2

The answer to this depends upon your own experiences.

Activity 10.3

We had in mind a situation when the researcher is conducting qualitative research, particularly focus groups and also when an agency first presents its proposal to a client in a beauty parade.

1   The writer or presenter is offering a means of taking in information at a glance therefore he or she is respecting the importance of the audience (not wasting their time).

2   The summary is contained where you would expect it, in the executive summary.

3   Flow chart

4   💰 💰 💰 💰 💰 💰

5   Repetition, rhetorical question, quotation, statistical evidence, exaggeration

6   To seek additional information, to seek clarification, to add information, to lead the discussion into another area, to display their own cleverness, to undermine the speaker.

7   A research report typically has the following elements: Title page; list of contents; executive summary; introduction/problem definition; research method (and limitations); research findings; conclusions; appendices.

8   Listening conditions, freedom from interruption and distraction, ventilation, heating and lighting, seating layout and audibility and visibility.

Index

80/20 principle, 25

ACORN, 79

ADMAP, 81
Adverting agencies, 50
Anecdotes, 198
Annotation, 120
Appearance, 196

Bias, 128, 150

Body language, 200
BRAD, 81
Broad objectives, 59
Business surveys, 128

Carelessness, 150

Cartoon completion, 112
CCTV, 97
Check boxes, 32
Closed questions, 163
Cluster sampling, 143
Competitor intelligence system, 80
Complaints, 23
Completeness checks, 33
Computerised forms, 31
Confusion of cause and effect, 150
Congeniality, 195
Consumer panel, 102
Consumer panels, 82
Contacts planning, 27
Content analysis, 119
Cookies, 23
Credibility, 195
Cues, 200
Customer database, 22
Customer databases, 22
Customer relationship management (CRM), 28
Customer retention, 24
Customer service, 23
Cut and paste, 119

Data analysis agencies, 49

Data cleansing, 31
Data fatigue, 152
Data mart, 35
Data mining, 34, 36
Data subjects, 38
Data warehouse, 34
Data warehousing, 34
Database management system (DMBS), 29
Database management system, 29
Database marketing, 22, 27

Database, 31
Decision making, 25
Decision support systems, 13
Decision-trees, 36
Definition, 198
Depth interviews, 137
depth, 110
Description, 198
Direct mail, 27
Directories, 79
Directory (Internet), 85
Discussion guide, 114
Duplication, 29, 33

Electronic Funds Transfer at Point of Sale (EFTPOS), 12

Electronic Point of Sale (EPOS), 12
E-mail, 26
Emphasis, 199
Environmental scanning, 80
ESOMAR, 50
Ethical issues, 62
Ethical responsibilities, 37
Exaggeration, 199
Executive interview, 111
Executive summary, 183
Existence checks, 32
Explanation, 198
Extranet, 11
Eye cameras, 96

Field agencies, 48

Fields, 31
Flat file system, 30
Focus groups, 114
Focus groups, 114, 116, 137
Format checks, 32
Friendly Martian, 112
Frugging, 152
Full service agency, 50
Funnelling, 171

Geodemographic information, 23

Google, 86
Group discussion, 114

Hall tests, 128

Halo effect, 168
Home audit panels, 82
Home interviews, 128
Humour, 199

ICC/ESOMAR code, 63

Impartially, 182
Independent consultants, 49
Information Age, 5
Information overload, 9
Information, 4
Insufficient data, 150
Interest, 195
Internet, 12, 26
Interviewer bias, 128
Interviews
Intranet, 11

Knowledge-based economy, 5

Leading questions, 165

Limitations, 91
Linking words, 198
List boxes, 32
List broker, 49

Management consultants, 50
Management process, 2, 178
Market intelligence, 80
Market Research Society (MRS), 50
Marketing decision support system, 13
Marketing decision support, 13
Marketing research and planning, 27
Marketing research, 14, 150
Mash up, 118
Mass customisation, 28
Mind maps, 119
Moderator, 115
Multidimensional data analysis, 35
Mystery shopping, 98

Narrow objectives, 59

Neural networks, 36
Non-probability sampling, 142
Non-response, 151

Observation, **94**, 95, 137

Observations, 95
Omission, 150
Omnibus survey, 134
Omnibus surveys, 83
Open questions, 164
Oral presentation, 55

Pareto, Vilfredo, 25

Pareto's law, 25
Participant observation, 96
Personal data, 37, 38

PESTEL, 5
Pilot test, 173
Population of interest, 140, **141**
Population, 140, 155
Portal, 86
Post-testing, 101
PowerPoint, 201
Pressure mats, 95
Pre-testing, 101
Primary data, 54
Probability sampling, 142
Product development and improvement, 27
Profiler, 50
Projective techniques, 111
Psychodrama, 112
Pupilometric cameras, 96
Purchase frequency, 25

Qualitative methods, 137

Qualitative research, 108
Quantitative data, 126
Quantitative methods, 137
Quantitative research, 126
Quasi-random sampling, 143
Questionnaire, 160
Questions, 198

Radio buttons, 31

Random, 143
Range checks, 32
Recording devices, 95
Records, 31
Relational database, 30
Reliable data, 12
Repertory grid, 137
Repetition, 199
Research brief, 57
Research brief, 57
Research proposal, 58
Research proposals, 58
Research questions, 59
Rhetorical questions, 199

Sample, **140**, 156

Sampling frame, 142
Sampling, 140
Search engines, 86
Secondary data, 54, **74**
Sentence completion, 112
Server logging software, 23
Service Level Agreement, 56
Shop surveys, 127
Simple random sample, 143
Snowball sampling, 144
Social networking, 117

The Chartered
Institute of Marketing

The Chartered
Institute of Marketing

The Chartered
Institute of Marketing

The Chartered
Institute of Marketing

Review form

Please help us to ensure that the CIM learning materials we produce remain as accurate and user-friendly as possible. We cannot promise to answer every submission we receive, but we do promise that it will be read and taken into account when we update this Study Text.

Name: _____   Address: _____

_____

_____

1. How have you used this Text?
(Tick one box only)

☐ Self study (book only)

☐ On a course: college_____

☐ Other _____

3. Why did you decide to purchase this Text?
(Tick one box only)

☐ Have used companion Assessment workbook

☐ Have used BPP Texts in the past

☐ Recommendation by friend/colleague

☐ Recommendation by a lecturer at college

☐ Saw advertising in journals

☐ Saw information on BPP website

☐ Other _____

2. During the past six months do you recall seeing/receiving any of the following?
(Tick as many boxes as are relevant)

☐ Our advertisement in *The Marketer*

☐ Our brochure with a letter through the post

☐ Our website www.bpp.com

4. Which (if any) aspects of our advertising do you find useful?
(Tick as many boxes as are relevant)

☐ Prices and publication dates of new editions

☐ Information on product content

☐ Facility to order books off-the-page

☐ None of the above

5. Have you used the companion Assessment Workbook?   Yes ☐   No ☐

6. Have you used the companion Passcards?   Yes ☐   No ☐

7. Your ratings, comments and suggestions would be appreciated on the following areas.

	Very useful	Useful	Not useful
Introductory section (How to use this text, study checklist, etc)	☐	☐	☐
Chapter introductions	☐	☐	☐
Syllabus learning outcomes	☐	☐	☐
Activities	☐	☐	☐
The Real World examples	☐	☐	☐
Quick quizzes	☐	☐	☐
Quality of explanations			
Index	☐	☐	☐
Structure and presentation	☐	☐	☐

	Excellent	Good	Adequate	Poor
Overall opinion of this Text	☐	☐	☐	☐

8. Do you intend to continue using BPP CIM products?   ☐ Yes   ☐ No

On the reverse of this page is space for you to write your comments about our Study Text. We welcome your feedback.

Please return to: CIM Publishing Manager, BPP Learning Media, FREEPOST, London, W12 8BR.

TELL US WHAT YOU THINK

Please note any further comments and suggestions/errors below. For example, was the text accurate, readable, concise, user-friendly and comprehensive?